ICWMC 2019

The Fifteenth International Conference on Wireless and Mobile Communications

June 30 – July 4, 2019

Rome, Italy

ICWMC 2019 Editors

Christos Bouras, Computer Engineering & Informatics Department, University of Patras, Greece

Meryeme Ayache, ENSIAS, University Mohamed 5 of Rabat, Morocco

Printed from e-media with permission by:

Curran Associates, Inc.
57 Morehouse Lane
Red Hook, NY 12571

Printed by Curran Associates, Inc. (2019)

International Academy, Research, and Industry Association (IARIA)
412 Derby Way
Wilmington, DE 19810

Phone: (408) 893-6407
Fax: (408) 527-6351

petre@iaria.org

Additional copies of this publication are available from:

Curran Associates, Inc.
57 Morehouse Lane
Red Hook, NY 12571 USA
Phone: 845-758-0400
Fax: 845-758-2633
Email: curran@proceedings.com
Web: www.proceedings.com

Table of Contents

ICWMC 2019

Foreword

The Fifteenth International Conference on Wireless and Mobile Communications (ICWMC 2019), held between June 30 – July 4, 2019 - Rome, Italy, followed on the previous events on advanced wireless technologies, wireless networking, and wireless applications.

ICWMC 2019 addressed wireless related topics concerning integration of latest technological advances to realize mobile and ubiquitous service environments for advanced applications and services in wireless networks. Mobility and wireless, special services and lessons learnt from particular deployment complemented the traditional wireless topics.

We take here the opportunity to warmly thank all the members of the ICWMC 2019 Technical Program Committee, as well as the numerous reviewers. The creation of such a high quality conference program would not have been possible without their involvement. We also kindly thank all the authors who dedicated much of their time and efforts to contribute to ICWMC 2019. We truly believe that, thanks to all these efforts, the final conference program consisted of top quality contributions.

Also, this event could not have been a reality without the support of many individuals, organizations, and sponsors. We are grateful to the members of the ICWMC 2019 organizing committee for their help in handling the logistics and for their work to make this professional meeting a success.

We hope that ICWMC 2019 was a successful international forum for the exchange of ideas and results between academia and industry and for the promotion of progress in the area of wireless and mobile communications.

We are convinced that the participants found the event useful and communications very open. We also hope that Rome provided a pleasant environment during the conference and everyone saved some time for exploring this beautiful city.

ICWMC 2019 Chairs

ICWMC Steering Committee

Carlos Becker Westphall, Universidade Federal de Santa Catarina, Brazil
Brian M. Sadler, Army Research Laboratory, USA
Magnus Jonsson, Halmstad University, Sweden
Afrand Agah, West Chester University of Pennsylvania, USA
David Sanchez, University of Las Palmas de Gran Canaria, Spain
David Navarro, Ecole Centrale de Lyon, France
Carl James Debono, University of Malta, Malta
Xiang Gui, Massey University, New Zealand
Zdenek Becvar, Czech Technical University in Prague, Czech Republic
Dragana Krstic, University of Niš, Serbia

ICWMC Industry/Research Advisory Committee

ICWMC 2019

Committee

ICWMC Steering Committee

Carlos Becker Westphall, Universidade Federal de Santa Catarina, Brazil
Brian M. Sadler, Army Research Laboratory, USA
Magnus Jonsson, Halmstad University, Sweden
Afrand Agah, West Chester University of Pennsylvania, USA
David Sanchez, University of Las Palmas de Gran Canaria, Spain
David Navarro, Ecole Centrale de Lyon, France
Carl James Debono, University of Malta, Malta
Xiang Gui, Massey University, New Zealand
Zdenek Becvar, Czech Technical University in Prague, Czech Republic
Dragana Krstic, University of Niš, Serbia

ICWMC Industry/Research Advisory Committee

Augusto Morales, Check Point Software Technologies, Spain
Sivakumar Sivaramakrishnan, vToggle Ltd., New Zealand
Christian Makaya, IBM T.J. Watson Research Center, USA
Rajat Kumar Kochhar, Ericsson, India
Christopher Nguyen, Intel Corp., USA

ICWMC 2019 Technical Program Committee

Afrand Agah, West Chester University of Pennsylvania, USA
Vaneet Aggarwal, Purdue University, USA
Hamed Al-Raweshidy, Brunel University London, UK
Hanan Al-Tous, United Arab Emirates University, AlAin, UAE
Adel Aldalbahi, King Faisal University, Al-Hassa, Saudi Arabia
Karine Amis, IMT Atlantique Bretagne-Pays de la Loire, France
Antonio Arena, University of Pisa, Italy
Radu Arsinte, Technical University of Cluj-Napoca, Romania
Carlos A. Astudillo Trujillo, State University of Campinas, Brazil
Shadi Atalla, University of Dubai, UAE
Meryeme Ayache, ENSIAS | University Mohamed 5 of Rabat, Morocco
Stylianos Basagiannis, United Technologies Research Centre, USA
A. M. A. Elman Bashar, Plymouth State University, USA
Carlos Becker Westphall, Universidade Federal de Santa Catarina, Brazil
Zdenek Becvar, Czech Technical University in Prague, Czech Republic
Luca Bedogni, University of Bologna, Italy
Chafika Benzaid, University of Sciences and Technology Houari Boumediene (USTHB), Algeria

Luis Bernardo, Universidade Nova de Lisboa, Portugal
Vincent Beroulle, Univ. Grenoble Alpes LCIS, France
Robert Bestak, Czech Technical University in Prague, Czech Republic
Archana Bhise, Mukesh Patel School of Technology, Management and Engineering, Mumbai, India
Jean-Marie Bonnin, Institut Mines Télécom / IMT Atlantique - Inria IRISA, France
Brik Bouziane, CESI school in Rouen, France
David Boyle, Imperial College London, UK
Maurizio Bozzi, University of Pavia, Italy
An Braeken, Vrije Universiteit Brussel, Belgium
Rodrigo Campos Bortoletto, São Paulo Federal Institute of Education, Science, and Technology, Brazil
Juan-Carlos Cano, Universidad Politécnica de Valencia, Spain
Fernando Cerdan, Polytechnic University of Cartagena, Spain
Hsing-Lung Chen, National Taiwan University of Science and Technology, Taiwan
Ray-Guang Cheng, National Taiwan University of Science and Technology, Taiwan
Riccardo Colella, University of Salento, Italy
Estefania Coronado, FBK CREATE-NET, Trento, Italy
Nicolae Crisan, Technical University of Cluj-Napoca, Romania
Heming Cui, University of Hong Kong, Hong Kong
Donatella Darsena, University of Naples "Parthenope", Italy
John Day, Boston University, USA
Sonia Heemstra de Groot, Eindhoven University of Technology, Netherlands
Carl James Debono, University of Malta, Malta
Enrico Del Re, Università di Firenze, Italy
Paulo da Fonseca Pinto, Universidade Nova de Lisboa, Portugal
Klaus David, University of Kassel, Germany
Rishabh Dudheria, New York Institute of Technology - Nanjing campus, China
Alban Duverdier, CNES (French Space Agency), France
Peter Ekler, Budapest University of Technology and Economics, Hungary
Imad Ez-zazi, National School of Applied Sciences of Tangier - University of Abdelmalek Essaadi, Morocco
Abraham O. Fapojuwo, University of Calgary, Canada
Ibraheem Mhmoud Fayed, National Telecommunication Institute (NTI) | Ministry of Communication and Information Technology (MCIT), Cairo, Egypt
Manuel Fernandez Veiga, University of Vigo | AtlanTTIC Research Center, Spain
Gianluigi Ferrari, University of Parma, Italy
Miguel Franklin de Castro, Federal University of Ceará, Brazil
Valerio Frascolla, Intel, Germany
Antoine Gallais, Université de Strasbourg - ICube (CNRS UMR 7357), France
Jordi Garcia, CRAAX Lab - UPC BarcelonaTech, Spain
Ana-Belen Garcia-Hernando, Universidad Politecnica de Madrid, Spain
Roberto Garello, Politecnico di Torino, Italy
Krishna C. Garikipati, Motorola Mobility - Chicago, USA
Chunhua Geng, Nokia Bell Labs, USA
Carlo Giannelli, University of Ferrara, Italy
Mikael Gidlund, Mid Sweden University, Sweden
Lazaros Gkatzikis, Huawei France Research Center, France
Chris Gniady, University of Arizona, USA
Tor-Morten Grønli, Kristiania University College, Norway
Diego Alberto Godoy, Centro de Investigación en Tecnologías de Información y Comunicaciones |

Universidad Gastón Dachary - Posadas, Misiones, Argentina
Javier Gozalvez, Universidad Miguel Hernandez de Elche, Spain
Anna Guerra, University of Bologna, Italy
Xiang Gui, Massey University, New Zealand
Fabrice Guillemin, Orange Labs, Lannion, France
Burhan Gulbahar, Ozyegin University, Istanbul, Turkey
Wibowo Hardjawana, University of Sydney, Australia
Hiroaki Higaki, Tokyo Denki University, Japan
Jalaa Hoblos, Penn State University, Erie, USA
Ibrahim Hokelek, TUBITAK BILGEM, Turkey
Song-Nam Hong, Ajou University, South Korea
Pengda Huang, Southern Methodist University, USA
Javed Iqbal, Sarhad University of Science and Technology, Peshawar, Pakistan
Dushantha Nalin K. Jayakody, National Research Tomsk Polytechnic University, Russia
Nigel Jefferies, Huawei Technologies, UK
Thomas Jell, Siemens Mobility GmbH, München, Germany
Terje Jensen, Telenor, Norway
Anish Jindal, Thapar University, India
Magnus Jonsson, Halmstad University, Sweden
Yunho Jung, Korea Aerospace University, South Korea
Adrian Kacso, University of Siegen, Germany
Georgios Kambourakis, University of the Aegean, Greece
Sarah Kamel, Télécom ParisTech, France
Junaid Ahmed Khan, INRIA AGORA (ex URBANET) | CITI Lab INSA Lyon, France
Wooseong Kim, Gachon University, S. Korea
Rajat Kumar Kochhar, Ericsson, Sweden
Peng-Yong Kong, Khalifa University, Abu Dhabi, United Arab Emirates
Leszek Koszalka, Wroclaw University of Science and Technology, Poland
Dragana Krstic, University of Niš, Serbia
Trupil Limbasiya, BITS Pilani - Goa Campus, India
Eirini Liotou, National and Kapodistrian University of Athens, Greece
Xin Liu, China University of Petroleum, China
Miguel López-Benítez, University of Liverpool, UK
Phuong Luong, Ecole de Technologie Superieure (ETS), Montreal, Canada
Stephane Maag, Institut Mines Telecom / Telecom SudParis, France
Pavel Mach, Czech Technical University in Prague, Czech Republic
Christian Makaya, IBM T.J. Watson Research Center, USA
Abdallah Makhoul, University Bourgogne - Franche-Comté, France
D. Manivannan, University of Kentucky, USA
Hamid Menouar, Qatar Mobility Innovations Center (QMIC), Qatar
Carlos Colman Meixner, University of California, Davis, USA
Jorge Mena, UCLA, USA
Angelos Michalas, TEI of Western Macedonia, Kastoria, Greece
Fabien Mieyeville, University Claude Bernard Lyon 1 - Polytech Lyon, France
Makoto Miyake, M-TEC Company Limited, Japan
Jolanta Mizera-Pietraszko, Intytut Informatyki | Uniwersytet Opolski, Poland
Augusto Morales, Check Point Software Technologies, Spain
Mário W. L. Moreira, Universidade da Beira Interior, Covilhã, Portugal

You-Chiun Wang, National Sun Yat-sen University, Taiwan
Mingkui Wei, Sam Houston State University, USA
Wei Wei, Xi'an University of Technology, China
Ouri Wolfson, University of Illinois at Chicago, USA
Pei Xiao, University of Surrey, UK
Ping Yang, State University of New York at Binghamton, USA
Tiguiane Yelemou, Polytechnic University of Bobo-Dioulasso, Burkina Faso
M. Erkan Yuksel, Mehmet Akif Ersoy University, Turkey
Kanwal Zaidi, Massey University, New Zealand
Sherali Zeadally, University of Kentucky, USA
Junqing Zhang, Queen's University Belfast, UK
Yan Zhang, Imec-NL, Netherlands
Bo Zhou, Shanghai Jiao Tong University, China
Yuxun Zhou, University of California, Berkeley, USA

Copyright Information

Proposal of a Null Subcarrier Allocation Method for CAZAC-OFDM Systems

Taketo Nasuno and Masahiro Muraguchi

Department of Electrical Engineering, Tokyo University of Science
6-3-1 Niijuku, Katsushika-ku, Tokyo, 125-0051, Japan
E-mail: 4315086@ed.tus.ac.jp, murag@ee.kagu.tus.ac.jp

Abstract— **A major drawback of Orthogonal Frequency Division Multiplexing (OFDM) signals is the extremely high Peak-to-Average Power Ratio (PAPR). Constant Amplitude Zero Auto Correlation (CAZAC) precoding can dramatically improve the PAPR of OFDM signals, i.e., up to the same PAPR value of single carrier signals with the same modulation scheme. One negative point of the CAZAC precoding technic is not being able to meet the current wireless standards, which usually require a null subcarrier allocated on the center of data subcarriers. In this paper, we demonstrate the CAZAC-OFDM which completely satisfies the 4G-LTE standard by using the proposed allocation method for a null subcarrier without degrading the PAPR and the Bit-Error-Rate.**

Keywords- OFDM; CAZAC; null subcarrier; PAPR;.

I. INTRODUCTION

In recent years, with the rapid spread of wireless LAN and mobile communication terminals, such as smart phones, tablets, etc., the demand for wireless communication is expanding. However, since the capacity of the data is also increasing, it is a problem that there are few available frequency bands. Therefore, research on Orthogonal Frequency Division Multiplex (OFDM) system is progressing because it is the modulation scheme that can provide high spectral efficiently. By using OFDM systems, high-speed communication can be realized under limited frequency bands as compared with other modulation schemes, and OFDM system is currently adopted in downlink of the mobile communication system [1]. On the other hand, OFDM has the demerits of the high Peak to Average Power Ratio (PAPR). The high PAPR causes a decrease in the average power of the transmission signal, resulting in lowering of the energy efficiency of the power amplifiers and the shortened operation time causes a serious problem in battery-powered wireless terminals.

A new PAPR reduction technique with Constant Amplitude Zero Auto Correlation (CAZAC) equalization was recently proposed [2].

Our research group have demonstrated that CAZAC precoding can reduce the PAPR without any degradation of BER performances [3], and have also provided available control procedure for PAPR and spectrum managements for the CAZAC-OFDM system [4]. Unfortunately, the CAZAC-OFDM is not able to meet the current wireless standards, which usually require a null subcarrier allocated on the center of data subcarriers. The main reason of this subcarrier which is named the DC-subcarrier is to avoid DC-offset for received signal processing ease. In an ordinary OFDM system, each subcarrier carries independent information. On the other hand, by using CAZAC precoding, every information-data is spreading over subcarriers and every subcarrier shares all information-data. This peculiar feature, however, hinders the allocation of a null subcarrier, whereas, in case of ordinary OFDMs, it is easily allocated a null subcarrier by inputting null-data instead of information-data.

This paper proposes a method for null subcarrier allocation in the Constant Amplitude Zero Auto Correlation OFDM systems (CAZAC-OFDM systems). The method is to replace the CAZAC precoding data for the center subcarrier by null-data. This means that the information carried by the center subcarrier is dropped. Fortunately, since the CAZAC-OFDM has a frequency diversity effect, the dropped information is effectively recovered.

We will demonstrate that the CAZAC-OFDM system with proposed null subcarrier allocation method fulfills the requirements of the PAPR and the Bit-Error-Rate for 4G-LTE standard.

Section 2 describes the OFDM system and Section 3 describes the CAZAC precoding technic and proposal system. Section 4 then performs simulation verification and concludes in Section 5.

II. OFDM SYSTEM

This section describes existing OFDM systems.

A. PAPR

OFDM system is a form of multicarrier modulation and a communication system by OFDM can use frequency efficiently. In an OFDM transmitter, an Inverse Fast Fourier Transform (IFFT) is performed after primary modulation of a data sequence. As a result, the value after primary modulation is placed on each subcarrier, and a spectrum is formed in which each subcarrier overlaps. Even if each subcarrier overlaps, due to mutual orthogonality, respectively demodulation is possible, so that frequency utilization efficiency is excellent.

The N th sample with the input signal X (length N) after mapping is defined as (1) [5].

$$x_n = \frac{1}{N}\sum_{k=0}^{N-1} X_k e^{j\frac{2\pi}{N}kn} \quad (1)$$

Where X_k is the frequency-domain signal, and N is the number of subcarriers, $j = \sqrt{-1}$. After IFFT, a guard interval is inserted in the baseband signal. The OFDM symbol is generated by the above procedure. In particular, the value after IFFT when n=0 in (1) disappears the imaginary part, and only the real part remains as (2).

$$x_n = \frac{1}{N}\sum_{k=0}^{N-1} X_k \tag{2}$$

The PAPR of the OFDM signal (1) can be expressed as

$$PAPR = \frac{\max\limits_{0\le n\le N-1} |x_n|^2}{\mathrm{E}[|x_n|^2]}, \tag{3}$$

where $\mathrm{E}[\cdot]$ is expectation operator. PAPR represents amplitude fluctuation of each symbol.

As shown from by (1), the OFDM signal is composed of a plurality of subcarrier signals, which causes an increase in amplitude fluctuation. A high PAPR signal increases the Input Back Off (IBO) at the power amplifier in order to amplify the transmit signal without distortion. Increasing in IBO causes decreasing the efficiency of PA.

Figure 1 shows the OFDM time domain signal. While OFDM can make effectively utilize the limited frequency domain, a very large peak power is generated in the time domain. The more OFDM uses subcarriers, the more PAPR will be increased.

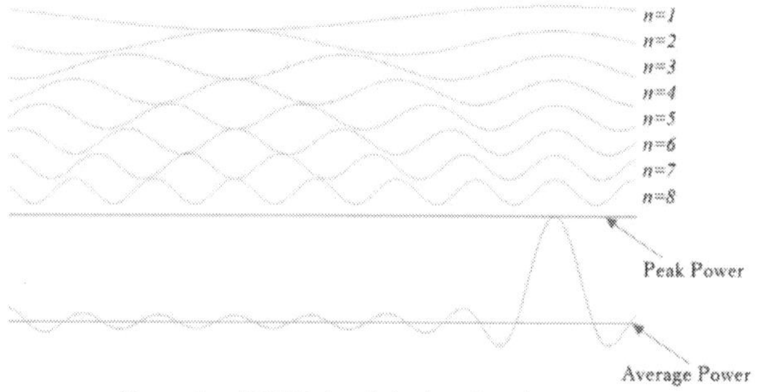

Figure 1. OFDM signals in time domain.

In order to reduce the PAPR, well-known techniques are clipping-and-filtering, partial transmit sequences (PTSs), and selected mapping (SLM)[6]. Clipping-and-filtering limits the peak amplitude of the transmission signal. However, non-linear distortion causes BER to degrade. PTS partitions input data into disjoint sub-blocks. Moreover, each sub-block are weighted by a phase factor. This technique chooses the phase factor to minimize the PAPR of combined signals. SLM generates multiple candidate data blocks. All data blocks represent the same information. Although PTS and SLM can be expected to create a certain reduction in PAPR, both techniques need side information in the receiver, which decreases spectral efficiency. The most practical solution to improving PAPR is to introduce single carrier frequency division multiplexing access (SC-FDMA). The 3GPP LTE system adopts SC-FDMA for uplink multiple access systems. However, SC-FDMA has not been considered to be suitable for next-generation high-speed communications. Therefore, we should reduce PAPR without any degradation of various performances

B. Null subcarrier

Communication standards that make use of OFDM, on the transmitting side, data is not placed on the relevant part beforehand, and zero padding is performed so that the real component is designed to be zero.

Figure 2 shows the transmission spectrum of OFDM with Null subcarrier inserted.

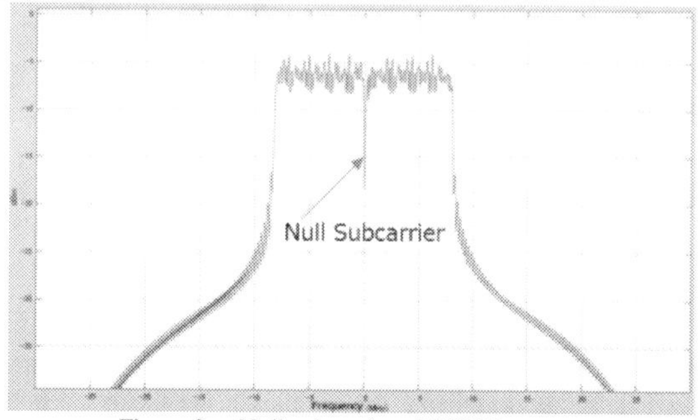

Figure 2. Null subcarrier of OFDM spectrum.

Since the data placed on the subcarrier corresponding to the part of 0Hz, which is the element which becomes the real part in the FFT processing on the receiving side is made null beforehand as the null subcarrier.

III. CAZAC-OFDM SYSTEM

This section describes the features of the CAZAC-OFDM system.

A. CAZAC precoding technique

Zadoff-Chu (ZC) sequence is one of the CAZAC sequence. The ZC sequence C_k of length L is defined as (4).

$$C_k = \begin{cases} exp\left(\frac{j\pi k(k-1)r}{L}\right) & (L \text{ is even}) \\ exp\left(\frac{j\pi (k-1)^2 r}{L}\right) & (L \text{ is odd}) \end{cases} \tag{4}$$

Where L is the length of the CAZAC sequence and r is the sequence number, $k = 1, 2, \cdots N^2$. L is a natural number, and r is a prime integer with respect to L.

CAZAC precoding uses a square matrix M generated from the equation in the case where L in (4) is an even number. The matrix equation is defined as (5).

$$M = \begin{bmatrix} c_1 & c_2 \cdots & c_N \\ c_{N+1} & c_{N+2}\cdots & c_{2N} \\ \vdots & \vdots \ \ddots & \vdots \\ c_{(N-1)N+1} & \cdots \ \cdots & c_{N^2} \end{bmatrix} \tag{5}$$

Where matrix M is the rearrangement of C_k in (4) in the row direction, and N is the number of subcarriers and $L = N^2, r = 1$. N is an even number, and L is also an even number.

Figures 3 and 4 show the block diagrams of CAZAC-OFDM transmitter and receiver, respectively. On the transmitting side of CAZAC-OFDM, CAZAC precoder is inserted before IFFT.

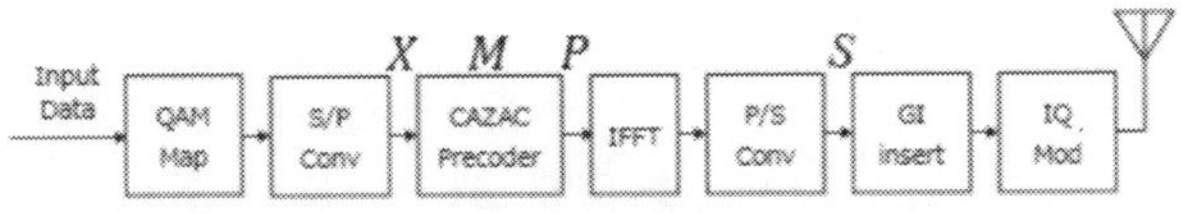

Figure 3. The transmitting side of CAZAC-OFDM

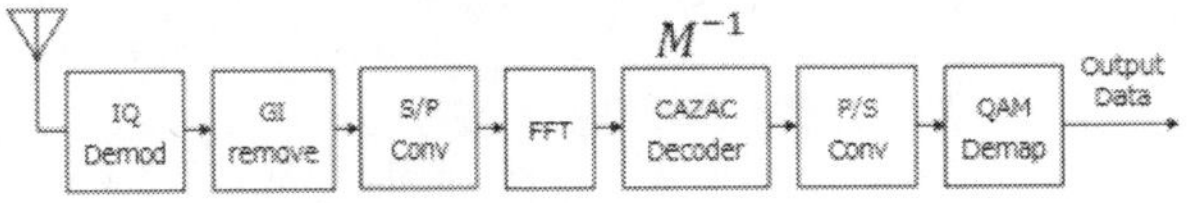

Figure 4. The receiving side of CAZAC-OFDM

CAZAC precoding signal P is generated by calculating the inner product of complex vector of QAM signal X and CAZAC matrix M like (6) [7]. S is the signal after inverse Fourier transform processing.

$$X_M = M \cdot X = \begin{bmatrix} c_1 & c_2 \cdots & c_N \\ c_{N+1} & c_{N+2} \cdots & c_{2N} \\ \vdots & \vdots \ \ddots & \vdots \\ c_{(N-1)N+1} & \cdots \ \cdots & c_{N^2} \end{bmatrix} \cdot \begin{bmatrix} X_1 \\ X_2 \\ \vdots \\ X_N \end{bmatrix} = \begin{bmatrix} P_1 \\ P_2 \\ \vdots \\ P_N \end{bmatrix} \quad (6)$$

While, on the receiving side of CAZAC-OFDM, CAZAC decoder is inserted after FFT and calculates the inner product of the received symbol Y in frequency domain and CAZAC inverse matrix M^{-1}.

According to Figure 3, X is QAM Vector, P is Modulation Vector for IFFT, M is CAZAC Matrix. Then S as

$$\begin{aligned} S(t_n) &= \frac{1}{N}\sum_{k=0}^{N-1} P_k e^{j2\pi kn/N} \\ &= \sum_{k=0}^{N-1}\left\{\sum_{m=0}^{N-1} e^{j\pi(m+kN)^2/L} X_m\right\} e^{j2\pi kn/N} \\ &= \sum_{m=0}^{N-1} e^{\frac{j\pi m^2}{N^2}} X_m \left\{\sum_{k=0}^{N-1} e^{\frac{j2\pi k(m+n)}{N}} e^{j\pi k^2}\right\} \end{aligned} \quad (7)$$

Where k is an integer not less than 0, and the following equation is developed.

$$exp(j\pi k^2) = \begin{cases} 1 & (k : \text{even}) \\ -1 & (k : \text{odd}) \end{cases} \quad (8)$$

To lead the (9) from the (8).

$$\exp(j\pi k^2) = (-1)^k \quad (9)$$

Substituting the (9) into the (7) lead to the (10).

$$S(t_n) = \sum_{m=0}^{N-1} e^{j\pi m^2/N^2} X_m \left\{\sum_{k=0}^{N-1}\{-e^{j2\pi(m+n)/N}\}^k\right\} \quad (10)$$

The inside of {} in (10) is the sum of the geometric progression. Therefore, (11) is derived.

$$\sum_{k=0}^{N-1}\{-e^{j2\pi(m+n)/N}\}^k = \begin{cases} N & (-e^{j2\pi(m+n)/N} = 1) \\ 0 & (-e^{j2\pi(m+n)/N} \neq 1) \end{cases} \quad (11)$$

When $2\pi(m+n)/N = 1$, $2(m+n)/N$ is an integer and odd number. Also, n and m are $0 \leq n \leq N-1$, $0 \leq m \leq N-1$. (12) follows on account of these relationships.

$$m = \frac{N}{2} - n \ (mod\ N) \quad (12)$$

(13) is derived from (10), (11) and (12).

$$S(t_n) = X\left(\left(\frac{N}{2} - n\right)_{mod\ N}\right) C\left(\left(\frac{N}{2} - n\right)_{mod\ N}\right) \quad (13)$$

From the above, we have theoretically derived $S(t_n)$ for arbitrary n. The time waveform of CAZAC-OFDM is obtained by phase-rotating the value after mapping such as Figure 5. Therefore, PAPR can be reduced to a single carrier equivalent without using side information and without degrading BER characteristics. This is ideal as an improvement to PAPR.

In OFDM systems, cyclic prefixes are used to prevent inter-symbol interference [8][9]. And certainly, this technique can use cyclic prefix without disadvantages.

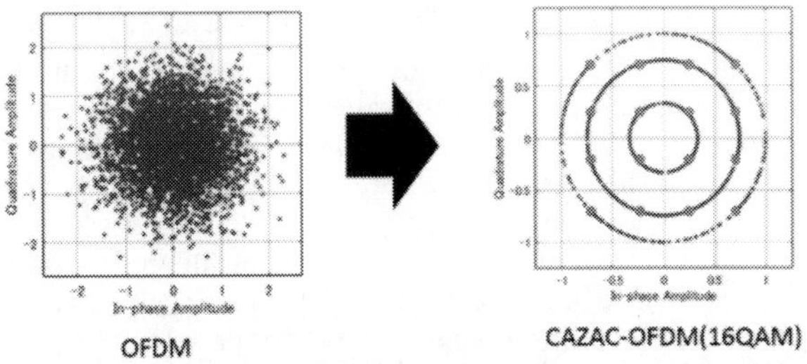

Figure 5. Time domain Signals with CAZAC precoder influenced by the value after mapping.

B. Frequency diversity effect of CAZAC-OFDM

By using CAZAC precoding for OFDM, it has a strong resistance to interference waves of a specific frequency. We consider the case where the signal of a specific subcarrier is lost due to frequency selective fading. In an ordinary OFDM system, each subcarrier has only one X component like Figure 6(a). Therefore, under the frequency selective fading, a specific subcarrier is strongly affected, and this specific data suffers serious damage like Figure 6 (b). As a result, BER deteriorates.

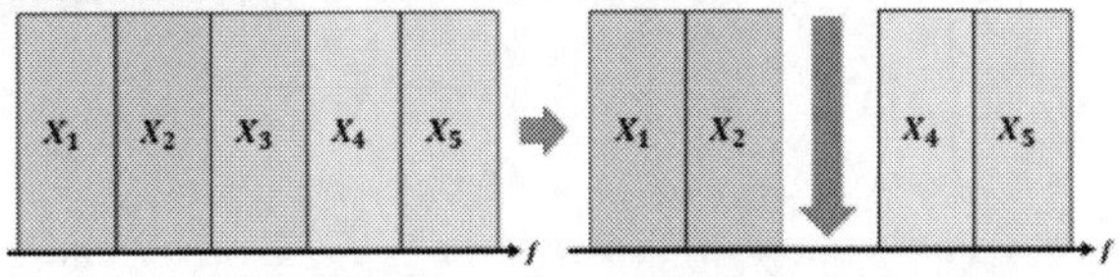

(a)Data X placement (b)Under frequency selective fading

Figure 6. The example of subcarrier deterioration of ordinary OFDM.

On the other hand, in a CAZAC-OFDM system, each subcarrier is possessing all X component averagely like Figure 7(a). Even if a narrow-band interference wave strongly affects a specific subcarrier, the influence of it is uniformly distributed to each data like Figure 7(b), and BER would be improved [10].

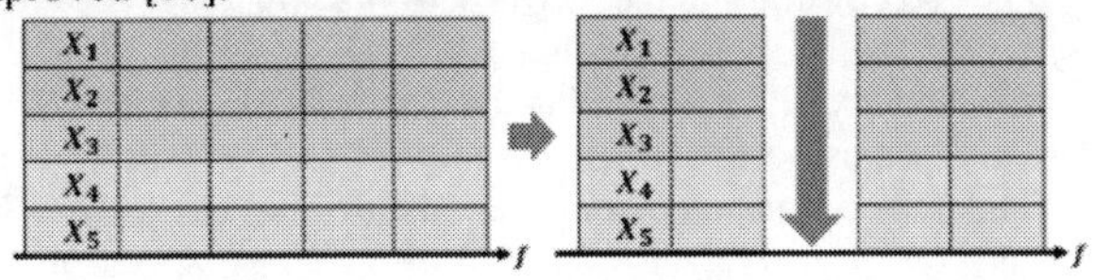

(a)Data X placement (b)Under frequency selective fading

Figure 7. The example of subcarrier deterioration of CAZAC-OFDM.

Thus, it's assumed that a CAZAC-OFDM system can reduce the influence of affected subcarriers by spreading X components to all subcarriers. This effect is due to the expression of CAZAC precoding signal P before IFFT. From (6), IFFT input signal for subcarrier is shown as (14).

$$\begin{aligned} P_n &= \sum_{k=0}^{N-1} C_{n(N+k)} X_k \\ &= C_{nN} X_0 + C_{n(N+1)} X_1 + C_{n(N+2)} X_2 + \cdots \\ &\quad + C_{n(2N-1)} X_{N-1} \end{aligned} \tag{14}$$

As shown in (14), P_n includes terms of all X components, i.e. $X_0, X_1, X_2, \ldots, X_{N-1}$. This means that each subcarrier is possessing all X component. Thus, the CAZAC-OFDM has a nature of spread-spectrum just like a CDMA.

C. *Null subcarrier allocation method for CAZAC-OFDM*

In CAZAC-OFDM, all subcarriers have all data components averagely. At the same time, it means that the null subcarrier can't be placed at the center of the frequency spectrum. Therefore, in this state OFDM cannot be applied to the current wireless standard.

In an ordinary OFDM system, zero-padding is performed on DC subcarrier in advance to obtain a null subcarrier, thereby setting the DC component to zero as (15).

$$X' = \begin{bmatrix} 0 \\ X_1 \\ \vdots \\ X_{N-1} \end{bmatrix} \tag{15}$$

On the other hand, in CAZAC-OFDM, if an operation as shown by (6) is performed on the original data information, when zero padding is performed in the same way as in ordinary OFDM, zero can't be generated in the CAZAC precoded signal as shown in (16), and it cannot be set as a null subcarrier.

$$\begin{aligned} X'_M = M \cdot X' &= \begin{bmatrix} c_1 & c_2 \cdots & c_N \\ c_{N+1} & c_{N+2} \cdots & c_{2N} \\ \vdots & \vdots \ \ddots & \vdots \\ c_{(N-1)N+1} & \cdots \ \cdots & c_{N^2} \end{bmatrix} \cdot \begin{bmatrix} 0 \\ X_1 \\ \vdots \\ X_{N-1} \end{bmatrix} \\ &= \begin{bmatrix} c_1 \cdot 0 + c_2 \cdot X_1 + \cdots c_N \cdot X_{N-1} = X'_{m1} \neq 0 \\ c_{N+1} \cdot 0 + c_{N+2} \cdot X_1 + \cdots c_{2N} \cdot X_{N-1} = X'_{m2} \neq 0 \\ \vdots \\ c_{(N-1)N+1} \cdot 0 + \cdots c_{N^2} \cdot X_{N-1} = X'_{mN} \neq 0 \end{bmatrix} \end{aligned} \tag{16}$$

Furthermore, if the size of the CAZAC matrix and the size of the IFFT do not match, the PAPR reduction effect can't be obtained. It means that IDFT must be performed including DC subcarriers. Therefore, the number of data subcarriers is increased by one compared to conventional OFDM. Thus, in order to use CAZAC-OFDM with the number of subcarriers of the current standard, it is necessary to use IDFT. Although the computational complexity $O(n^2)$ of the DFT is larger than the computational complexity $O(n\log n)$ of the FFT, it can be ignored considering the progress of the processor.

In the proposed system, DC subcarrier is set as null subcarrier while maintaining the orthogonality of the CAZAC sequence by performing the process of setting P_1 in (6) to zero. This process means that one data is lost, but CAZAC-OFDM can reduce adverse influence of affected subcarriers by spreading influence to all subcarriers. By using this frequency diversity effect of CAZAC-OFDM, lost data is demodulated.

IV. Simulation Results and Discussions

This chapter describes simulation specifications and results.

A. *Simulation specification*

To evaluate the performance of the proposed method, simulation was performed according to the specifications in Table 1. The simulation is performed in MATLAB using communications system toolbox. We compared the CCDF characteristics between ordinary OFDM and proposed method using the number of subcarriers used in the IEEE802.11ac standard. Next, the BER characteristics were compared while changing the value of the signal-to-noise ratio (SNR) of AWGN. At this time, fading is not taken into consideration. After that, we carried out the same comparison using the number of subcarriers used in the 4G-LTE standard.

For the forward error correction code and decoding, convolutional codes with coding rate $R = 1/2$, constraint length $K = 7$ and Viterbi decoding were applied.

Looking at Table 1, the number of data subcarriers in the conventional OFDM is one less than the number of proposed systems because transmission is performed without carrying data on DC subcarriers. On the other hand, although the DC subcarrier is set to be zero in the proposed system, it is demodulated using the frequency diversity effect, so it does not decrease the number of data subcarriers. Thus, the data rate of the proposed method is slightly improved as compared with ordinary OFDM.

TABLE I. Simulation Specification

Wireless Standards	IEEE802.11ac		4G-LTE	
Modulation	64QAM-OFDM		64QAM-OFDM	
DFT size	469		1201	
Method	Proposal	Conventional	Proposal	Conventional
Number of Data subcarriers	469	468	1201	1200
Bandwidth	160MHz		20MHz	
FEC	Convolutional code		Convolutional code	
Channel Model	AWGN		AWGN	

Figure 8 shows the configuration of the transmitter and receiver of the proposed system. One of the signals after CAZAC precoding processing is set to 0 so that only the center frequency of the signal after IDFT drops.

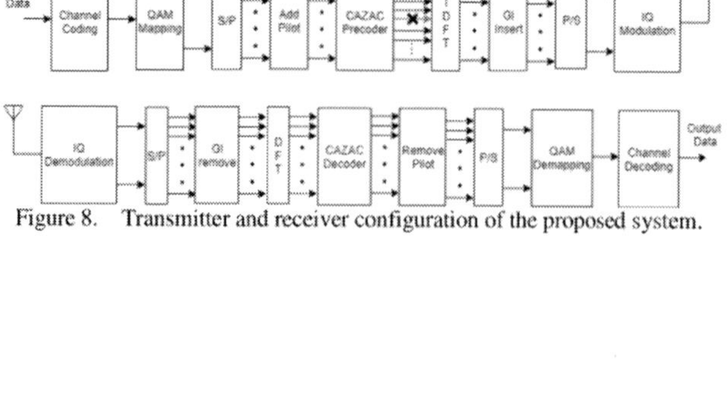

Figure 8. Transmitter and receiver configuration of the proposed system.

B. Simulation Results

First, we compare the OFDM and the proposed system for the CCDF characteristics and BER characteristics using the number of subcarriers used in the IEEE802.11ac standard as Figures 9 and 10. Here, conventional CAZAC-OFDM means it has no null subcarrier.

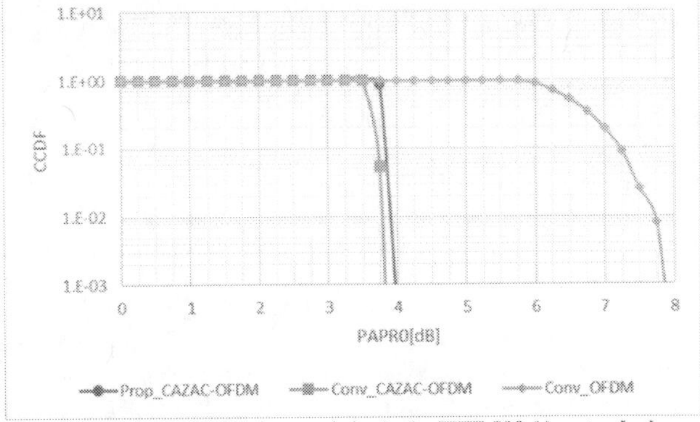

Figure 9. CCDF characteristics in the IEEE 802.11ac standard

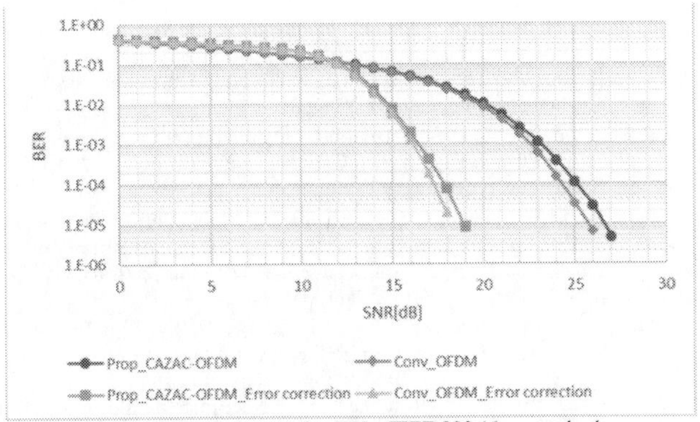

Figure 10. BER characteristics in the IEEE 802.11ac standard

Looking at Figure 9, by using the Null subcarrier allocation method like the proposed system, it is found that the proposed method can obtain CCDF characteristics almost the same as the ideal CAZAC-OFDM which does not adopt the DC subcarrier as Null. Therefore, it can be said that the proposed method can make the DC subcarrier Null without impairing the PAPR reduction effect of CAZAC-OFDM, and PAPR can be improved by about 4 dB when compared with CCDF characteristics of conventional OFDM.

Looking at Figure 10, at first, the CAZAC precoding process does not adversely affect the error correction by the convolutional code. Next, comparing the BER characteristics of ordinary OFDM and the proposed method, we can see that the BER of the proposed method is slightly deteriorating. This is because the data of the DC subcarrier is lost when the DC subcarrier is set to Null, and therefore the influence thereof appears even if the frequency diversity effect is used.

From the above results, it can be said that the proposed method in the IEEE802.11ac standard is a method which can obtain slight improvement of data rate and dramatic improvement of CCDF characteristics in exchange for slight deterioration of BER characteristic compared to conventional OFDM.

Next, similar comparisons using the number of subcarriers used in the 4G-LTE standard are shown in Figures 11 and 12. At this time, the spectrum of the proposed system with null subcarrier arranged is shown in the figure 13.

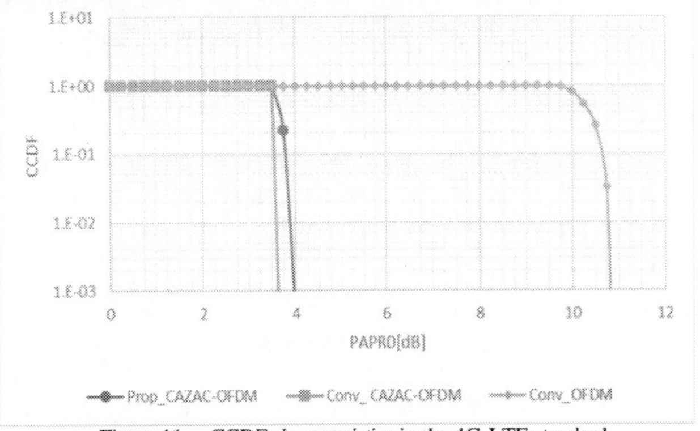

Figure 11. CCDF characteristics in the 4G-LTE standard

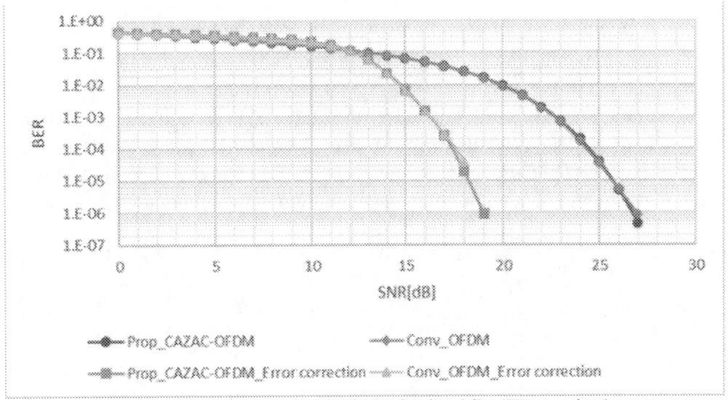

Figure 12. BER characteristics in the 4G-LTE standard

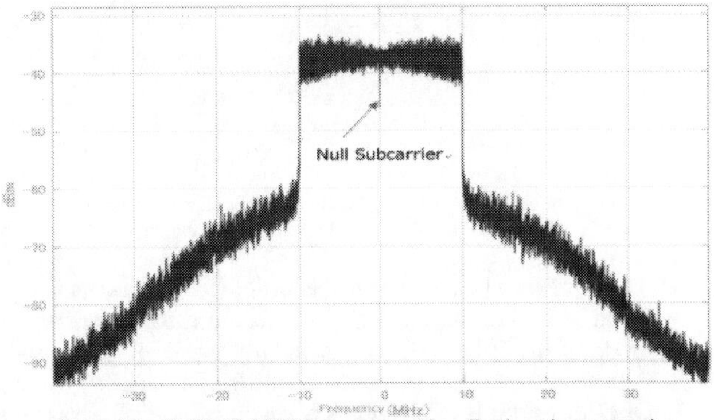

Figure 13. CAZAC-OFDM spectrum with null subcarrier arranged

Comparing Figure 11 with Figure 9, CAZAC-OFDM shows no change in CCDF characteristics even if the number of subcarriers increases. This is because CAZAC-OFDM uses the power pattern of QAM mapping as the output power after IFFT processing without depending on the number of subcarriers. On the other hand, since the conventional OFDM multiplexes a plurality of subcarriers intact, the peak power thereof increases with an increase in the number of subcarriers.

Therefore, the PAPR also increases with the number of subcarriers, which shows that the PAPR is very high in the 4G-LTE standard where the number of subcarriers is 1200. It means that PAPR can be improved as the number of subcarriers increases compared with OFDM in the proposed method, and here we can see that PAPR can be improved by about 7dB.

Looking at Figure 12, It was found that the BER performance of the proposed method is almost consistent with that of ordinary OFDM regardless of whether or not error correction is performed. Compared to Figure 10, it can be said that the frequency diversity effect by CAZAC precoding becomes more powerful as the number of subcarriers is larger, and in the 4G-LTE standard, the negative influence generated when the DC subcarrier is made Null is ignored. From the above results, it can be said that the proposed method in the 4G-LTE standard can improve the data rate slightly and dramatically improve the CCDF characteristics while maintaining the same BER characteristic as the conventional OFDM.

From these results, it was found that the BER characteristics differed depending on the number of subcarriers. Here, it is evaluated how much the deterioration degree of the BER characteristic with respect to the number of subcarriers under the simulation specification similar to Table 1 is. The difference in SNR at the error rate 10^{-3} point when only the number of data subcarriers is changed is shown in Figure 14. We evaluated using 234, 468 data subcarriers used in the IEEE802.11ac standard, 1200 subcarriers used in the 4G-LTE standard and subcarriers between them.

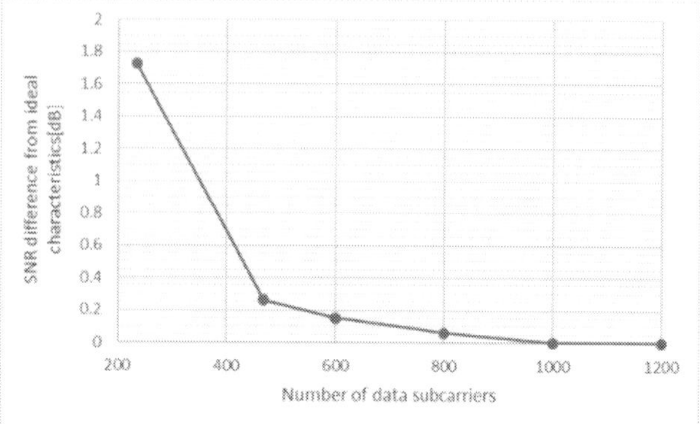

Figure 14. Degree of degradation of BER characteristics with respect to the number of data subcarriers

From this figure, when the proposed method is applied using 234 subcarriers, which is the medium-band transmission mode of the IEEE 802.11ac standard, the BER performance will be deteriorated by about 1.76 dB compared to ordinary OFDM. And it is difficult to say that it is practical. It is about 0.26 dB worse in the case of 468 subcarriers which is the broadband transmission mode, which can be said to be a practical range considering that PAPR can be greatly improved if this degree is deteriorated. And at 1000 subcarriers, the degradation of BER characteristics was not completely seen.

It has resulted that only advantages are obtained in mobile communication exceeding 1000 subcarriers and terrestrial digital broadcasting. In recent years, communication using a large number of subcarriers tends to be performed in order to enable further high-speed communication, including a wireless LAN. This is a promising trend for the proposed system.

V. CONCLUSIONS

In CAZAC-OFDM that reduces high PAPR while taking advantage of OFDM, PAPR can be reduced while zero DC component by applying Null subcarrier placement method utilizing frequency diversity effect. It means that CAZAC-OFDM can be adapted to current wireless standards. Moreover, it is confirmed that the deterioration of the BER characteristic decreases as the number of subcarriers increases. As a result, in the 4G-LTE standard, we confirmed that the proposed system can be used without degrading BER while suppressing PAPR to the equivalent of single carrier. These results meet recent trends that are changing from narrowband transmission to broadband transmission in order to transmit data with large amount of information at high speed.

REFERENCES

[1] A. Ghosh, R. Ratasuk, B. Mondal, N.Mangalvedhe, and T.Thomas,"LTE-advanced:Next-generationWireless Broadband Technology," IEEE Wireless Communications, vol. 17, no. 3, June 2010, pp. 10–22.

[2] Z. Feng, et al , "Performance-enhanced direct detection optical OFDM transmission with CAZAC equalization", in 2015 IEEE Photonics Technology Letters, pp.1507-1510

[3] K. Miyazawa, T. Kimura and M. Muraguchi, "Proposal of visible light OFDM system with CAZAC equalization" in 2017 23rd Asia-Pacific Conference on Communications (APCC), pp.491-496

[4] Y. Sugai, Y. Shirato, T. Kimura and M. Muraguchi, "PAPR and Spectral Control Procedure for OFDM Wireless Systems Using CAZAC Equalization," The Fourteenth Advanced International Conference on Telecommunications (AICT) 2018, pp.75-80, July 2018.

[5] I. Baig and V. Jeoti, "PAPR Reduction in OFDM Systems: Zadoff-Chu Matrix Transform Based Pre/Post-Coding Techniques," in Proc. of the 2nd International Conference on Computational Intelligence, Communication Systems and Networks, pp. 373-377, July 2010.

[6] H. Seung, Hee and L. Jae, Hong, "An Overview of Peak-to-average Power Ratio Reduction Techniques for Multicarrier Transmission," IEEE Wireless Communications, vol. 12, no. 2, Apr. 2005, pp. 56–65.

[7] R. Ishioka, T. Kimura and M. Muraguchi, "A Proposal for a New OFDM Wireless System using a CAZAC Precoding Scheme," Proc. AICT 2017, pp. 47-51, June 2017.

[8] D. Darsena, G. Gelli, L. Paura, F. Verde, "A constrained maximum-SINR NBI-resistant receiver for OFDM systems", IEEE Trans. Signal Process., vol. 55, pp. 3032-3047, June 2007.

[9] D. Darsena, F. Verde, "Minimum-mean-output-energy blind adaptive channel shortening for multicarrier SIMO transceivers", IEEE Trans. Signal Process., vol. 55, pp. 5755-5771, Jan. 2007.

[10] K. Miyazawa, T. Kimura, M. Muraguchi, "Proposal of visible light OFDM system with CAZAC equalization," 23rd Asia-Pacific Conference on Communications (APCC), pp.491-496, Dec. 2017

A New Technique of Symbol Synchronization for OFDM Systems with CAZAC Precoding

Ryoju Tachikawa and Masahiro Muraguchi
Dept. of Electrical Engineering
Tokyo University of Science
6-3-1 Niijuku, Katsushika-ku, Tokyo, 125-8585, Japan
e-mail: 4315076@ed.tus.ac.jp, murag@ee.kagu.tus.ac.jp

Abstract— **As Orthogonal Frequency Division Multiplex (OFDM) signal is essentially a sum of multiple subcarrier signals aligned in frequency domain, its waveform in time domain is a waveform that changes like Gaussian noise, and thus the amplitude of time-domain waveform has high Peak-to-Average Power Ratio (PAPR). Constant Amplitude Zero Auto-Correlation (CAZAC) waveform precoding transforms from an OFDM waveform into a waveform kind of single-carrier modulation signal. In this paper, a new technique of symbol synchronization for OFDM systems with CAZAC precoding is proposed. By the CAZAC precoding, the waveform of one OFDM symbol can be changed to the waveform of Zadoff-Chu sequence by inputting proper data sequence. Here, the Zadoff-Chu sequence, known as one of CAZAC sequence, has excellent autocorrelation characteristics and is utilized as a strong tool for symbol synchronization in 4G-LTE systems.**

Keywords- OFDM; Zadoff-Chu sequence; CAZAC precorder; symbol synchronization;

I. Introduction

Currently, OFDM modulation scheme is mainly used in wireless communication systems: Wi-Fi, 4G-LTE, digital terrestrial broadcasting, etc. OFDM signals have high spectrum efficiency. However, as OFDM signal is essentially a sum of multiple subcarrier signals aligned in frequency domain, its waveform in time domain is a waveform that changes like Gaussian noise, and thus the amplitude of time domain waveform has high PAPR.

To reduce the PAPR, many techniques have been proposed: Selected Mapping (SLM), Active Constellation Extension (ACE), Partial Transmit Sequence (PTS), etc. [1]. The technique that PAPR was improved drastically in CAZAC-OFDM which used CAZAC precoding have been proposed [2]-[4]. CAZAC precoder makes the PAPR of multilevel quadrature amplitude modulation (M-QAM) OFDM signals into the PAPR of M-QAM single-carrier signals.

CAZAC-OFDM has an extremely unique time-domain waveforms of transmitted signals. The feature of the waveforms is that it consists of signals of which the phase of mapping data is rotated. Here, the mapping data means I-Q modulation data for subcarriers. In addition, the amount of phase rotation and the time ordering are uniquely determined. Thus, processing data sequence properly, the waveform of one OFDM symbol can be generated optionally.

OFDM systems require exact timing estimation on the receiver side [5]. If OFDM symbols are demodulated without exact timing, phase rotation and distortion in amplitude occurred. It results in much degradation of the bit-error rates. Therefore, most of OFDM systems employ preamble blocks and cyclic-prefix periods for synchronization.

In this paper, a new technique of symbol synchronization of OFDM systems with CAZAC precoding is proposed [6]. By using CAZAC precoding, the time-domain waveform of one OFDM symbol can be changed to the waveform of Zadoff-Chu sequence by inputting proper data sequence. Here, the Zadoff-Chu sequence, known as one of CAZAC sequence, has constant amplitude and excellent autocorrelation characteristics and is utilized as a tool for symbol synchronization in 4G-LTE systems [7]-[9]. If we accord the length of Zadoff-Chu sequence with the length of one OFDM symbol, for example, 64 Fast Fourier Transform (FFT) points, the OFDM symbol consisting of Zadoff-Chu sequence can be used for one unit of preamble sequence. Moreover, the technique is expected to be used in both of packet and continuous mode OFDM systems. By replacing data symbols with the Zadoff-Chu symbols periodically, the technique can apply to the synchronization for continues mode OFDM systems, such as digital terrestrial broadcasting systems.

The rest of this paper is organized as follows. In Section 2, we describe OFDM system, CAZAC-OFDM system and proposed system. In Section 3, we describe performance evaluation and computer simulation results. Finally, we conclude this paper in Section5.

II. Proposed System

In this section, we describe OFDM system, CAZAC-OFDM system and proposed system. We first describe OFDM system and then, we explain CAZAC precoding technique. Next, we explain proposed system.

A. *OFDM System*

In OFDM system, N-point inverse Fast Fourier Transform (IFFT) is taken for the transmitted symbols $\boldsymbol{X} = [X_0, X_1, \dots, X_{N-1}]^T$, so as generate $\boldsymbol{x} = [x_0, x_1, \dots, x_{N-1}]^T$, the samples for the sum of N orthogonal subcarrier signals. Let $\boldsymbol{y}$ donate the received sample that corresponds to $\boldsymbol{x}$ with the additive noise w (i.e.,$\boldsymbol{y} = \boldsymbol{x} + \boldsymbol{w}$). Taking the N −point FFT of the received samples, $\boldsymbol{y} = [y_0, y_1, \dots, y_{N-1}]^T$, the noisy version of transmitted symbols $\boldsymbol{Y}_l = [y_0, y_1, \dots, y_{N-1}]^T$ can be obtained in the receiver.

As all subcarriers are of the finite duration T, the spectrum of the OFDM signal can be considered as the sum of the frequency-shifted sinc functions in the frequency domain as illustrated in Figure 1, where the overlapped neighboring sinc functions are spaced by $1/T$. As the OFDM signals are orthogonal, they are inter-carrier interference (ICI)-free. The OFDM scheme also inserts a guard interval in the time domain, which mitigates the inter-symbol interference (ISI) between OFDM symbols [5].

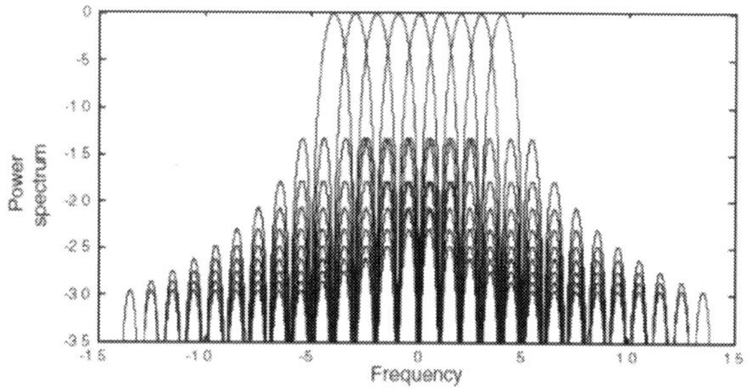

Figure 1. Power spectrum of OFDM signal

B. CAZAC-OFDM

CAZAC sequence is constant amplitude and provides a good cross-correlation property. Therefore, CAZAC sequence is used in wireless communication systems such as channel estimation and time synchronization. The Zadoff-Chu (ZC) sequence c_k which is one of the CAZAC sequences is represented as

$$c_k = e^{\frac{j\pi k^2}{N^2}} \tag{1}$$

Where $k = 1,2, \dots, N^2 - 1$ donates the sequence index. In this paper, CAZAC $N \times N$ precoding matrix M is represented as

$$\boldsymbol{M} = \begin{bmatrix} c_1 & \cdots & c_N \\ c_{N+1} & \cdots & c_{2N} \\ \vdots & \ddots & \vdots \\ c_{(N-1)N+1} & \cdots & c_{N^2} \end{bmatrix} \tag{2}$$

In CAZAC-OFDM system, we precode by multiplying this matrix $\boldsymbol{M}$ before IFFT.

Time signal in CAZAC-OFDM is obtained by multiplying matrix $\boldsymbol{M}$ before IFFT. The time signal x_n can be represented as

$$x_n = X\left(\left(\frac{N}{2} - n\right)_{mod\ N}\right) C\left(\left(\frac{N}{2} - n\right)_{mod\ N}\right) \tag{3}$$

where $X(n)$ is a value after data mapping. Therefore, the time signal in CAZAC-OFDM is a value after data mapping phase rotated (Figure 2).

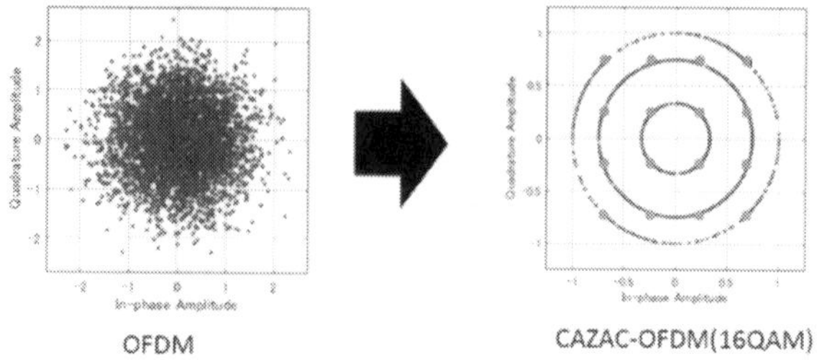

Figure 2. Plots on complex phase plane of OFDM and CAZAC-OFDM

C. Zadoff-Chu Sequence

ZC sequence is currently used in the following three applications in LTE/LTE-advanced.

1). Reference sequence of uplink reference signal

It is required that the uplink reference signal has highly autocorrelation and the power fluctuation is small in the time domain. Therefore, ZC sequence having the characteristic that the power is constant in the frequency domain and the time domain is used.

2). Main Sync Signal for Cell Search

The cell search is the following before doing the terminal to communicate with LTE network.

· detect and synchronize cells in the network

· receive and decode necessary information for communication within the cell and appropriate operation.

The ZC sequence is used as the main synchronization signal to assist these cell searches.

3). A Random Access Preamble

Random access is what the terminal does in order to establish uplink synchronization. By sending the random access preamble to the base station by the terminal, the base station estimates the transmission timing of the terminal. As this random access preamble, the ZC sequence is used [7]-[9].

D. Synchronizing Symbol Timing

Synchronizing symbol timing is synchronization processing to obtain OFDM symbols of the reference. The process decides FFT window position. After establishing the synchronization, we can demodulate that received OFDM signals. In packet mode, preamble signals as short as possible is transmitted before the data to establish symbol timing synchronization. It can be roughly classified into an autocorrelation type using a repetitive signal section and a cross correlation type using a matched filter of a preamble provided in a demodulator (Figure 3) [5][10].

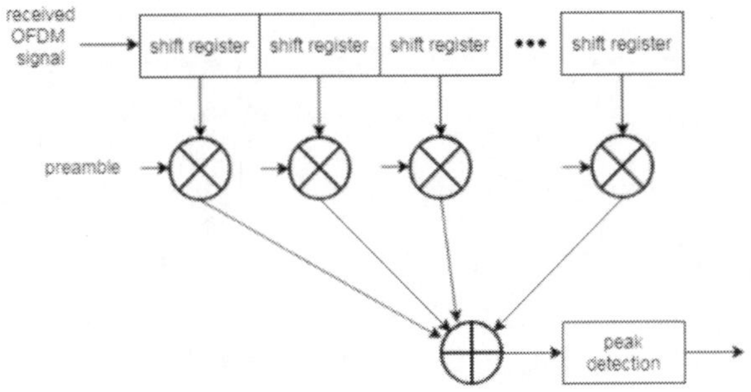

Figure 3. Cross correlation type

E. Transmission Mode

When the OFDM signals continue for a long time, this scheme is called continuous mode. In this case, some time is allowed for establishing frequency and symbol timing synchronization in the receiver. Therefore, establishing the synchronizations gradually is possible by using pilot signals embed in OFDM signals. A schematic of the signal in continuous mode is shown in Figure 4.

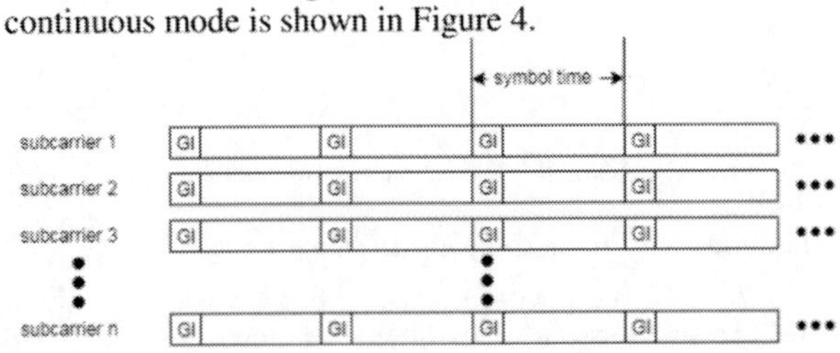

Figure 4. Continuous mode signal

On the other hand, OFDM signals separated by a certain time are transmitted and received in packet mode which are applied in wireless LAN and mobile communication. In the receiver, it is necessary to wait at all times and establish synchronizations in a short period of time. Signals to establish synchronizations called preamble are assigned in packet mode. By using this preamble for synchronizations, we can execute synchronization processing quickly and accurately, which are required for packet mode. A schematic of the signal in packet mode is shown in Figure 5.

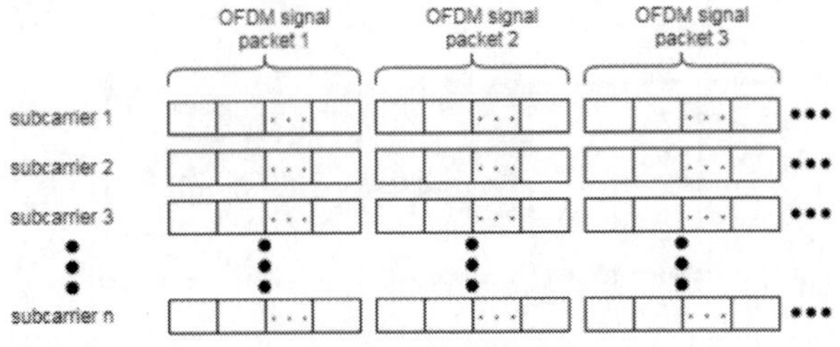

Figure 5. Packet mode signal

F. Oversampling

PAPR for the discrete-time base band signal $x[n]$ may not be the same as that fore the continuous-time base band signal $x(t)$. In fact, the PAPR for $x[n]$ is lower than that for $x(t)$, simply because $x[n]$ may not have all peaks of $x(t)$. In practice, the PAPR for the continuous-time baseband signal can be measured only after implementing the actual hardware, including digital-to-analog convertor (DAC). In other words, measurement of the PAPR for the continuous-time baseband signal is not straight forward. Therefore, there must be some means of estimating the PAPR from the discrete-time signal $x[n]$. Fortunately, it is known that $x[n]$ can show almost the same PAPR as $x(t)$ if it is L-times interpolated (oversampled) where $L \geq 4$.

It inserts $(L-1)$ zeros between the samples of $x[n]$ to yield $w[m]$ as follows:

$$w[m] = \begin{cases} x[m/L], & for\ m = 0, \pm L, \pm 2L, \dots \\ 0, & elsewhere \end{cases} \quad (4)$$

A low pass filter (LPF) is used to construct the L −times-interpolated version of $x[n]$ from $w[m]$. For the LPF with an impulse response of $h[m]$, the L-times-interpolated output $y[m]$ can be represented as

$$y[m] = \sum_{k=-\infty}^{\infty} h[k]w[m-k] \quad (5)$$

Figures 6 and 7 illustrate the signals and their spectra appearing in the oversampling process with a sampling frequency of 2kHz to yield a result of interpolation with $L = 4$. Referring to these figures, the IFFT output signal $x[n]$ can be expressed in terms of the L −times interpolated version as

$$x'[m] = \frac{1}{\sqrt{L \cdot N}} \sum_{k=0}^{L \cdot N-1} X'[k] \cdot e^{\frac{j2\pi m \Delta f k}{L \cdot N}}, \quad (6)$$
$$m = 0,1,\dots,NL-1$$

with

$$X'[k] = \begin{cases} X[k], & for\ 0 \leq k < \frac{N}{2}\ and\ NL - \frac{N}{2} < k < NL \\ 0, & elsewhere \end{cases} \quad (7)$$

where N, Δf, and $X[k]$ donate the FFT size (or the total number of subcarriers), the subcarrier spacing and the complex symbol carried over a subcarrier k, respectively.

In the case of 4-times oversampling, the time waveform has a form obtained by interpolating between the original two signal points with three points [5].

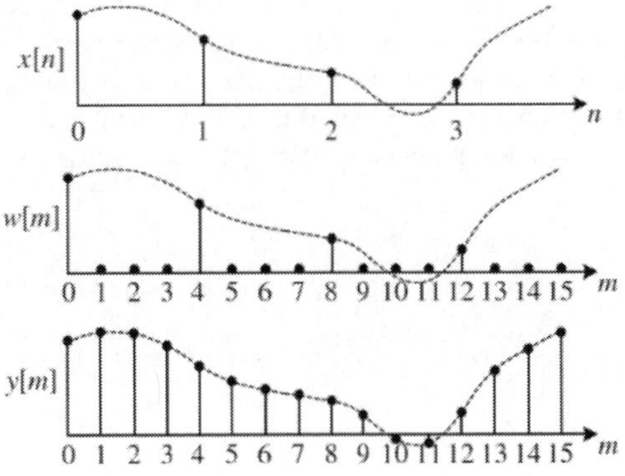

Figure 6. Interpolation with $L = 4$ in the time domain

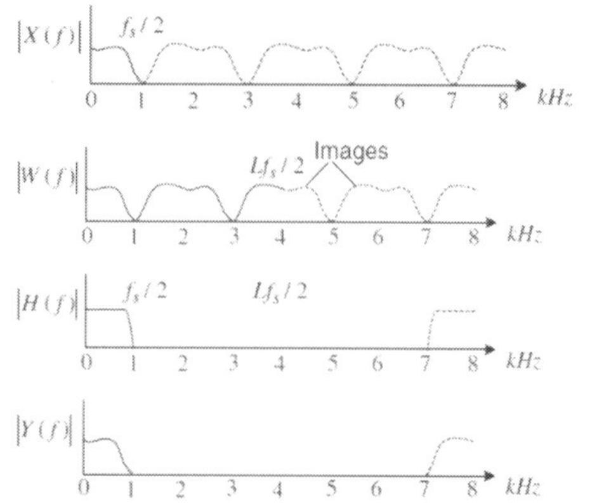

Figure 7. Interpolation with $L = 4$ in the frequency domain

G. Processed Preamble

Using the characteristics of the transmission waveform of CAZAC-OFDM shown in (1), we estimated the symbol timing by inserting a preamble which becomes the ZC sequence after CAZAC precoding and IFFT. From (1), the relation between before and after modulation of CAZAC-OFDM on the transmission side is as shown in the Figure 8. From (1) and (3), the amount of phase rotation θ at each subcarrier is represented as

$$\theta = \pi \frac{\left(\left(\frac{N}{2} - n\right)_N\right)^2}{N^2} \tag{8}$$

From these, we can shape the time waveform to desired waveform by processing CAZAC precoding and IFFT after reversing the order and giving the opposite phase rotation in advance. Then, rather than sending the preamble from the physical layer, it can treat the same way as data and send the preamble as a transmission waveform. In the conventional packet mode transmission system, when transmitting a preamble, it is transmitted using another route as shown Figure 9. Therefore, the switching operation is required at the time of transmission of data and the transmission of data. However, if the above process is used, the preamble can be transmitted without switching. Therefore, it is expected that the preamble can be embedded and used for synchronization not only in the packet mode but also in the continuous mode. In other words, it is possible to use the same system when synchronization processing and data is transmitted.

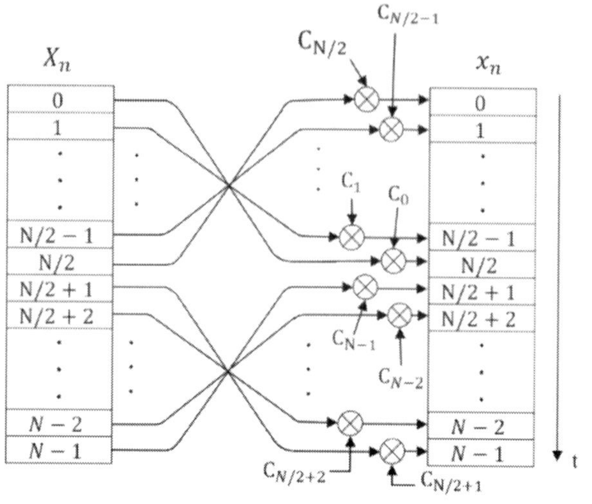

Figure 8. Schematic diagram of the symbol configuration before and after modulation of CAZAC-OFDM

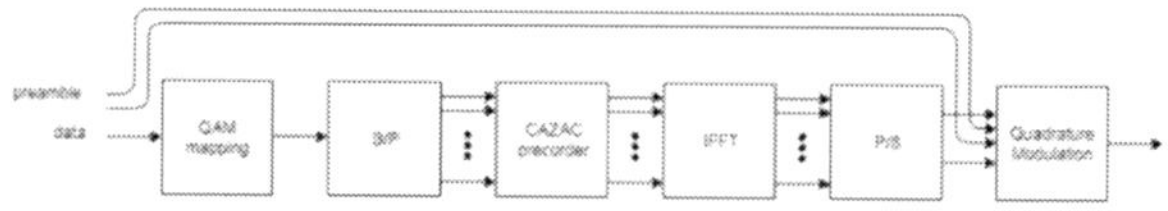

Figure 9. Conventional transmitter model

H. Proposed Flame Configuration

Proposed flame configuration is as shown in the Figure 10. The preamble is transmitted for three periods at first. Subsequently, data is transmitted. Data is demodulated by the timing decided from the preamble. Used preamble is ZC sequence and is represented as

$$ZC = \exp\left(-j\pi \frac{(k-1)^2}{64}\right) (k = 1,2,\ldots,64) \tag{9}$$

The autocorrelation property of this sequence is as shown in the shown Figure 11. In this simulation, we assume the frequency synchronization and time synchronization to be perfectly synchronized. Therefore, the preamble is used for symbol synchronization.

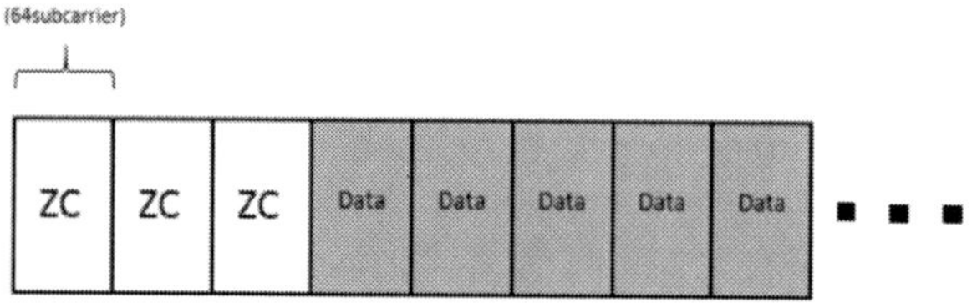

Figure 10. Proposed flame configuration(time domain)

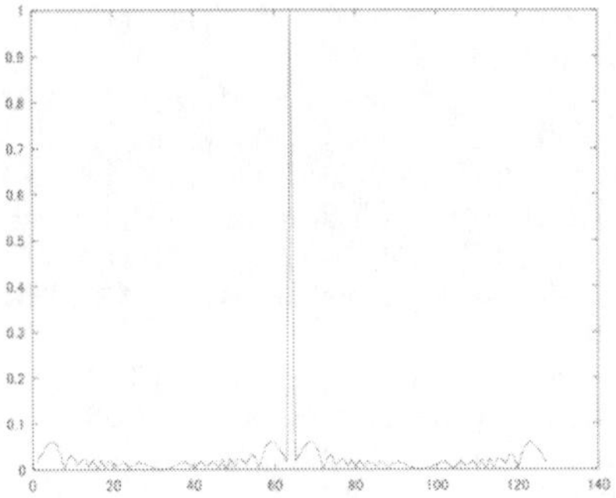

Figure 11. Autocorrelation properties of the ZC sequence

I. *Transmitter and Receiver Model*

Proposed transmitter and receiver model are as shown in the Figures 12 and 13. In the receiver, we prepared the ZC sequence and cross-correlated with the received preamble. The timing of the peak was detected, and the symbol timing was estimated.

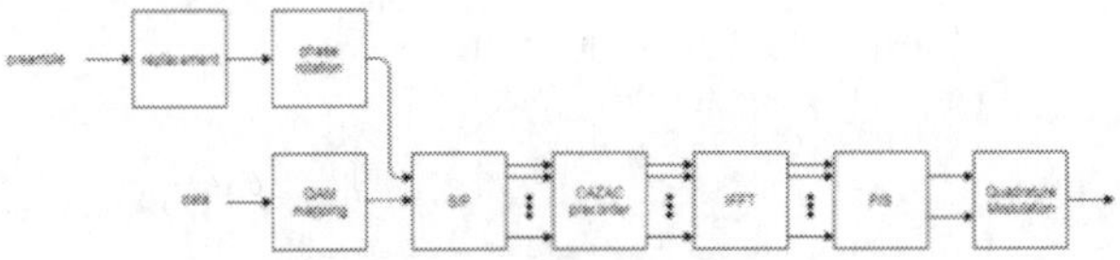

Figure 12. Transmitter model

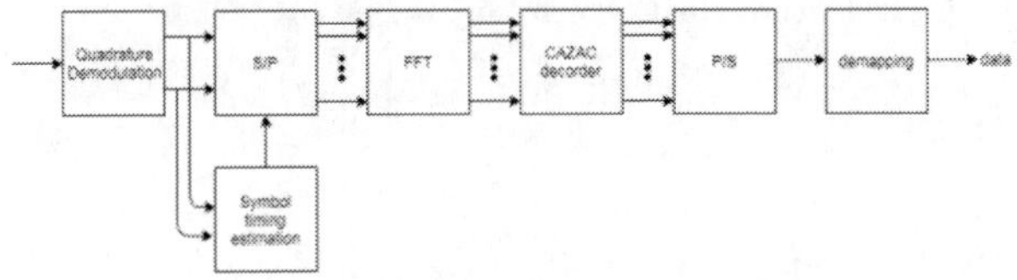

Figure 13. Receiver model

III. Performance Evaluation

In this section, we describe performance evaluation of proposed system. We present simulation results to discuss the performance of the proposed synchronization technique.

A. *Setup*

In order to evaluate the performance of the proposed system, we simulated by MATLAB. Table 1 summarizes the simulation specifications. Bandwidth, symbol length and guard interval are based on the specification of IEEE802.11a. We also do 4-times oversampling at the same time. Therefore, prepared the ZC sequence was expanded fourfold as in the Figure 14. With the above simulation specifications, we examined whether synchronization is established while changing the SNR.

TABLE I. Simulation Specification

Modulation	16QAM-CAZAC-OFDM
Bandwidth	20MHz
Carrier frequency	600MHz
Number of subcarriers	64
Symbol time	4μs
Guard interval time	0.8μs
Channel model	AWGN
Length of the ZC sequence	64

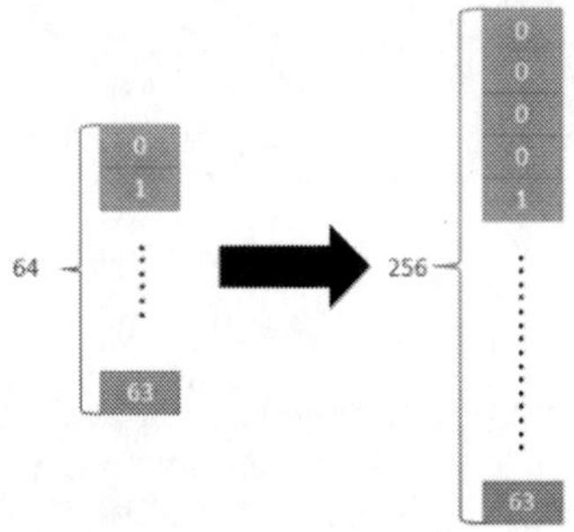

Figure 14. Expansion of the ZC sequence

B. *Simulation Results*

Figure 15 plots the probabilities of synchronizations versus SNR. In the 4-times oversample, the probability of synchronizations is 1 when the SNR is 13 dB or more. Here, the BER characteristic in conventional 16-QAM-CAZAC-OFDM and proposed system is as shown in Figure 16. The BER in proposed system has characteristics similar to that of conventional CAZAC-OFDM. The BER at which the signal can be reproduced using error correction code is 10^{-3} or less becomes reproducible in the range of 13dB or more. In that range, we confirmed that the probability of synchronization can be 1 in 4-times oversample. We confirmed that BER does not deteriorated if synchronization is established. We confirmed that we can establish synchronization using the autocorrelation property of the ZC sequence.

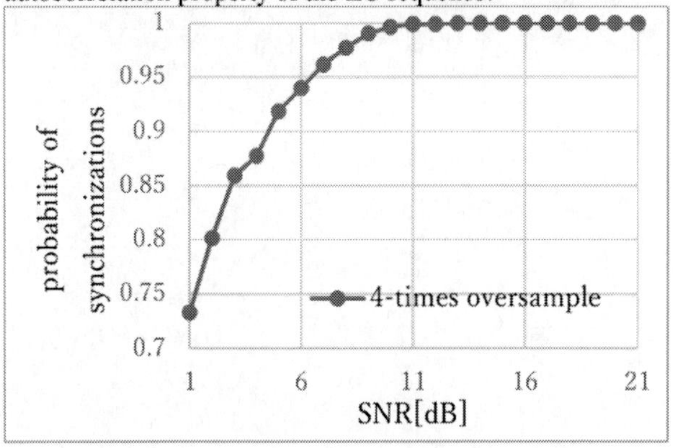

Figure 15. Probabilities of synchronizations versus SNR

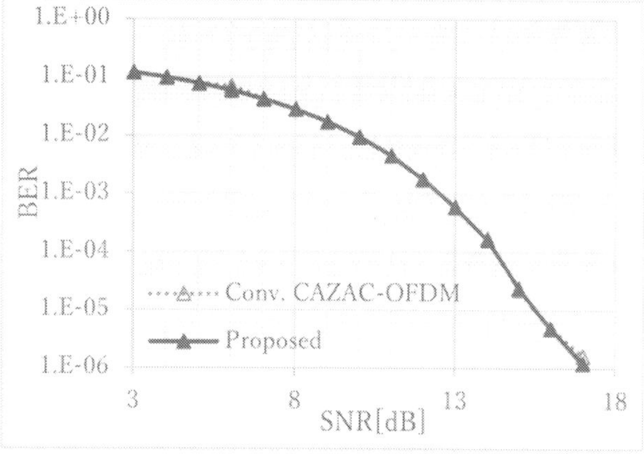

Figure 16. BER performances of the 16QAM-CAZAC-OFDM

IV. CONCLUSION

In this paper, we proposed a new technique of symbol synchronization of OFDM systems with CAZAC precoding. CAZAC-OFDM is one of the useful PAPR reduction techniques. Here, we also showed that the waveform of one OFDM symbol can be changed to the waveform of ZC sequence by processing data sequence properly. Using this technique, we demonstrated that a symbol synchronization can be established. Since the preamble can be treated as data, synchronization can be established using the preamble not only in the packet mode but also in the continuous mode. We have confirmed that once the synchronization is established, the BER does not deteriorate.

REFERENCES

[1] S. H. Han and J. H. Lee "An Overview of Peak-to-Average Power Ratio Reduction Techniques for Multicarrier Transmission", IEEE Wireless Communications, vol. 12, no.2, pp. 56-65, Apr. 2005.

[2] R. Ishioka, T. Kimura and M. Muraguchi, "A Proposal for a New OFDM Wireless System using a CAZAC Equalization Scheme," Proc. AICT 2017, June 2017, pp. 47-51.

[3] Y. Sugai, Y. Shirato, T. Kimura and M. Muraguchi, "PAPR and Spectral Control Procedure for OFDM Wireless Systems Using CAZAC Equalization," Proc. AICT 2018, July 2018, pp. 75-80.

[4] T. Onoda, T. Kimura and M. Muraguchi, "Proposal of Power Saving Techniques for Wireless Terminals Using CAZAC-OFDM Scheme," Proc. AICT 2018, July 2018, pp. 115-120.

[5] Y. S. Cho, J. Kim, W. Y. Yang and C. G. Kang, "MIMO-OFDM Wireless Communications with MATLAB", John Wiley & Sons (Asia) Ltd , 2010

[6] M. M. U. GUL, S. Lee and X. Ma "Robust synchronization for OFDM employing Zadoff-Chu sequence", 2012 46th Annual Conference on Information Sciences and Systems (CISS), pp. 1-6, Mar. 2012.

[7] H. Zarrinkoub "Understanding LTE with MATLAB", John Wiley & Sons Ltd, 2014

[8] C.Gessner, A. Roessler and M.Kottkamp "UMTS Long Term Evolution (LTE) – Technology Introduction Application Note" ROHDE&SCHWARZ, 2012

[9] J. Zyren and W. McCoy, "Overview of the 3GPP Long Term Evolution Physical Layer", Freescale, 2007

[10] T. M. Schmidl and D. C. Cox "Robust frequency and timing synchronization for OFDM", IEEE Transactions on Communications, pp. 1613-1621, Dec.1997

Comparison of 4G and 5G Network Simulators

Christos Bouras*†, Georgios Diles†, Apostolos Gkamas ‡, Andreas Zacharopoulos†
*Computer Technology Institute and Press "Diophantus", Patras, Greece
†Computer Engineering and Informatics Dept., University of Patras, Greece
‡University Ecclesiastical Academy of Vella, Ioannina, Greece
Email: bouras@cti.gr, diles@ceid.upatras.gr, gkamas@aeavellas.gr, st1003768@ceid.upatras.gr

***Abstract*—Network simulation is a technique of utmost importance to evaluate new network performance, verify new algorithms and analyze various network topologies. It is used to find results to be expected from a hardware setup without the need for actual implementation. For this reason, there is a plethora of Network Simulation Software applied to different scenarios to evaluate theories and hypotheses. The aim of this paper is to study the most common Simulators regarding the deployment of 5G networks, provide a detailed comparison featuring their main advantages and showcasing potential defects and support the academic community, offering the required data to help choose the necessary one.**

***Keywords*–Simulator; Comparison; 4G; 5G.**

I. Introduction

The exponential increase in mobile data traffic has driven current wireless networks towards their limits and as a result, researchers should be highly motivated to create powerful next-generation mobile networks, based on the current networks trends and needs of that era. It is indicative that due to popularization of smart devices and development of Internet services that the industry faces during the 4th Generation mobile networks (4G) era, advancements in mobile networks to accommodate such demand has become necessary. Considering that the mobile data traffic flow is expected to increase a thousand percent by the end of this decade, the current research on this generation of mobile networks and the next (5G) is actively moving with a high pace. Vendors and operators are already involved in 5G testing and trials, which is soon expected to lead to a finalized standard.

Network technology is advancing rapidly as well and, accompanied by expansion of network scale, have made it extremely hard to analyse networks. It goes without saying that testing algorithms and protocols is extremely important since their launching in large scale is prohibitive because of uncertainty of its outcome. Network schemes can be tested either by analytical modelling or with the help of simulation tools. Although analytical modelling can indeed have very realistic results, it does not come without drawbacks, most notably the lack of precision regarding energy and memory needs and can be proven to be very expensive.

On the other hand, network simulation is used to imitate over time the operation of a real-world system enabling the observation of services and applications the network could support. It allows the researchers to model a network's behaviour given the proposed changes, either with the use of mathematical formulas to calculate the interaction between the various entities of the network, or actually recording and recapping information that emerge from it. It provides the capability to manipulate most of the environment attributes to evaluate the system behaviour under different circumstances and allows the comparison between alternatives to optimize network performance. These developments make network simulators an important requirement for scientific researchers around the globe. It comes with relatively low cost and small to no risk, enabling researchers to decide and predict on network behaviour with greater convenience, compared to practical networks. As a consequence, there have been attempts to create diverse softwares for network simulation to test new algorithms and simulate network behaviour. But choosing the most suitable simulator for each occasion is not always an easy decision.

Picking the right simulation tool is a subject that has been troubling scientists for many years. Actually, it is not the first attempt to compare simulation software, as there have been a couple published in recent years. Challenges of system-level simulation and performance evaluation and the importance of creating a stable and reliable tool for 5G in consideration of the new needs and technologies that emerge are discussed in [1]. One example is the work presented in [2] and [3], where the comparison of popular network simulators is shown.

A performance analysis which includes open source platforms simulating a MANET routing protocol is presented in [4]. There are researches testing different routing protocols [5] in different simulators with different network parameters to evaluate the performance of network protocols. A more detailed comparison, in which in addition to open simulators, commercial platforms are also included, is presented in [6].

In this paper, we analyse both commercial and open source state-of-the-art simulators presenting performance comparison regarding 4G and 5G networks in an attempt to provide reference to the scientific community when there is a need to choose the right software for simulation. Currently, the majority of the state of the art simulation tools follow discrete event simulation methodology. This is the reason why, we will only focus on this technique. In [7], researchers discussed current simulators with different characteristics in different aspects. Here, we study some of the most popular simulation tools that follow discrete event simulation like ns-3, OMNeT++, Riverbed and NetSim. The motivation behind this paper is to provide comprehensive review of various Simulators, available for scientists allowing advanced research on 4G and 5G Networks.

The rest of the paper is structured as follows. Section II manifests importance and difficulties of simulation. In Section III, the simulation tools are presented while the cumulative comparison follows in Section IV where the simulators' features and advantages are discussed. Finally in Section V, we draw up our conclusions.

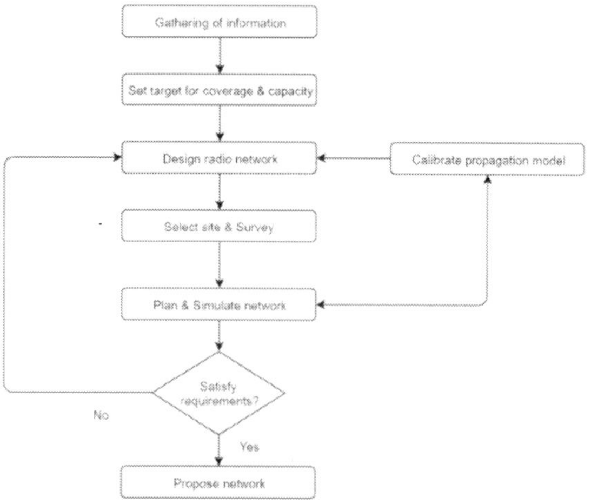

Figure 1. Network Simulation

II. Network Simulation

Creating the desirable network in a real time scenario is challenging as researchers' needs and requirements may vary depending on the situation. For that reason, there is a great number of softwares that can be used in every case. In any case, one feature is certain and non-negotiable, all of the simulation softwares have to enable a user to represent a network topology, specify the nodes on the network, and of course the links and the traffic between them. Of course, there may be simulators of much higher complexity that permit specification of every detail regarding the protocols they wish to use for handling traffic in a network laying quite solid foundations for future real time implementation. Simulators may come with text-based applications that can provide a not very intuitive interface, which could nevertheless allow evolved tools for customising or with graphical applications capable of granting users an easy and fast way to visualization of the the workings of the environment they wish to examine.

The simulation of wireless networks is even more complicated due to the nature of wireless networks. The basic concept of wireless network simulation can be found in Figure 1.

Differentiating simulators is most commonly based in terms of speed, accuracy, cost and convenience of use. The majority of the simulators provide a multi-protocol and modularity framework. There are some network simulators in companies that are developed exclusively for business, while others are developed by research institutes and/or universities to be used for researching purposes. In general, commercial software is not open, more expensive but can provide more protocol and model support while the other simulators are free, but may not be as applicable.

The criteria based on which the different types of simulators will be judged regard system performance, ease of learning and ease of use, the presence of Graphical Interface support, availability of the tool, etc. There are general information as well as properties of the softwares. They can be found gathered in Table 1 in Section IV.

III. Simulators and their Features

The following section presents the main simulators studied, their main properties, the major strengths and most important weaknesses. As mentioned above, the softwares in question follow discrete-event simulation. This methodology means that the operation of the system is modeled as a discrete sequence of events in time and its behavior can be simulated by modeling the events in the system where user has to set the scenarios in the right order. Also, they are chosen due to their popularity and widespread use.

A. ns-3

The ns-3 is a discrete-event network simulator developed mainly to be used for research and educational purposes. Based on the development on ns-2, the ns-3 project was launched in 2006 and is licensed under the GNU GPLv2 license, and is applicable for development and research for free. It should be noted that although ns-3 was based on NS2, it is to not be mistaken as an updated version of it, rather than as an attempt to replace it, meaning that ns-3 does not provide backward compatibility with NS2. It defines a model of working procedure of packet data networks, and provides an engine for simulation.

Without deviating from its predecessor and base, ns-3 uses two key languages in C++ and Python. While the simulator is developed exclusively in C++ with optional python bindings, this allows the users the freedom to choose between C++ and Python for the scripts of simulation they write. It should be noted that in any case, both languages work very effectively on ns-3. The specified software also provides Graphical Interface for the results' visual presentation, with the use of animators. Finally, ns-3 comes with a powerful library enabling the users to do have the desired outcome, allowing them to edit ns-3 itself.

The main features of Network Simulator 3, which also differentiate it from NS2 include:

1) Different software core: ns-3 has its core written entirely in C++ and with Python scripting interface [8].
2) Virtualization support: Implements the use of lightweight Virtual Machines.
3) Software integration: allow the inclusion of more open-source networking software which means that the simulation models do not have to be rewritten.
4) Attention to realism: real computers are emulated in more detail by protocol entities.

Due to its features, ns-3 displays several strengths, such as:

- High modularity.
- A lot more flexibility in comparison to most simulation softwares.
- Easier and more credible model validation via ported code support.
- Enable simulation for a plethora of protocols.
- Wide range of use for expanding or enhancing existing networks.
- Allows Software integration.

However, it also has some weaknesses:

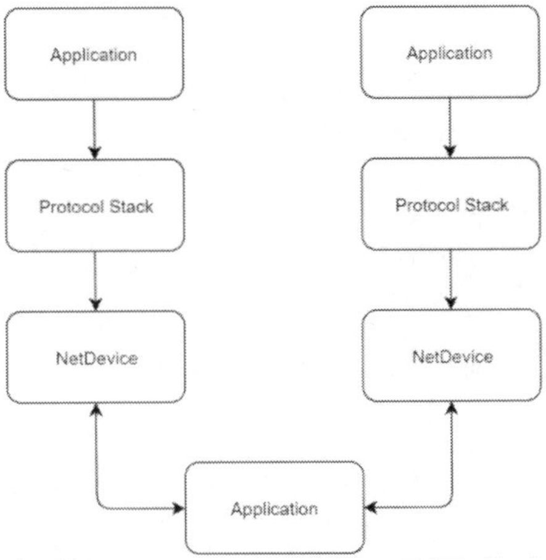

Figure 2. Architecture of ns-3

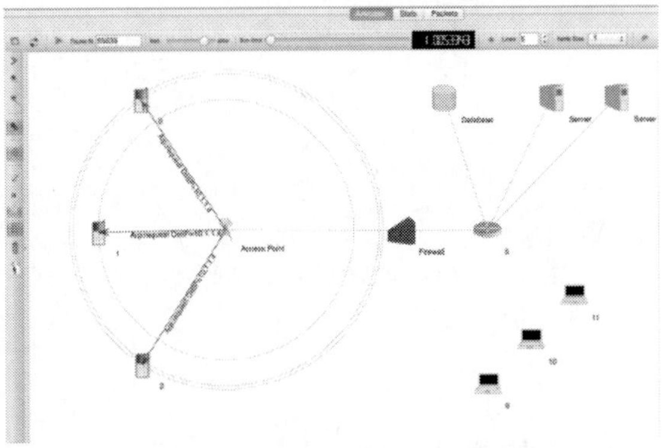

Figure 3. An example of NetAnim [8]

- ns-3 still suffers from lack of credibility.
- ns-3 attempts to replicate the successful approach of NS2 but the latter was used by many organizations that contributed by adding to models and components [6].
- There is an imperative need of active maintainers who will respond to the user questions, write adequate documentation, fix reported bugs, and ensure the correct service of the system.
- The aforementioned maintainers are also needed in order to have financial advantage of ns-3 like other commercially released simulators.

The basic structure of ns-3 architecture layers is shown in Figure 2. In Figure 3, an example of NetAnim interface is shown, a software exetutable that allows display of topology and animation of packet flow [8].

B. *OMNeT++*

Publicly available since 1997, OMNeT++ [9] is an extensible, modular, discrete event simulation software [10]. Although it can successfully model complex IT systems, multiprocessors, distributed hardware architectures, it is more often used for computer networks simulation, both wireless and wired. It is written thoroughly in C++. Using the software under

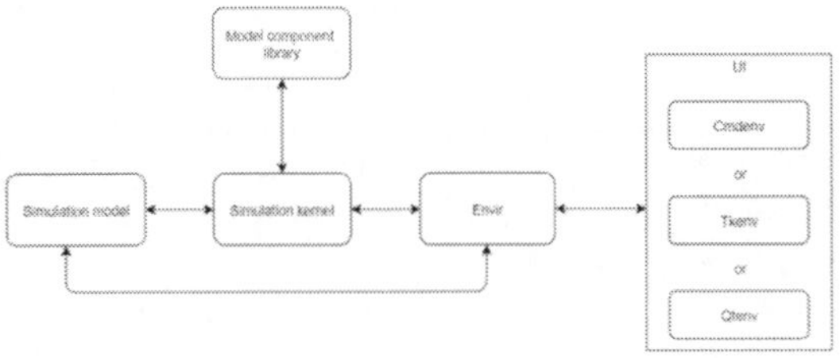

Figure 4. Structure of OMNeT++ simulator

the Academic Public License makes it free for non-benefit or academic use. Its free disposal combined with the tool's extensibility and the amount of available online documentations have made it very popular in the academic community. The motivation behind the development of OMNeT++ is to bridge the gap between research-oriented, free simulators like ns-3 and commercial alternatives like Riverbed that are much more high-priced. It is a component-based architecture and components (called modules) are programmed entirely in C++. They are then assembled into larger components and models with the use of NED, a language of higher level. Its modular architecture allows the simulation kernel to be easily embedded into almost every application.

The software has great GUI support and the simulation environment also offers a compiler for the NED topology description language (nedc), graphical network editor for NED files (GNED), GUI for simulation execution (Tkenv), command-line user interface for simulation execution (Cmdenv) [9] [11].

The most important feature of the simulator is that the modules are assembled by reusable components to be combined in different ways. Another important feature is that OMNet++ is basically a framework approach, providing the groundwork to develop various simulations models to meet different application areas requirements, which subsequently follow their release cycles. Currently, it is on version 5.4.1.

The simulator's strengths can be summarized as follows:

- Makes it easier to trace and debug.
- Can be used to model most hardware with accuracy.
- It offers wide GUI support via a complete, robust environment.
- Provides Reusable modules that can be combined in different ways

While its weaknesses include:

- The mobility extension can be found somewhat incomplete.
- It offers poor analysis and management of typical performance.

The structure of OMNeT++ simulation system can be found in Figure 4 and an example of simulation in Figure 5.

C. *Riverbed Modeler*

OPNET (Optimized Network Engineering Tools) Modeler is the development environment of OPNET simulator and is targeted for both research purposes and development. It was

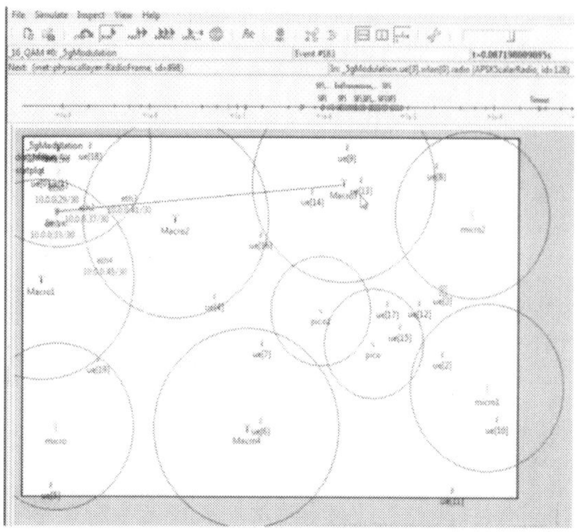

Figure 5. Example of simulation on OMNeT++

one of the most popular commercial simulation softwares by the end of 2008 and being in the market for such a long period, it managed to occupy a large share of it. Nowadays, it is part of Riverbed Modeler. Its flexibility allows it to be highly useful in studying communication applications, protocols and networks. It offers the users vast and impressive visual interface, due to its commercial nature. Using the graphical editor interface, the users are able to build whole network topology and entities from the application layer all the way to the physical layer and the mapping from the graphical design to the implementation of the real systems is created using Object-Oriented programming. All topologies configuration and simulation results can be presented very intuitively and visually. The users also have the freedom to adjust the parameters and quickly repeat experiments using the graphical interface, performing tests for various scenarios [11]. Riverbed is based on a mechanism called discrete event system.

According to the authors of [7], OPNET can be used to carry through with three functions:

1) modeling: it provides a vary intuitive and visually rich GUI, allowing users to develop a great variety of models.
2) simulating: It uses three different technologies.
3) analysis: the results originating from the simulation process can be presented and analysed using the simulators tools, such as user friendly charts, animations or statistics.

Important features of the Riverbed system is that the organisation of the networks is accomplished via hierarchical structure plus the fact that graphical interface and programming tools are available to users to define protocols or packet format.

Some strengths of the system include:

- Fast discrete event analytical simulation engine [6].
- Reduces simulation runtime by utilizing parallel and distributed capabilities [12].
- Allows quick correlation of graphical result with network behavior and easy interpretation.

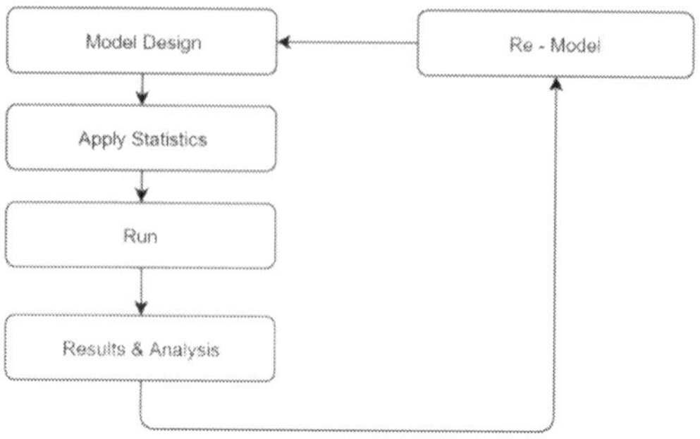

Figure 6. Simulation Workflow of Riverbed Modeler

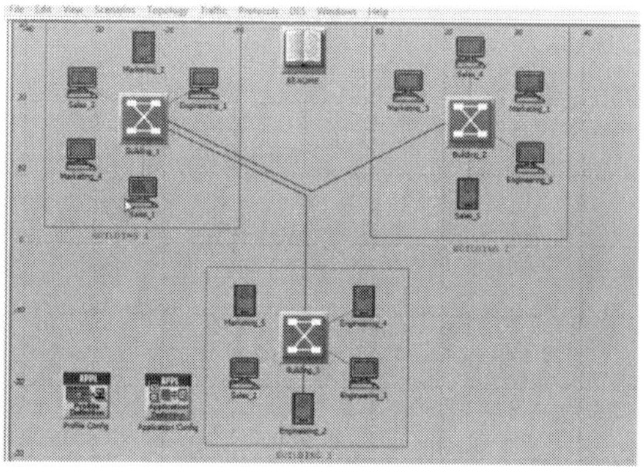

Figure 7. GUI of Riverbed Modeler

While some weaknesses could be:

- It only supports a small number of nodes within a single device.
- Simulation is inadequate in case there are long periods where nothing happens.
- Provided GUI might be powerful but its use it rather complicated.
- Sampling resolution sets the limit for the result accuracy.

The simulation workflow of Riverbed modeler can be found in Figure 6 and the Graphical Interface in Figure 7.

D. NetSim

NetSim is a stochastic discrete event simulator targeted for experimentation and research on networks. Its a leading network simulation software for protocol modelling and simulation, allowing us to analyze computer networks with unmatched depth, power and flexibility [13]. It is developed in 1997 by Tetcos . Its native development environment, acts as the interface between Users code and NetSims protocol libraries and simulation kernel [14]. NetSim is available as Pro, Standard or Academic versions and is built on a common design framework of high level architecture and code. Every version has of course different features, supports different options and has a different price. NetSim is more versatile than most of the other softwares and robust with an excellent and easy to use graphical interface. It should be noted that It is capable to provide performance metrics at abstraction levels

TABLE I. TABLE FOR COMPARISON OF SIMULATORS.

	ns-3	OMNeT++	Riverbed	NetSim
License Type	Open Source	Open Source (study & research)	Commercial	Proprietary
Language Supported	C++ & Python	C++	C & C++	C++ & Java
Supported OS	Linux, Mac OS Windows	Linux, Mac OS Windows	Linux, Windows	Windows
GUI Support	Good	Good	Excellent	Excellent
Document Available	Yes	Yes	Yes	Yes
Ease of Use	Hard	Easy	Easy	Easy
Simulation Event Type	Discrete event	Discrete event	Discrete event	Stochastic Discrete event
Available Module	Wired,Wireless Adhoc,WSN	Wired,Wireless Adhoc,WSN	Wired,Wireless Adhoc,WSN	Wired & Wireless SN
Scalability	Limited	Enough	Large	Enough
Availability of analysis tool	Yes	Yes	Yes	No
Communication with other modules	No	No	Yes	No
Network visualization tool	Yes	Yes	Yes	Yes
Possibility to design and modify scenarios	Yes	Yes	Yes	Yes
5G native support	Yes	No	No	No

from network to node and creates a packet trace with all of the necessary details. Its main limitation is that it is follows a single process discrete event simulation methodology. This means that it uses a single event queue for the needs of the simulation and at any given time, it contains one entry for each station on the network. Currently, it is on Version 10.

The major benefits are (a) programmability, (b) architectural accuracy, and (c) flexibility.

NetSim's strengths include:

- It offers a powerful, user friendly GUI that makes its use rather simple.
- Allows data packet flow visualization using its built-in animator.
- Users can extract performance analysis metrics in various levels.
- Its analysis framework offers various graphical options and enables intra and inter-protocol performance comparison.

Some weaknesses could be identified:

- All of the versions are commercial, meaning there is no free way of usage.
- It is a single process discrete event simulator.

The graphical interface of Netsim can be found in Figure 8 .

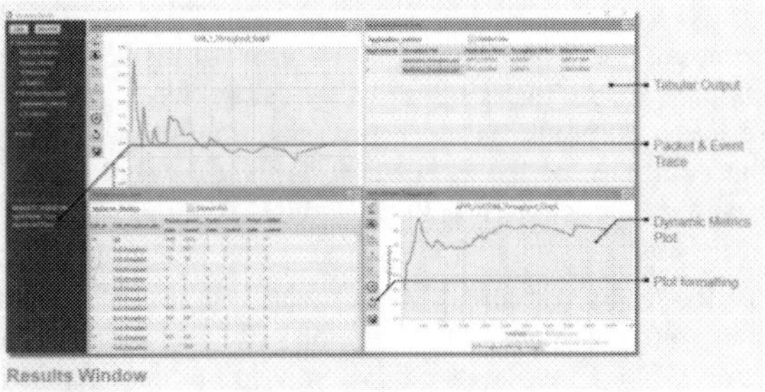

Figure 8. GUI of Netsim [13]

IV. CUMULATIVE COMPARISON

The simulation comparison is shown in Table I, where the criteria are presented and whether they are fulfilled. The comparison is based on both general information as well as properties of the softwares.

The general information that can be found on the upper section of the table, e.g. supported language & OS, license type, GUI support and technical properties of the softwares are compiled under the middle rule, e.g. simulation event type, scalability and network visualization tool.

All the simulators studied in this paper support tools that help the visualization of the network. They also allow scenarios redesign and modification through parameters change and can create trace files. They offer complete documentation and are user friendly, easy to use with ns-3 proving to be the most challenging to learn. The modularity of OMNeT++ is a big advantage, although it leaves the user with quite a big amount of work to done because of the lack of protocols offered. When it comes to communication with other simulators, Riverbed Modeler supports this feature while Omnet++, ns-3 and NetSim do not. Because of its proprietary nature, it is only natural that Riverbed can afford to simulate networks of much larger scale.

On the other hand, ns-3 is open source, OMNeT++ may not entirely be free but offers academic version for non commercial use and NetSim offers a cheaper, alternative version for students. This means that for these versions, the simulation scale ability is more limited. Of course, the commercial versions of the latter two softwares, can support large scale simulations. ns-3 and OMNeT++ can be deployed in all widely used

Operating Systems, contrary to Riverbed and NetSim. As far as GUI support is compared, the graphical environment offered by all of them are found more than adequate. Of course, OMNeT++ and NetSim offer vast and powerful GUI support with many more features and abilities like analysis framework and graphical options. Riverbed on the other hand, does provide an excellent GUI but it can be judged quite complicated and not so user-friendly.

It should be noted that all the simulators are supported by a great community but, ns-3 being open source means that there are less maintainers to respond to questions or fix reported bugs and abnormalities. However, it is extremely widespread and is being used by so many students, scientists and academics that the on-line community can help and offer great support for most issues.

More specifically, according to [15] a Google Scholar search of the ns-3 simulator results since 2017 (excluding patents and citations) yields over 2000 links (with some false positives). In addition the IEEE digital library lists 145 ns-3 publications for 2017, and the ACM digital library lists 2579 publications matching the search term ns-3 in 2017. In addition, there are organized Workshops on ns-3 and the related proceedings are published in the ACM digital library. The above facts ensure the important acceptance of ns-3 simulator as network research tool. In addition to ns-3, also OMNeT++ has an active community which have organized 5 OMNeT++ Community Summits until 2018. As result, if we compare the above simulators in terms of research community support seems that ns-3 and OMNeT++ have the most active research community which organize relative workshops about the evolution of the simulation softwares. This seems logical based on the fact that both ns-3 and OMNet++ can be obtained at no cost.

If we discuss about 5G Networks simulations native support, only ns-3 simulator supports 5G Networks simulations and OMNET++, Riverbed, NetSim do not provide native support for 5G Networks simulations. ns-3 supports 5G Networks simulations through 'mmWave Cellular Network Simulator module' [16]. This module includes a number of detailed statistical channel models as well as the ability to incorporate real measurements or raytracing data. The physical and medium access control layers are modular and highly customizable. The module is interfaced with the core network of the ns-3 Long Term Evolution (LTE) module for full-stack simulations of end-to-end connectivity, and advanced architectural features, such as dual-connectivity, are also available.

Especially for 5G Networks simulations there are specialized simulators, such as NYUSIM [17]. NYUSIM is a novel channel simulation software, which can be used to generate realistic temporal and spatial channel responses to support realistic physical-layer and link-layer simulations and design for fifth generation (5G) cellular communications. NYUSIM has been built upon the statistical spatial channel model for broadband millimeter wave (mmWave) wireless communication systems.

V. Conclusion and Future Work

Network simulation is an effective, low cost and small risk method. However, it is necessary and this why it is extensively performed by scientists in all kinds of fields to validate the research carried out. Network simulation can prove to be an essential mechanism on the hands of researchers for the analysis on network behaviour and evaluation on possible network design and will remain increasingly important following the networks' growing complexity and scale.

This paper contains a general overview of a number of tools used for standard network simulation, along with a comparison between them with respect to various parameters. The study confirms that picking a suitable, required and efficient simulator for the specific job of a research work can be quite demanding but bears the according results. Each simulator comes with its advantages and disadvantages and can be useful or even necessary in different cases and the choice of a fitting software should be done based on the study motive.

References

[1] Y. Wang, J. Xu, and L. Jiang, "Challenges of system-level simulations and performance evaluation for 5g wireless networks," IEEE Access, vol. 2, 2014, pp. 1553–1561.

[2] V. Mishra and S. Jangale, "Analysis and comparison of different network simulators," International Journal of Application or Innotvation in Engineering and Management (IJAIEM). Special Issue for International Technological Conference-2014 2014.

[3] X. Zhou and H. Tian, "Comparison on network simulation techniques," in 2016 17th International Conference on Parallel and Distributed Computing, Applications and Technologies (PDCAT), Dec 2016, pp. 313–316.

[4] A. R. Khan, S. M. Bilal, and M. Othman, "A performance comparison of open source network simulators for wireless networks," in 2012 IEEE International Conference on Control System, Computing and Engineering, Nov 2012, pp. 34–38.

[5] C. E. Perkins, E. M. Royer, S. R. Das, and M. K. Marina, "Performance comparison of two on-demand routing protocols for ad hoc networks," IEEE Personal Communications, vol. 8, no. 1, Feb 2001, pp. 16–28.

[6] M. Kabir, S. Islam, M. Hossain, and S. Hossain, "Detail comparison of network simulators," International Journal of Scientific and Engineering Research, vol. 5, no. 10, October 2014, pp. 16–28.

[7] J. Pan and R. Jain, "A survey of network simulation tools: Current status and future developments," Email: jp10@ cse. wustl. edu, vol. 2, no. 4, 2008, p. 45.

[8] www.nsnam.org, "ns-3 network simulator," https://www.nsnam.org/, 2019, [Online; retrieved 24-April-2019].

[9] www.omnetpp.org, "Omnet++ official site," https://www.omnetpp.org/, 2019, [Online; retrieved 24-April-2019].

[10] A. Varga and R. Hornig, "An overview of the omnet++ simulation environment," in In Proceedings of the 1st international conference on Simulation tools and techniques for communications, networks and systems & workshops, p. 60. ICST (Institute for Computer Sciences, Social-Informatics and Telecommunications Engineering, 2008.

[11] G. Borboruah and G. Nandi, "A study on large scale network simulators," International Journal of Computer Science and Information Technologies, vol. 5, no. 6, 2014, pp. 7318–7322.

[12] www.riverbed.com, "Riverbed modeler," https://www.riverbed.com/gb/products/steelcentral/steelcentral-riverbed-modeler.html, 2019, [Online; retrieved 24-April-2019].

[13] www.tetcos.com, "Netsim official developer," https://www.tetcos.com/, 2018, [Online; accessed 9-August-2018].

[14] S. Siraj, A. Gupta, and R. Badgujar, "Network simulation tools survey," International Journal of Advanced Research in Computer and Communication Engineering, vol. 1, no. 4, 2012, pp. 199–206.

[15] www.nsnam.org, "Statistics," https://www.nsnam.org/about/statistics/, 2018, accessed: 07-December-2018.

[16] M. Mezzavilla et al., "End-to-end simulation of 5g mmwave networks," IEEE Communications Surveys Tutorials, vol. 20, no. 3, thirdquarter 2018, pp. 2237–2263.

[17] S. Sun, G. R. MacCartney and T. S. Rappaport, "A novel millimeter-wave channel simulator and applications for 5G wireless communications," 2017 IEEE International Conference on Communications (ICC), Paris, 2017, pp. 1-7.

Partial-Diffusion Least Mean-Square Estimation Over Networks Under Noisy Information Exchange

Wael M. Bazzi
Electrical Engineering Department
American University in Dubai
Dubai, UAE
Email: wbazzi@aud.edu

Vahid Vadidpour, Amir Rastegarnia, Azam Khalili
Department of Electrical Engineering
Malayer University
Malayer, Iran, 65719-95863
Email: {vahidpour, rastegarnia, khalili}@malayeru.ac.ir

Abstract— **Partial diffusion scheme is an effective method for reducing computational load and power consumption in adaptive network implementation. The Information is exchanged among the nodes, usually over noisy links. In this paper, we consider a general version of Partial-Diffusion Least-Mean-Square (PDLMS) algorithm in the presence of various sources of imperfect information exchanges. Like the established PDLMS, we consider two different schemes to select the entries, sequential and stochastic, for transmission at each iteration. Our objective is to analyze the aggregate effect of these perturbations on general PDLMS strategies. Simulation results demonstrate that considering noisy link assumption adds a new complexity to the related optimization problem and the trade-off between communication cost and estimation performance in comparison to ideal case becomes unbalanced. Our simulation results substantiate the effect of noisy links on PDLMS algorithm and verify the theoretical analysis.**

Keywords- adaptive networks; diffusion adaptation; noisy informatin exchange; partial diffusion; sequential, stochastic.

I. INTRODUCTION

Due to limited electrical power and bandwidth resources for inter-node communication over a practical Wireless Sensor Networks (WSN) or ad hoc networks, data transmission through radio communication links can become prohibitively expensive for realizing a collaborative task. Generally speaking, although benefits of diffusion strategies achieved by increasing inter-node communications, they are compromised by the communication cost. As a result, since various nodes can have various numbers of neighbors, they may require disparate hardware or consume power dissimilarity [1]–[4]. Therefore, reducing the communication cost while maintaining the benefits of cooperation is of practical importance.

There have been several attempts to reduce the communication cost without considerable degradation of the estimation and compromising the cooperation benefits in diffusion algorithms. Among them diffusion least mean-square (LMS), such as reducing the dimension of the estimates [5]–[7], selecting a subset of the entries of the estimates [1] [2] [8] [9], set-membership filtering [10][11], or partial updating [12] have been reported in [13]–[15]. Among these methods, we focus on [1] which LMS algorithm for adaptive distribute estimation has been formulated and analyzed by utilizing partial-diffusion. In [1], an adapt-then-combine (ATC) Partial-Diffusion Least-Mean-Square (PDLMS) algorithm is proposed for distributed estimation over adaptive networks in which, at each iteration, each node transmits a subsets of the entries of intermediate estimate vector to its neighbors.

In the PDLMS strategy proposed in [1], the weight estimates that are exchanged among the nodes can be subject to perturbations over communication links. The effect of link noise during the exchange of weight estimates, already appear for the diffusion algorithm in the works [16]–[20]. It should be noted that since our objective is to minimize the inter-node communications, the nodes only exchange their intermediate estimates with their neighbors. Therefore, we allow for noisy exchange just during the two combination steps. We subsequently study the performance of this general case utilizing the energy conservation argument. We established its stability and convergence in the mean and mean-square senses. We also derive a theoretical expression for the steady-state Mean-Square-Deviation (MSD) and verify its accuracy via numerical simulations.

The main contributions in this paper include:

- Focusing on [1] which involves transmission of a subset of entries of the inter-node estimate vectors named partial diffusion, we provide a more general algorithmic structure of which [1] is just a special case. To achieve this, we consider the fact that the weight estimates exchanged among the nodes can be subject to quantization errors and additive noise over communication links. We also consider two different schemes for selecting the weight vector entries for transmission at each iteration. We allow for noisy exchange during the two combination steps only. It should be noted that since our objective is to minimize the inter-node communication, the nodes only exchange their intermediate estimates with their neighbors;
- Using the energy conservation argument [21] we analyze the stability of algorithms in mean and mean square senses under certain statistical conditions.
- We illustrate the comparable convergence performance of PDLMS algorithm with noisy links using different numerical examples.

This paper is organized as follows. In Section II, we formulate the PDLMS under noisy information exchange. The performance analyses are examined in Section III. We provide simulation results in Section IV and draw conclusions in Section V.

A. Notation

We adopt the lowercase letters to denote vectors, uppercase letter for matrices, normal font for nonrandom (deterministic) quantities, and the boldface letters for random quantities. The notation $(.)^*$ refers to conjugate transposition, $Tr(.)$ refer to the trace of its matrix argument, $\otimes$ for the Kronecker product, and $vec(.)$ for a vector formed by stacking the columns of its matrix argument. We shall also use $col(...)$ to denote a column vector formed by stacking its arguments on top of each other and $diag(...)$ to denote a (block) diagonal matrix formed from its argument. All vectors in our treatment are column vectors, with the exception of regression vectors, $\boldsymbol{u}_{k,i}$.

II. Partial Diffusion Algorithms with Imperfect Information Exchange

Consider a connected network consisting of N nodes. At time instant $i \geq 0$, each node k has access to scalar measurements $\boldsymbol{d}_k(i)$ and $1 \times M$ regression data vectors $\boldsymbol{u}_{k,i}$. The data across all nodes are assumed to be related to an unknown $M \times 1$ vector w^o via linear regression model of the form [17]:

$$\boldsymbol{d}_k(i) = \boldsymbol{u}_k(i) w^o + \boldsymbol{v}_k(i) \tag{1}$$

where $\boldsymbol{v}_k(i)$ denotes the measurement noise with zero mean and variance $\sigma_{v,k}^2$ and the vector w^o refers to the parameter of interest.

We are now interested in solving optimization problems of the type:

$$\min_w \textstyle\sum_{k=1}^{N} \mathbb{E}\left|\boldsymbol{d}_k(i) - \boldsymbol{u}_{k,i}\boldsymbol{w}\right|^2 \tag{2}$$

The nodes in the network would like to estimate w^o by solving the equation above in adaptive and collaborative manners. We review the diffusion adaptation strategies with imperfect information exchange below.

A. Diffusion Adaptation with Imperfect Information Exchange

Consider the following general adaptive diffusion strategies with $C = I_N$ corresponding to the case in which the nodes only share the weight estimates for $i \geq 0$ [21]:

$$\boldsymbol{\phi}_{k,i} = \textstyle\sum_{l \in N_k} a_{1,lk} \boldsymbol{w}_{l,i-1} \tag{3}$$

$$\boldsymbol{\psi}_{k,i} = \boldsymbol{\phi}_{k,i-1} + \mu_k \boldsymbol{u}_{k,i}^* \left[\boldsymbol{d}_k(i) - \boldsymbol{u}_{k,i}\boldsymbol{\phi}_{k,i-1}\right] \tag{4}$$

$$\boldsymbol{w}_{k,i} = \textstyle\sum_{l \in N_k} a_{2,lk} \boldsymbol{\psi}_{l,i} \tag{5}$$

The scalars $\{a_{1,lk}, a_{2,lk}\}$ are non-negative real coefficients corresponding to the (l,k) entries of $N \times N$ combination matrices $\{A_1, A_2\}$, respectively. The role of these combination matrices is in convergence behavior of the diffusion strategy (3)-(5). These coefficients are zero whenever node $l \notin \mathcal{N}_k$, where $\mathcal{N}_k$ denotes the neighborhood of node k. These matrices are assumed to satisfy the conditions:

$$A_1^T \mathbb{1}_N = \mathbb{1}_N, \qquad A_2^T \mathbb{1}_N = \mathbb{1}_N \tag{6}$$

where the notation $\mathbb{1}$ denotes an $N \times 1$ column vector with all its entries equal to one.

We model the noisy data received by node k from its neighbor l as follows (see Figure 1):

$$\boldsymbol{w}_{lk,i-1} = \boldsymbol{w}_{l,i-1} + \boldsymbol{v}_{lk,i-1}^{(w)} \tag{7}$$

$$\boldsymbol{\psi}_{lk,i} = \boldsymbol{\psi}_{l,i} + \boldsymbol{v}_{lk,i}^{(\psi)} \tag{8}$$

where $\boldsymbol{v}_{lk,i-1}^{(w)}$ $(M \times 1)$ and $\boldsymbol{v}_{lk,i}^{(\psi)}$ $(M \times 1)$ are vector noise signal. They are temporally white and spatially independent random process with zero mean and covariance given by $\left\{R_{v,lk}^{(w)}, R_{v,lk}^{(\psi)}\right\}$. The quantities $\left\{R_{v,lk}^{(w)}, R_{v,lk}^{(\psi)}\right\}$ are all zero if $l \notin \mathcal{N}_k$ or when $l = k$. It should be noted that the subscript lk indicates that l is the source and k the sink, the flow of information is from l to k.

Using the perturbed data (7) and (8), the adaptive strategy (3)-(5) becomes

$$\boldsymbol{\phi}_{k,i} = \textstyle\sum_{l \in N_k} a_{1,lk} \boldsymbol{w}_{lk,i-1} \tag{9}$$

$$\boldsymbol{\psi}_{k,i} = \boldsymbol{\phi}_{k,i-1} + \mu_k \boldsymbol{u}_{k,i}^* \left[\boldsymbol{d}_k(i) - \boldsymbol{u}_{k,i}\boldsymbol{\phi}_{k,i-1}\right] \tag{10}$$

$$\boldsymbol{w}_{k,i} = \textstyle\sum_{l \in N_k} a_{2,lk} \boldsymbol{\psi}_{lk,i} \tag{11}$$

B. Partial-Diffusion with Impeferct Information Exchange

In order to lower the level of inter-node communication required among the nodes, we utilize partial-diffusion strategy proposed in [1], to transmit L out of M entries of the intermediate estimates at each time instant where the integer L is fixed and pre-specified. Again, we develop a more general class of PDLMS of which [1] is a special case. The selection of to-be-transmitted entries at node k and time instant i can be portrayed by an $M \times M$ diagonal entry-selection matrix, denoted by $\boldsymbol{\Lambda}_{k,i}$, that has L ones and $M - L$ zeros on its diagonal. The position of ones states the selected entries. Multiplication of an intermediate estimate vector by this matrix replaces its non-selected entries with zero.

According to (9) and (11) that can also be expressed as:

$$\boldsymbol{\phi}_{k,i} = a_{1,kk}\boldsymbol{w}_{k,i-1} + \textstyle\sum_{l \in N_k \setminus \{k\}} a_{1,lk}\left[\boldsymbol{\Lambda}_{l,i-1}\boldsymbol{w}_{lk,i-1} + (I_M - \boldsymbol{\Lambda}_{l,i-1})\boldsymbol{w}_{lk,i-1}\right] \tag{12}$$

$$\boldsymbol{\psi}_{k,i} = \boldsymbol{\phi}_{k,i-1} + \mu_k \boldsymbol{u}_{k,i}^* \left[\boldsymbol{d}_k(i) - \boldsymbol{u}_{k,i}\boldsymbol{\phi}_{k,i-1}\right] \tag{13}$$

$$\boldsymbol{w}_{k,i} = a_{2,kk}\boldsymbol{\psi}_{k,i} + \textstyle\sum_{l \in N_k \setminus \{k\}} a_{2,lk}\left[\boldsymbol{\Lambda}_{l,i}\boldsymbol{\psi}_{lk,i} + (I_M - \boldsymbol{\Lambda}_{l,i})\boldsymbol{\psi}_{lk,i}\right]$$

(14)

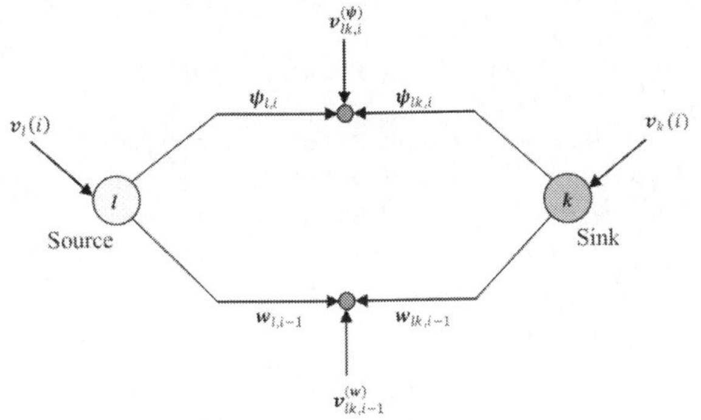

Figure 1. Several additive nise sources perturb the exchange of information from node l to node k.

Each node needs the information of all entries of its neighbors' intermediate estimate vectors for the consultation phase. However, when the intermediate estimates are broadcast partially ($0 < L < M$), nodes have no access to the non-communicated entries. To resolve this indistinctness, we allow the nodes utilize their own intermediate estimates entries instead of ones from the neighbors that have not been communicated, i.e., at node k, substitute

$$\left(I_M - \boldsymbol{\Lambda}_{l,i-1}\right)\boldsymbol{w}_{k,i-1} \qquad \forall l \in \mathcal{N}_k \setminus \{k\} \tag{15}$$

for

$$\left(I_M - \boldsymbol{\Lambda}_{l,i-1}\right)\boldsymbol{w}_{lk,i-1} \qquad \forall l \in \mathcal{N}_k \setminus \{k\} \tag{16}$$

and

$$\left(I_M - \boldsymbol{\Lambda}_{l,i}\right)\boldsymbol{\psi}_{k,i} \qquad \forall l \in \mathcal{N}_k \setminus \{k\} \tag{17}$$

for

$$\left(I_M - \boldsymbol{\Lambda}_{l,i}\right)\boldsymbol{\psi}_{lk,i} \qquad \forall l \in \mathcal{N}_k \setminus \{k\} \tag{18}$$

Based on this approach together with using perturbed data as introduced in (7) and (8), we formulate general PDLMS under noisy exchange as follows:

$$\begin{aligned}\boldsymbol{\phi}_{k,i} = {} & a_{1,kk}\boldsymbol{w}_{k,i-1} \\ & + \textstyle\sum_{l\in\mathcal{N}_k\setminus\{k\}} a_{1,lk}\big[\boldsymbol{\Lambda}_{l,i-1}\boldsymbol{w}_{l,i-1} + (I_M - \\ & \boldsymbol{\Lambda}_{l,i-1})\boldsymbol{w}_{k,i-1}\big] + \textstyle\sum_{l\in\mathcal{N}_k\setminus\{k\}} a_{1,lk}\boldsymbol{\Lambda}_{l,i-1}\boldsymbol{v}_{lk,i-1}^{(w)}\end{aligned} \tag{19}$$

$$\boldsymbol{\psi}_{k,i} = \boldsymbol{\phi}_{k,i-1} + \mu_k \boldsymbol{u}_{k,i}^{*}\left[\boldsymbol{d}_k(i) - \boldsymbol{u}_{k,i}\boldsymbol{\phi}_{k,i-1}\right] \tag{20}$$

$$\begin{aligned}\boldsymbol{w}_{k,i} = {} & a_{2,kk}\boldsymbol{\psi}_{k,i} \\ & + \textstyle\sum_{l\in\mathcal{N}_k\setminus\{k\}} a_{2,lk}\big[\boldsymbol{\Lambda}_{l,i}\boldsymbol{\psi}_{l,i} + (I_M - \\ & \boldsymbol{\Lambda}_{l,i})\boldsymbol{\psi}_{k,i}\big] + \textstyle\sum_{l\in\mathcal{N}_k\setminus\{k\}} a_{2,lk}\boldsymbol{\Lambda}_{l,i}\boldsymbol{v}_{lk,i}^{(\psi)}\end{aligned} \tag{21}$$

Remark: The probability of transmission for all the entries at each node is equal and state as [1], [9]

$$p = {}^{L}/_{M} \tag{22}$$

Moreover, the entry selection matrices, $\boldsymbol{\Lambda}_{k,i}$, do not rely on any data/parameter with the exception of L and M.

Introduce the following aggregate $M \times 1$ zero mean noise signals:

$$\boldsymbol{v}_{k,i-1}^{(w)} \triangleq \textstyle\sum_{l\in\mathcal{N}_k\setminus\{k\}} a_{1,lk}\boldsymbol{\Lambda}_{l,i-1}\boldsymbol{v}_{lk,i-1}^{(w)} \tag{23}$$

$$\boldsymbol{v}_{k,i}^{(\psi)} \triangleq \textstyle\sum_{l\in\mathcal{N}_k\setminus\{k\}} a_{2,lk}\boldsymbol{\Lambda}_{l,i}\boldsymbol{v}_{lk,i-1}^{(\psi)} \tag{24}$$

These noises correspond to the cumulative effect on node k of all selected exchange noises from the neighbors of node k while exchanging the estimates $\{\boldsymbol{w}_{l,i-1}, \boldsymbol{\psi}_{l,i}\}$ in the course of the two consultation steps. The $M \times M$ covariance matrices of these noises are given by:

$$R_{v,k}^{(w)} \triangleq \textstyle\sum_{l\in\mathcal{N}_k\setminus\{k\}} a_{1,lk}^2\boldsymbol{\Lambda}_{l,i-1}R_{v,lk}^{(w)} \tag{25}$$

$$R_{v,k}^{(\psi)} \triangleq \textstyle\sum_{l\in\mathcal{N}_k\setminus\{k\}} a_{2,lk}^2\boldsymbol{\Lambda}_{l,i}R_{v,lk}^{(\psi)} \tag{26}$$

Thus, the PDLMS algorithm, Adapt Then Combine (ATC) approach, under noisy information exchange takes the following form:

TABLE I. PDLMS ALGORITHM UNDER NOISY INFORMATION EXCHANGE

Initialization:
Start with $\boldsymbol{w}_{k,-1} = 0$ and given non-negative real coefficient $\{a_{lk}\}$, $A_1 = I_N$ and $A_2 = A$, satifying (6),
for $i \geq 0$, every node k computes
Step 1: Incremental Phase
$\boldsymbol{\psi}_{k,i} = \boldsymbol{w}_{k,i-1} + \mu_k \boldsymbol{u}_{k,i}^{*}[\boldsymbol{d}_k(i) - \boldsymbol{u}_{k,i}\boldsymbol{\phi}_{k,i-1}]$
Step 2: Diffusion Phase
$\boldsymbol{w}_{k,i} = a_{kk}\boldsymbol{\psi}_{k,i} + \sum_{l\in\mathcal{N}_k\setminus\{k\}} a_{lk}[\boldsymbol{\Lambda}_{l,i}\boldsymbol{\psi}_{lk,i} + (I_M - \boldsymbol{\Lambda}_{l,i})\boldsymbol{\psi}_{lk,i}]$

C. Entry Selection Method

In order to select L out of M entries of the intermediate estimates of each node at each iteration, the methods we utilized are comparable to the selection processes in stochastic and sequential *partial-update* schemes [12], [22], [23]. Here, we just review these methods namely *sequential* and *stochastic* partial-diffusion.

In sequential partial-diffusion the entry selection matrices, $\boldsymbol{\Lambda}_{k,i}$, is a diagonal matrix:

$$\boldsymbol{\Lambda}_{k,i} = \begin{bmatrix} r_{1,i} & \cdots & 0 \\ \vdots & \ddots & \vdots \\ 0 & \cdots & r_{M,i} \end{bmatrix}, \quad r_{\ell,i} = \begin{cases} 1 & if\ \ell \in \mathcal{I}_{(i \bmod \bar{B})+1} \\ 0 & otherwise \end{cases} \tag{27}$$

with $\bar{B} = \lceil M/L \rceil$. The number of selection entries at each iteration is limited by L. The coefficient subsets $\mathcal{I}_i$ are not unique as long as they meet the following requirements [12]:

1. Cardinality of $\mathcal{I}_i$ is between 1 and L;
2. $\cup_{r=1}^{\bar{B}} \mathcal{I}_r = \mathcal{S}$ where $\mathcal{S} = \{1,2,\dots,M\}$;
3. $\mathcal{I}_r \cap \mathcal{I}_p = \emptyset, \forall r, p \in \{1,\dots,\bar{B}\}$ and $r \neq p$.

The description of the entry selection matrices, $\boldsymbol{\Lambda}_{k,i}$, in stochastic partial-diffusion is similar to that of sequential one. The only difference is as follows. At a given iteration, $\boldsymbol{i}$, sequential case one of the set $\mathcal{I}_r, r = 1, \dots, \bar{B}$ is chosen in a predetermined fashion, whereas for stochastic case, one of the sets $\mathcal{I}_r$ is sampled at random from $\{\mathcal{I}_1, \mathcal{I}_2, \dots, \mathcal{I}_{\bar{B}}\}$. One might ask why these methods are considered to organize these selection matrices. To answer this question, it is worth mentioning that the nodes need to recognize which entries of their neighbors' intermediate estimates have been propagated at each iteration. These schemes bypass the need for addressing (position in the vector) [1], [9].

III. Steady-State Performance Analysis

We now move on to examine the behavior of the general PDLMS implementations (19)-(21), and the influence of the mentioned perturbations on its convergence and steady-state performance. For this reason, we shall study the convergence of the weight estimates both in the mean and mean-square senses. In order to make the analysis tractable, we introduce the following assumptions on statistical properties of the measurement data and noise signals.

Assumptions:

1. The regression data $\boldsymbol{u}_{k,i}$ are temporally white and spatially independent random variables with zero mean and covariance matrix $R_{u,k} \triangleq \mathrm{E}\boldsymbol{u}_{k,i}^*\boldsymbol{u}_{k,i} \geq 0$.
2. The noise signal $\boldsymbol{v}_k(i)$, $\boldsymbol{v}_{k,i-1}^{(w)}$ and $\boldsymbol{v}_{k,i}^{(\psi)}$ are temporally white and spatially independent random variable with zero mean and covariance $\sigma_{v,k}^2$, $R_{v,k}^{(w)}$ and $R_{v,k}^{(\psi)}$, respectively. In addition, the quantities $\left\{R_{v,lk}^{(w)}, R_{v,lk}^{(\psi)}\right\}$ are all zero if $l \notin N_k$ or when $l = k$.
3. The regression data $\{\boldsymbol{u}_{m,i_1}\}$, the model noise signals $\boldsymbol{v}_n(i_2)$, and the link noise signals $\boldsymbol{v}_{l_1k_1,j_1}^{(w)}$ and $\boldsymbol{v}_{l_2k_2,j_2}^{(\psi)}$ are mutually independent random variables for all indexes $\{i_1, i_2, j_1, j_2, k_1, k_2, l_1, l_2, m, n\}$.
4. The step-sizes, μ_k $\forall k$, are small enough such that their squared values are negligible.

We are interested in examining the evolution of the weight-error vectors. To do so, we let:

$$\widetilde{\boldsymbol{w}}_{k,i} \triangleq w^o - \boldsymbol{w}_{k,i} \tag{28}$$

We import the information from across the network into block vectors and matrices as follows:

$$\boldsymbol{\mathcal{R}}_{u,i} \triangleq diag\{\boldsymbol{u}_{1,i}^*\boldsymbol{u}_{1,i}, \boldsymbol{u}_{2,i}^*\boldsymbol{u}_{2,i}, \dots, \boldsymbol{u}_{N,i}^*\boldsymbol{u}_{N,i}\} \tag{29}$$

$$\boldsymbol{s}_i \triangleq diag\{\boldsymbol{u}_{1,i}^*\boldsymbol{v}_1(i), \boldsymbol{u}_{2,i}^*\boldsymbol{v}_2(i), \dots, \boldsymbol{u}_{N,i}^*\boldsymbol{v}_N(i)\} \tag{30}$$

$$\boldsymbol{v}_i^{(w)} \triangleq col\left\{\boldsymbol{v}_{1,i}^{(w)}, \boldsymbol{v}_{2,i}^{(w)}, \dots, \boldsymbol{v}_{N,i}^{(w)}\right\} \tag{31}$$

$$\boldsymbol{v}_i^{(\psi)} \triangleq col\left\{\boldsymbol{v}_{1,i}^{(\psi)}, \boldsymbol{v}_{2,i}^{(\psi)}, \dots, \boldsymbol{v}_{N,i}^{(\psi)}\right\} \tag{32}$$

$$\mathcal{M} \triangleq diag\{\mu_1 I_M, \dots, \mu_N I_M\} \tag{33}$$

$$\widetilde{\boldsymbol{w}}_i \triangleq col\{\widetilde{\boldsymbol{w}}_{1,i}, \dots, \widetilde{\boldsymbol{w}}_{N,i}\} \tag{34}$$

Subsequently, some algebra demonstrates that

$$\boxed{\begin{aligned}\widetilde{\boldsymbol{w}}_i = {} & \boldsymbol{\mathcal{A}}_{2,i}(I_{NM} - \mathcal{M}\boldsymbol{\mathcal{R}}_{u,i})\boldsymbol{\mathcal{A}}_{1,i-1}\widetilde{\boldsymbol{w}}_{i-1} \\ & -\boldsymbol{\mathcal{A}}_{2,i}(I_{NM} - \mathcal{M}\boldsymbol{\mathcal{R}}_{u,i})\boldsymbol{v}_{i-1}^{(w)} - \boldsymbol{\mathcal{A}}_{2,i}\mathcal{M}\boldsymbol{s}_i - \boldsymbol{v}_i^{(\psi)}\end{aligned}} \tag{35}$$

where

$$\boldsymbol{\mathcal{A}}_{r,i} = \begin{bmatrix} \mathrm{A}_{1,1,i} & \cdots & \mathrm{A}_{1,N,i} \\ \vdots & \ddots & \vdots \\ \mathrm{A}_{N,1,i} & \dots & \mathrm{A}_{N,N,i} \end{bmatrix}, \forall r \in \{1,2\} \tag{36}$$

$$\mathbf{A}_{p,q,i} = \begin{cases} I_M - \sum_{l\epsilon N_p\setminus\{p\}} a_{r,lp}\boldsymbol{\Lambda}_{l,i} & if\ q = p \\ a_{r,qp}\boldsymbol{\Lambda}_{q,i} & if\ q\epsilon N_p \setminus \{p\} \\ O_M & other\ wise \end{cases} \tag{37}$$

A. Mean Performance

Taking expectation of both sides of (35) under *Remark* and *Assumptions*, we find that the mean error vector evolves according to the following recursion:

$$\mathbb{E}\widetilde{\boldsymbol{w}}_i = \mathcal{Q}_2\mathrm{E}(I_{NM} - \mathcal{M}\mathcal{R}_u)\mathcal{Q}_1\mathbb{E}\widetilde{\boldsymbol{w}}_{i-1} \tag{38}$$

where

$$\mathcal{Q}_1 = \mathbb{E}[\boldsymbol{\mathcal{A}}_{1,i}], \quad \mathcal{Q}_2 = \mathbb{E}[\boldsymbol{\mathcal{A}}_{2,i-1}] \tag{39}$$

From (38), we observe that in order for the recursion to be stable in the mean sense, the matrix $\mathcal{Q}_2\mathrm{E}(I_{NM} - \mathcal{M}\mathcal{R}_u)\mathcal{Q}_1$ should be stable [24]. Picking $\mathcal{Q}_1$ and $\mathcal{Q}_2$ which all their entries are real non-negative and all their rows add up to unity [1]. Therefore, in the light of lemma 1 of [25], mean stability and asymptotic unbiasedness of the algorithm is guaranteed if the matrix $I_{NM} - \mathcal{M}\mathcal{R}_u$ is stable or equivalently if

$$|\lambda_{max}\{I_{NM} - \mathcal{M}\mathcal{R}_u\}| < 1 \tag{40}$$

where $\lambda_{max}\{.\}$ refers to the largest eigenvalue of a matrix. The set of the eigenvalue of $I_{NM} - \mathcal{M}\mathcal{R}_u$ is the union of the set of the eigenvalue of $I_M - \mu_k R_{u,k}$ $\forall k$ [25]. Thus, (40) is satisfied when $|\lambda_{max}\{I_M - \mu_k R_{u,k}\}| < 1, \forall k$ or $|1 - \mu_k\lambda_{max}\{R_{u,k}\}| < 1$, $\forall k$. These inequalities determine the stability bounds for step-sizes as

$$0 < \mu_k < \frac{2}{\lambda_{max}\{R_{u,k}\}} \quad \forall k \tag{41}$$

B. Mean-Square Performance

The weighted variance relation for the error vector $\tilde{\boldsymbol{w}}_i$ can be obtained from the error recursion (35) as:

$$\mathbb{E}\|\tilde{\boldsymbol{w}}_i\|_\Sigma^2 = \mathbb{E}\|\tilde{\boldsymbol{w}}_{i-1}\|_{\Sigma'}^2 + \mathbb{E}\left(\boldsymbol{s}_i^* \mathcal{M} \mathcal{A}_{2,i}^T \Sigma \mathcal{A}_{2,i} \mathcal{M} \boldsymbol{s}_i\right) + \mathbb{E}\left(\boldsymbol{v}_{i-1}^{*(w)} \mathcal{H}_i^* \Sigma \mathcal{H}_i \boldsymbol{v}_{i-1}^{(w)}\right) + \mathbb{E}\left(\boldsymbol{v}_i^{*(\psi)} \Sigma \boldsymbol{v}_i^{(\psi)}\right) \quad (42)$$

where Σ is an arbitrary positive semi-definite Hermitian matrix of size $NM \times NM$ and

$$\mathcal{H}_i \triangleq \mathcal{A}_{2,i}\left(I_{NM} - \mathcal{M}\mathcal{R}_{u,i}\right) \quad (43)$$

Furthermore, the matrix Σ' can be expressed as

$$\Sigma' \triangleq \mathbb{E}\boldsymbol{\mathcal{B}}_i^* \Sigma \boldsymbol{\mathcal{B}}_i \quad (44)$$

with

$$\boldsymbol{\mathcal{B}}_i \triangleq \mathcal{A}_{2,i}\left(I_{NM} - \mathcal{M}\mathcal{R}_{u,i}\right)\mathcal{A}_{1,i-1} \quad (45)$$

The variance relation becomes

$$\mathbb{E}\|\tilde{\boldsymbol{w}}_i\|_\Sigma^2 = \mathbb{E}\|\tilde{\boldsymbol{w}}_{i-1}\|_{\Sigma'}^2 + \left(vec^T\{\mathcal{G}\}\mathcal{D}_2 + vec^T(\mathcal{H}R_v^{(w)}\mathcal{H}^*)\mathcal{D}_2 + vec^T\left(R_v^{(\psi)}\right)\right) vec(\Sigma) \quad (46)$$

where

$$\mathcal{D}_1 = \mathbb{E}\left(\mathcal{A}_{1,i-1}^T \otimes \mathcal{A}_{1,i-1}^T\right) \quad (47)$$

$$\mathcal{D}_2 = \mathbb{E}\left(\mathcal{A}_{2,i}^T \otimes \mathcal{A}_{2,i}^T\right) \quad (48)$$

$$\mathcal{G} = \mathcal{M}\mathbb{E}[\boldsymbol{s}_i \boldsymbol{s}_i^*]\mathcal{M} = diag\{\mu_1 \sigma_{v,1}^2 R_{u,1}, \ldots, \mu_N \sigma_{v,N}^2 R_{u,N}\} \quad (49)$$

$$\mathcal{H} \triangleq \mathbb{E}\left[I_{NM} - \mathcal{M}\mathcal{R}_{u,i}\right] = I_{NM} - \mathcal{M}\mathcal{R}_u \quad (50)$$

$$R_v^{(w)} \triangleq \mathbb{E}\boldsymbol{v}_{i-1}^{(w)} \boldsymbol{v}_{i-1}^{*(w)} = diag\left\{R_{v,1}^{(w)}, \ldots, R_{v,N}^{(w)}\right\} \quad (51)$$

$$R_v^{(\psi)} \triangleq \mathbb{E}\boldsymbol{v}_i^{(\psi)} \boldsymbol{v}_i^{*(\psi)} = diag\left\{R_{v,1}^{(\psi)}, \ldots, R_{v,N}^{(\psi)}\right\} \quad (52)$$

Therefore, the steady-state weighted variance relation (46) becomes

$$\lim_{i\to\infty} \mathbb{E}\|\tilde{\boldsymbol{w}}_i\|^2_{unvec\left[\left(\mathrm{I}_{N^2M^2} - \mathcal{D}_1\left[\mathbb{E}\left(I_{NM} - \mathcal{R}_{u,i}\mathcal{M}\right)\otimes\left(I_{NM} - \mathcal{R}_{u,i}\mathcal{M}\right)\right]\mathcal{D}_2\right) vec(\Sigma)\right]}$$

$$= \left(vec^T\{\mathcal{G}\}\mathcal{D}_2 + vec^T\left(\mathcal{H}R_v^{(w)}\mathcal{H}^*\right)\mathcal{D}_2 + vec^T\left(R_v^{(\psi)}\right)\right) vec(\Sigma) \quad (53)$$

It is known that a recursion of type (53) is stable and convergent if the matrix $\mathcal{D}_1\left[\mathbb{E}\left(I_{NM} - \mathcal{R}_{u,i}\mathcal{M}\right)\otimes\left(I_{NM} - \mathcal{R}_{u,i}\mathcal{M}\right)\right]\mathcal{D}_2$ is stable [24], [26]. All the entries of $\mathcal{D}_1$ and $\mathcal{D}_2$ are real non-negative and all its columns sum up to one. Moreover, the eigenvalue of $\mathcal{T}\otimes\mathcal{T}$ are square of the eigenvalue of $\mathcal{T}$. Therefore, stability of this matrix has the same conditions as the stability of $I_{NM} - \mathcal{R}_u\mathcal{M}$. This means that choosing the step-sizes is accordance with (41) makes the algorithm stable likewise in the mean-square sense hence convergent to steady state.

The network MSD is defined as:

$$\mathrm{MSD}^{\mathrm{network}} \triangleq \lim_{i\to\infty} \frac{1}{N}\sum_{k=1}^N \mathbb{E}\left\|\tilde{\boldsymbol{w}}_{k,i}\right\|^2 \quad (54)$$

Since we are free to choose Σ, we select it as $\mathrm{I}_{N^2M^2} - \mathcal{D}_1\left[\mathbb{E}\left(I_{NM} - \mathcal{R}_{u,i}\mathcal{M}\right)\otimes\left(I_{NM} - \mathcal{R}_{u,i}\mathcal{M}\right)\right]\mathcal{D}_2 = vec(I_{NM}/N)$ then the expression (53) gives

$$\mathrm{MSD}_{\mathrm{imperfect}}^{\mathrm{network}} = \frac{1}{N}\left[vec(\mathcal{G})\mathcal{D}_2 + vec(\mathcal{H}R_v^w\mathcal{H}^*)\mathcal{D}_2 + vec\left(R_v^{(\psi)}\right)\right]^T \left(I_{N^2M^2} - \mathcal{F}\right)^{-1} \mathrm{vec}(I_{NM}) \quad (55)$$

IV. Numerical Studies

In order to illustrate the PLDMS strategies performance under noisy information exchange, we present some simulation results in this section.

A. Simulation

We consider an adaptive network with a random topology and $N = 10$ where each node is, in average, connected to two other nodes. The unknown parameter w^o of length $M = 8$ is randomly generated. We adopt a uniform step-size, $\mu_k = 0.01$, The measurements were generated according to model (1), and regressors, $\boldsymbol{u}_{k,i}$, were chosen Gaussian i.i.d with randomly generated different diagonal covariance matrices, $R_{u,k}$. The additive noises at nodes are zero mean Gaussian with variances $\sigma_{v,k}^2$ and independent of the regression data. The traces of the covariance matrix regressors and the noise variances at all nodes, $Tr\left(R_{u,k}\right)$ and $\sigma_{v,k}^2$, are shown in Figure 2.

We also use white Gaussian link noise signals such that $R_{v,lk}^{(w)} = \sigma_{w,lk}^2 I_M$ and $R_{v,lk}^{(\psi)} = \sigma_{\psi,lk}^2 I_M$. All link noise variances $\{\sigma_{w,lk}^2, \sigma_{\psi,lk}^2\}$ are randomly generated. The average power of each type of link noise across the network is 35 dB less than that of the model noise. In Figure 3, we plot the experimental network MSD curves for ATC case ($A_1 = I_N$) of PDLMS algorithm using both sequential and stochastic partial diffusion schemes under noisy information exchange for different numbers of entries at each iteration, M. We use uniform weights for $\{a_{1,lk}, a_{2,lk}\}$ at combination phase at this stage. In Figure 4, we compare network MSD learning curve of PDLMS for both ATC and CTA, Combine Then Adapt, cases ($A_2 = I_N$) under ideal and noisy links.

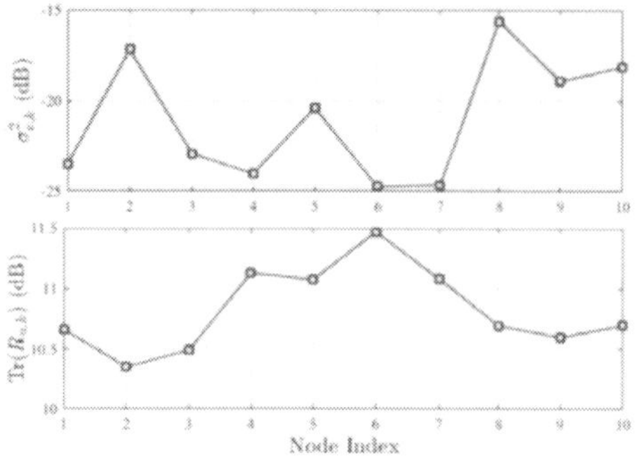

Figure 2. Covariance matrix trace of the input signal and the variance of the noise at each node.

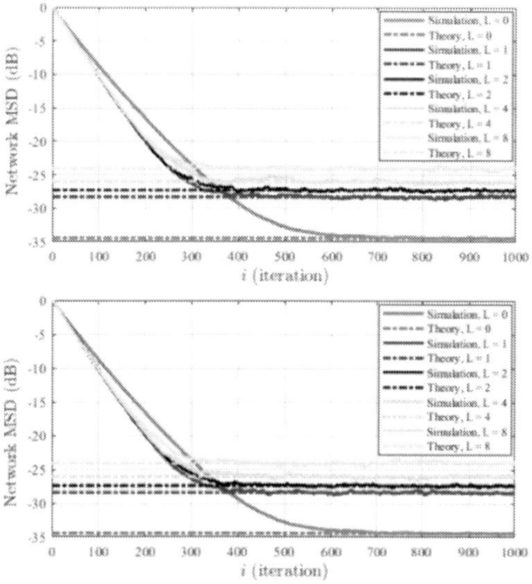

Figure 3. Network MSD learning curve of PDLMS for ATC under noisy links (top) sequential and (bottom) stochastic.

B. Discussion

From the simulation results, we make the following observations:

In [1], authors emphasized that the PDLMS algorithm delivers a trade-off between communications cost and estimation performance. However, noisy links add a new complexity to the network optimization problem. In addition, in the presence of noisy links, the trade-off between communication cost and estimation performance becomes unbalanced. This is because as more entries are broadcast at each iteration, more perturbed weight estimates are interred in consultant phase.

The sequential partial-diffusion schemes outperform the stochastic partial-diffusion. Finally, the adaptive ATC strategy outperforms the adaptive CTA strategy for both perfect and imperfect cases.

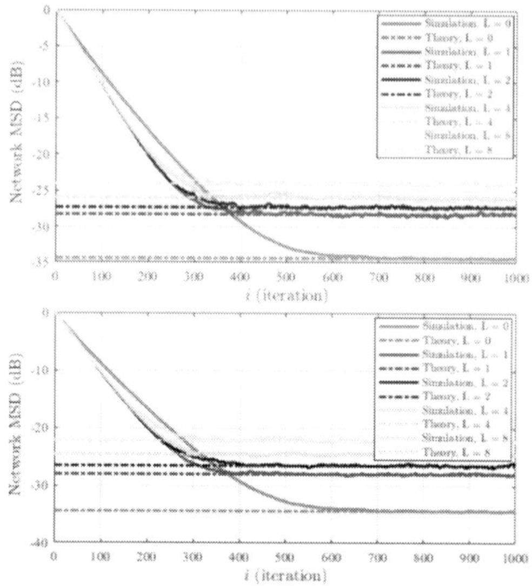

Figure 4. Comparison of network MSDs of sequential PDLMS algorithm for (top) ATC and (bottom) CTA under noisy information exchange

V. CONCLUSION

In this work, we presented a general form of PDLMS algorithms, formulated the ATC and CTA versions of PDLMS under noisy Links, and investigated the performance of partial-diffusion algorithms under several sources of noise during information exchange for both sequential and stochastic schemes. We also illustrated that the PDLMS strategy could still stabilize the mean and mean-square convergence of the network with noisy information exchange. We derived analytical expressions for network learning curve MSD. The important result is that the noisy links are the main factor in performance degradation of a diffusion LMS strategy running in a network with imperfect communication. Furthermore, there is no direct relation between the MSD performance and number of selected entries under imperfect information exchange. The performance degradation incurred by noisy links depends not only on the link noise variances, $\sigma^2_{w,lk}$ and $\sigma^2_{\psi,lk}$, but also on the other parameters of the network, i.e., the measurement and state noise variances, the network topology, and combination weights. These topics will be addressed in future work.

REFERENCE

[1] R. Arablouei, S. Werner, Y.-F. Huang, and K. Dogancay, "Distributed least mean-square estimation with partial diffusion," *Signal Process. IEEE Trans.*, vol. 62, no. 2, pp. 472–484, 2014.

[2] V. Vahidpour, A. Rastegarnia, A. Khalili, and S. Sanei, "Analysis of partial diffusion recursive least squares adaptation over noisy links," *IET Signal Process.*, 2017.

[3] V. Vahidpour, A. Rastegarnia, A. Khalili, and S. Sanei, "Partial

Diffusion Kalman Filtering for Distributed State Estimation in Multiagent Networks," *Neural Networks Learn. Syst. IEEE Trans.*, 2019.

[4] E. E. Tsiropoulou, S. T. Paruchuri, and J. S. Baras, "Interest, energy and physical-aware coalition formation and resource allocation in smart IoT applications," in *2017 51st Annual Conference on Information Sciences and Systems (CISS)*, 2017, pp. 1–6.

[5] M. O. Sayin and S. S. Kozat, "Compressive diffusion strategies over distributed networks for reduced communication load," *Signal Process. IEEE Trans.*, vol. 62, no. 20, pp. 5308–5323, 2014.

[6] M. O. Sayin and S. S. Kozat, "Single bit and reduced dimension diffusion strategies over distributed networks," *Signal Process. Lett. IEEE*, vol. 20, no. 10, pp. 976–979, 2013.

[7] S. Chouvardas, K. Slavakis, and S. Theodoridis, "Trading off complexity with communication costs in distributed adaptive learning via Krylov subspaces for dimensionality reduction," *Sel. Top. Signal Process. IEEE J.*, vol. 7, no. 2, pp. 257–273, 2013.

[8] R. Arablouei, K. Dogancay, S. Werner, and Y.-F. Huang, "Adaptive distributed estimation based on recursive least-squares and partial diffusion," *Signal Process. IEEE Trans.*, vol. 62, no. 14, pp. 3510–3522, 2014.

[9] V. Vahidpour, A. Rastegarnia, A. Khalili, W. M. Bazzi, and S. Sanei, "Analysis of Partial Diffusion LMS for Adaptive Estimation Over Networks with Noisy Links," *IEEE Trans. Netw. Sci. Eng.*, 2017.

[10] J. R. Deller Jr and Y. F. Huang, "Set-membership identification and filtering for signal processing applications," *Circuits, Syst. Signal Process.*, vol. 21, no. 1, pp. 69–82, 2002.

[11] S. Gollamudi, S. Nagaraj, S. Kapoor, and Y.-F. Huang, "Set-membership filtering and a set-membership normalized LMS algorithm with an adaptive step size," *Signal Process. Lett. IEEE*, vol. 5, no. 5, pp. 111–114, 1998.

[12] K. Dogancay, *Partial-update adaptive signal processing: Design Analysis and Implementation*. Academic Press, 2008.

[13] S. Werner, T. Riihonen, and Y.-F. Huang, "Energy-efficient distributed parameter estimation with partial updates," in *Green Circuits and Systems (ICGCS), 2010 International Conference on*, 2010, pp. 36–40.

[14] S. Werner and Y.-F. Huang, "Time-and coefficient-selective diffusion strategies for distributed parameter estimation," in *Signals, Systems and Computers (ASILOMAR), 2010 Conference Record of the Forty Fourth Asilomar Conference on*, 2010, pp. 696–697.

[15] A. Malipatil, Y.-F. Huang, and S. Werner, "An SMF approach to distributed average consensus in clustered sensor networks," in *Signal Processing Advances in Wireless Communications, 2009. SPAWC'09. IEEE 10th Workshop on*, 2009, pp. 81–85.

[16] R. Abdolee and B. Champagne, "Diffusion LMS algorithms for sensor networks over non-ideal inter-sensor wireless channels," in *Distributed Computing in Sensor Systems and Workshops (DCOSS), 2011 International Conference on*, 2011, pp. 1–6.

[17] A. Khalili, M. A. Tinati, and A. Rastegarnia, "Performance analysis of distributed incremental LMS algorithm with noisy links," *Int. J. Distrib. Sens. Networks*, vol. 2011, 2011.

[18] A. Khalili, M. A. Tinati, A. Rastegarnia, and J. Chambers, "Steady-state analysis of diffusion LMS adaptive networks with noisy links," *Signal Process. IEEE Trans.*, vol. 60, no. 2, pp. 974–979, 2012.

[19] A. Khalili, M. A. Tinati, A. Rastegarnia, and J. A. Chambers, "Transient analysis of diffusion least-mean squares adaptive networks with noisy channels," *Int. J. Adapt. Control Signal Process.*, vol. 26, no. 2, pp. 171–180, 2012.

[20] X. Zhao, S.-Y. Tu, and A. H. Sayed, "Diffusion adaptation over networks under imperfect information exchange and non-stationary data," *Signal Process. IEEE Trans.*, vol. 60, no. 7, pp. 3460–3475, 2012.

[21] A. H. Sayed, "Adaptive Filters. Hoboken." NJ: John Wiley & Sons, 2008.

[22] A. H. Sayed, "Diffusion adaptation over networks," *Acad. Press Libr. Signal Process.*, vol. 3, pp. 323–454, 2013.

[23] M. Godavarti and A. O. Hero III, "Partial update LMS algorithms," *Signal Process. IEEE Trans.*, vol. 53, no. 7, pp. 2382–2399, 2005.

[24] C. D. Meyer, *Matrix analysis and applied linear algebra*, vol. 2. Siam, 2000.

[25] F. S. Cattivelli and A. H. Sayed, "Diffusion LMS strategies for distributed estimation," *Signal Process. IEEE Trans.*, vol. 58, no. 3, pp. 1035–1048, 2010.

[26] K. M. Abadir and J. R. Magnus, *Matrix algebra*, vol. 1. Cambridge University Press, 2005.

Malicious Node Detection Method against Message Flooding Attacks in Sparse Mobile Ad-Hoc Networks

Takuya Idezuka*, Tomotaka Kimura†, Kouji Hirata‡, and Masahiro Muraguchi*
* Faculty of Engineering, Tokyo University of Science, Tokyo 125-8585, Japan
Email: 4318504@ed.tus.ac.jp, murag@ee.kagu.tus.ac.jp
† Faculty of Science and Engineering, Doshisha University, Kyoto 610-0321, Japan
Email: tomkimur@mail.doshisha.ac.jp
‡ Faculty of Engineering, Kansai University, Osaka 564-8680, Japan
Email: hirata@kansai-u.ac.jp

***Abstract*—In recent years, many store-carry-forward routing schemes have been proposed for sparse mobile ad-hoc networks, which are the most representative networks in Delay/Disruption Tolerant Networking (DTN) environments. In general, store-carry-forward routing schemes are designed under an assumption that all nodes in the network are cooperative. Therefore, they are highly vulnerable to malicious behaviors. In this paper, we propose a malicious node detection method for message flooding attacks in which malicious nodes generate a lot of unnecessary messages to exhaust network resources. Our proposed method detects suspicious nodes in a distributed manner. Specifically, each node records suspicious scores for other nodes in the network. Whenever two nodes encounter each other, their suspicious scores are updated based on the number of messages received from the encounter nodes. Therefore, the increase in the suspicious score indicates that the scored node frequently generates and forwards the messages. After each node sufficiently updates suspicious scores, it identifies malicious nodes based on their suspicious scores. Through simulation experiments, we show the effectiveness of the proposed method.**

Keywords–DTN; store-carry-forward routing; sparse mobile ad-hoc networks; message flooding

I. INTRODUCTION

In recent years, Delay/Disconnected Tolerant Networking (DTN) technologies attract attention for realizing communications under poor communication environments [1] [2], where a path from a source node to a destination node does not exist for most of the time. A representative example of poor communication environments is a sparse mobile ad-hoc network, where the node density is very sparse. To deliver messages in the sparse mobile ad-hoc network, we use store-carry-forward routing, which is a typical example of DTN technologies. In store-carry-forward routing, when a node generates or receives messages, it stores them in its buffer. After that, the node carries them until it encounters another node. When this happens, the node forwards the messages to the encounter node. By repeating this procedure, the messages eventually reach their destination nodes.

Epidemic Routing is the earliest proposed store-carry-forward routing [3]. In Epidemic Routing, whenever a node having a message encounters another node, it always forwards a copy of the message. The node receiving the copy further spreads copies of the message over the network. If there are sufficient network resources, Epidemic Routing has the excellent delay performance, though it consumes a lot of network resources compared with other store-carry-forward routing schemes. Therefore, many improvements of Epidemic Routing have been proposed in the past [1] [4]–[6].

Most of these store-carry-forward routing schemes are designed under an assumption that all nodes in the network are cooperative and do not behave maliciously. The store-carry-forward routing is vulnerable to uncooperative behaviors, and this degrades the system performance, such as delivery delay and consumption of network resources. Therefore, to deliver messages safely using store-carry-forward routing, security issues should be considered.

To date, the behavior of some malicious attacks (e.g., black hole attacks [7], gray hole attacks [8], and fake packet attacks [9]) have been analyzed and their countermeasures have been proposed [10]. In [11], the authors analyze the behavior of message flooding attacks shown in Figure 1, where malicious nodes frequently generate a lot of unnecessary messages and spread them over the network to prevent delivering legitimate messages that cooperative nodes generate. Through Markov analysis and simulation experiments, the authors revealed how message flooding attacks affect the system performance. Because network resources are very limited in sparse mobile ad-hoc networks, the malicious node can exhaust the network resources even when malicious nodes generate slightly more messages than cooperative nodes. Therefore, countermeasures against message flooding attacks should be considered.

In this paper, we propose a detection method to identify malicious nodes that launch the message flooding attack. Our proposed method detects suspicious nodes in a distributed manner. Specifically, each node records suspicious scores for other nodes in the network. Whenever two nodes encounter each other, their suspicious scores are updated based on the number of messages received from the encounter nodes. Therefore, the increase of the suspicious score indicates that the scored node frequently generates and forwards the messages. After each node sufficiently updates suspicious scores, it identifies malicious nodes based on their suspicious scores. If our proposed method can identify malicious nodes, each node does not receive messages from the malicious nodes when it encounters them. By doing this, even when the malicious nodes generate a lot of unnecessary messages, we can prevent exhausting the network resource. In this paper, through simulation experiments, we show the effectiveness of our detection method.

The remainder of this paper is organized as follows. Section II describes the system model. In Section III, we explain our

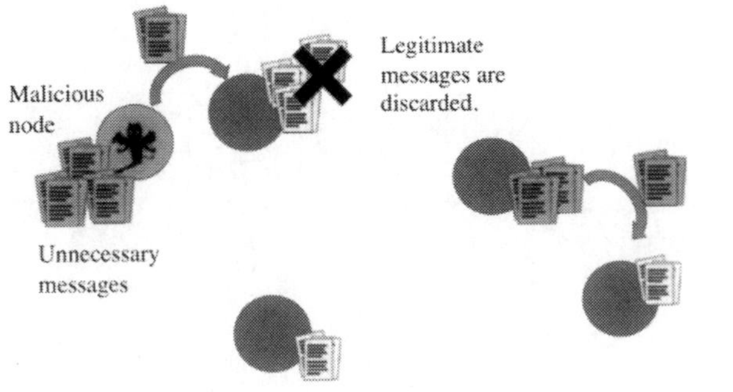

Figure 1. Message Flooding Attacks ($B = 3$).

proposed method against message flooding attacks. In Section IV, the performance of our proposed method is discussed with the results of the simulation experiments. Finally, we conclude the paper in Section V.

II. System Model

We assume that there are N mobile nodes including a malicious node that launches the message flooding attack. We call nodes except for the malicious node *cooperative nodes*. Here, let $\mathcal{N}$ and $\mathcal{N}_C$ denote the sets of the nodes in the network and the cooperative nodes, respectively. The ID of the malicious node is denoted by M. By definition, $\mathcal{N} = \mathcal{N}_C \cup \{M\}$. Encounters between two cooperative nodes occur according to a Poisson process with rate $\lambda_{v,w}$ $(v, w \in \mathcal{N}_C,\ v \neq w)$. Encounters between the malicious node M and a cooperative node also occur according to a Poisson Process with rate $\lambda_{M,v}$ $(v \in \mathcal{N}_C)$. Note that in [12], the exponential inter-meeting time assumption was validated in some random mobility models, such as the random waypoint and the random direction.

Each node independently generates messages and delivers them to their destination nodes using Epidemic Routing. Specifically, each cooperative node generates a message according to a Poisson process with rate Λ_C. On the other hand, the malicious node generates unnecessary messages according to a Poisson process with rate Λ_M $(\Lambda_C < \Lambda_M)$. Therefore, the malicious node generates messages more frequently than the cooperative nodes. Note that, in this paper, we regard nodes that frequently generates messages as malicious nodes even if the nodes are cooperative. These nodes exhaust the network resources, and thus they should be detected.

Furthermore, we assume that each node has the buffer and can store at most B messages. When messages are generated or received, if the buffer is full, all the messages cannot be stored in the buffer. Therefore, buffer overflow would occur. To prevent buffer overflow, when the number of messages is $B+1$ or more, B messages with high priority are selected, and the reminder of the messages are discarded. In this paper, each node adopts First-In First-Out (FIFO) queuing discipline. That is, it gives high priority to messages whose holding time in the buffer is short. In Figure 1, each node can store at most $B = 3$ messages in the buffer. The cooperative node that has three legitimate messages receives the copy of the unnecessary message from the malicious node, so that it discards the legitimate message with long holding time.

The drawback of Epidemic Routing is that copies of messages remained in the network after they have been delivered to their destination nodes. The nodes with the message copies cannot know that the messages are delivered to their destination nodes. To overcome this issue, a vaccine recovery method is proposed to delete the unnecessary copies [4]. In the vaccine recovery method, immediately after a message reaches the destination node, the destination node generates an *anti-packet*. The anti-packet is spread over the network using Epidemic Routing. When a node receives the anti-packet, the node deletes the message from its buffer if it has a copy of the message corresponding to the anti-packet. By doing this, it has been shown that we can delete the copies of messages remaining in the network and reduce the network resources largely. Therefore, in this paper, we adopt the vaccine recovery method to delete unnecessary message copies.

III. Our Proposed Method

Each node $v \in \mathcal{N}_C$ has the suspicious score matrix $X^{(v)} = [x_{i,j}^{(v)}]$ to identify the malicious node. The size of the suspicious score matrix $X^{(v)}$ is $N \times N$, and $x_{i,j}^{(v)}$ indicates the suspicious score of node i that node j evaluates. The suspicious scores are updated when nodes encounter each other. At the nth encounter of nodes v, w, after the messages are exchanged, node v records the number $N_{v,w}^{(n)}$ of the received messages and the encounter time $t_{v,w}^{(n)}$. Node w also records $N_{w,v}^{(n)}$ and $t_{w,v}^{(n)}$. $x_{v,w}^{(v)}$ is then updated as follows:

$$x_{v,w}^{(v)} := \frac{x_{v,w}^{(v)} t_{v,w}^{(n-1)} + C_{v,w}^{(n)}}{t_{v,w}^{(n)}}, \tag{1}$$

$$\begin{aligned} C_{v,w}^{(n)} &= \int_{t_{v,w}^{(n-1)}}^{t_{v,w}^{(n)}} N_{v,w}^{(n-1)} \exp(-\alpha \cdot (t - t_{v,w}^{(n-1)}))dt \\ &= N_{v,w}^{(n-1)} \alpha \{1 - \exp(-\alpha(t_{v,w}^{(n)} - t_{v,w}^{(n-1)}))\}, \end{aligned} \tag{2}$$

where α $(\alpha > 0)$ indicates the attenuation parameter, and $C_{v,w}^{(n)}$ increases with the number $N_{v,w}^{(n-1)}$ of the received messages. Node w also updates $x_{w,v}^{(w)}$. Note that the suspicious score $x_{v,w}^{(v)}$ represents the estimation of the time-average number of the messages received from node w (see Figure 2). Therefore, the increase in the suspicious score $x_{v,w}^{(v)}$ means that node v receives many messages frequently from node w, and thus node v can regard node w as the candidates of malicious nodes.

Moreover, nodes v, w exchange their suspicious score vectors $\boldsymbol{x}^{(v)} = (x_{v,1}^{(v)}, x_{v,2}^{(v)}, \cdots, x_{v,N}^{(v)})$ and $\boldsymbol{x}^{(w)} = (x_{w,1}^{(w)}, x_{w,2}^{(w)}, \cdots, x_{w,N}^{(w)})$ when they encounter. After that, nodes v and w updates their suspicious score vectors $\boldsymbol{x}^{(v)}$ and $\boldsymbol{x}^{(w)}$, respectively.

$$x_{w,i}^{(v)} := x_{w,i}^{(w)}, \quad (i \in \mathcal{N}) \tag{3}$$

$$x_{v,j}^{(w)} := x_{v,j}^{(v)}, \quad (j \in \mathcal{N}). \tag{4}$$

After each node v sufficiently updates and exchanges the suspicious scores, it calculates the total suspicious score to distinguish between the cooperative and the malicious nodes. Node v calculates the total suspicious score $S_k^{(v)}$ as follows:

$$S_k^{(v)} = \sum_{i \in \mathcal{N} \setminus \{v\}} x_{i,k}^{(v)}. \tag{5}$$

When $S_k^{(v)}$ is larger than the threshold value t_h, node v regards node k as the malicious nodes. In our proposed method, the

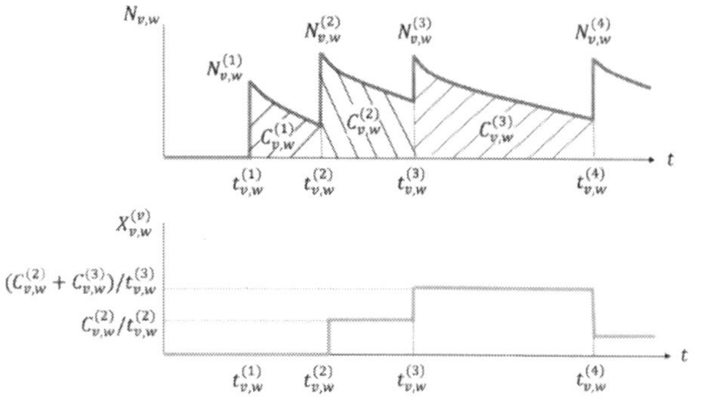

Figure 2. Suspicious Score.

threshold value t_h is defined as follows:

$$t_h = \mu^{(v)} + 2\sigma^{(v)}, \tag{6}$$

where $\mu^{(v)}$ and $\sigma^{(v)}$ are the average and the standard deviation of the total suspicious scores. Formally, $\mu^{(v)}$ and $\sigma^{(v)}$ are defined as follows:

$$\mu^{(v)} = \frac{\sum_{k \in \mathcal{N} \setminus \{v\}} S_k^{(v)}}{N-1}, \tag{7}$$

$$\sigma^{(v)} = \sqrt{\frac{\sum_{k \in \mathcal{N} \setminus \{v\}} (S_k^{(v)} - \mu^{(v)})^2}{N-1}}. \tag{8}$$

IV. Performance Evaluation

To show the effectiveness of our proposed method, we conducted the simulation experiments. In this section, we explain the simulation model, and then we show the results of the simulation experiments.

A. Simulation Model

There are 99 cooperative nodes and a malicious node in the network. $\mathcal{N} = \{0, 1, \ldots, 99\}$. The ID of the malicious node is fixed to be $M = 50$. The message generation rate of each cooperative node Λ_C is set to be 0.01. The message generation rate Λ_M is chosen from $\{0.5, 1, 3, 5, 10\}$. Messages are delivered according to Epidemic Routing incorporated with the vaccine recovery method. The rate of encountering two cooperative nodes $\lambda_{v,w}$ $(v, w \in \mathcal{N}_C, v \neq w)$ is set to be 0.01. This means that as a unit time, we choose the mean inter-meeting time $1/(98\lambda) \approx 1$ of a cooperative node to any other cooperative nodes. The rate $\lambda_{M,v}$ of encountering the malicious node and the cooperative node is set to be 0.01 or 0.1. The size of buffer B is set to be 10. For a warm-up period in each simulation experiment, the nodes generate and distribute 10,000 messages. Unless stated otherwise, the message generation rate Λ_M is set to be 5 and the total suspicious score $S_k^{(v)}$ $(v, k \in \mathcal{N}_C, v \neq k)$ is calculated after 10,000 unit times are elapsed.

B. Results

Figure 3 shows the total suspicious scores $S_k^{(0)}$ $(k = 1, 2, \ldots, 99)$ that node 0 evaluates. The total suspicious score $S_{50}^{(0)}$ of the malicious node $M = 50$ is higher than the threshold value t_h. On the other hand, the total suspicious scores $S_k^{(0)}$ $(k \in \mathcal{N}_C)$ are smaller than the threshold value t_h. Therefore, node 0 can estimate that node 50 is malicious and other nodes are cooperative. This result indicates that our proposed method can differentiate the malicious node from the cooperative nodes.

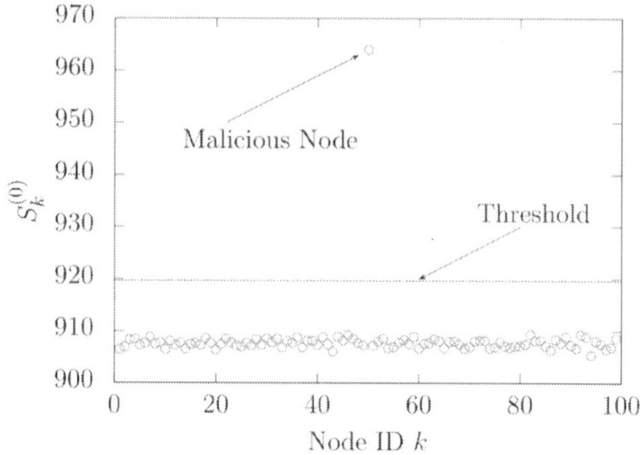

(a) $\lambda_{M,v} = 0.1$

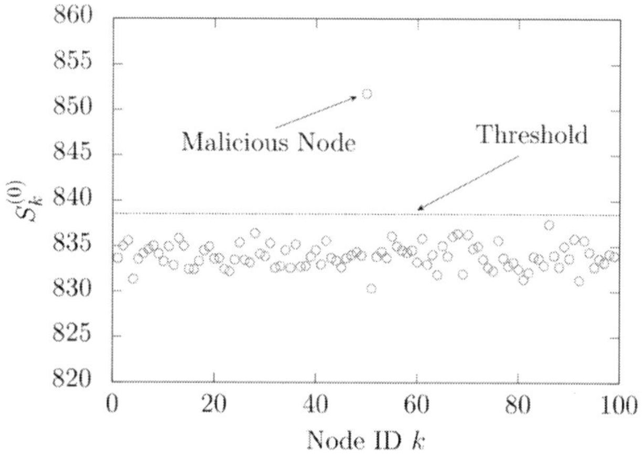

(b) $\lambda_{M,v} = 0.01$

Figure 3. Total suspicious score $S_k^{(0)}$.

Figure 4 shows the total suspicious score $S_{50}^{(0)}$ as a function of the elapsed time t. For small t, the total suspicious score $S_{50}^{(0)}$ is smaller than the threshold value t_h, and thus node 0 cannot identify the malicious node. On the other hand, for large t $(t > 100)$, the total suspicious score $S_{50}^{(0)}$ exceeds the threshold value t_h. Therefore, when the suspicious scores are sufficiently updated, our proposed method can identify the malicious node.

Figure 5 shows the total suspicious score as a function of the message generation rate Λ_M of the malicious node. For $\Lambda_M > 1$, $S_{50}^{(0)}$ and $S_1^{(0)}$ are larger and smaller than the threshold value t_h, respectively. Our proposed method can detect the malicious node when the malicious node frequently generates messages. However, for $\Lambda_M = 0.5$, the total suspicious score of the malicious node $S_{50}^{(0)}$ and the cooperative node $S_1^{(0)}$ are smaller than the threshold value t_h. This result indicates that our proposed method cannot identify the malicious node when the malicious node generates slightly more messages than the cooperative nodes.

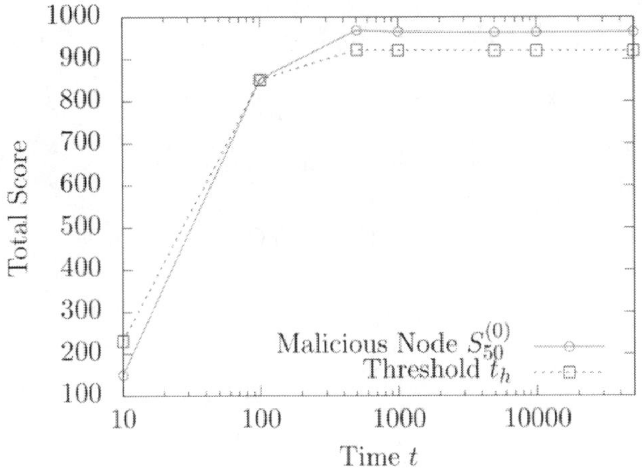

Figure 4. Total suspicious score as a function of elapsed time t.

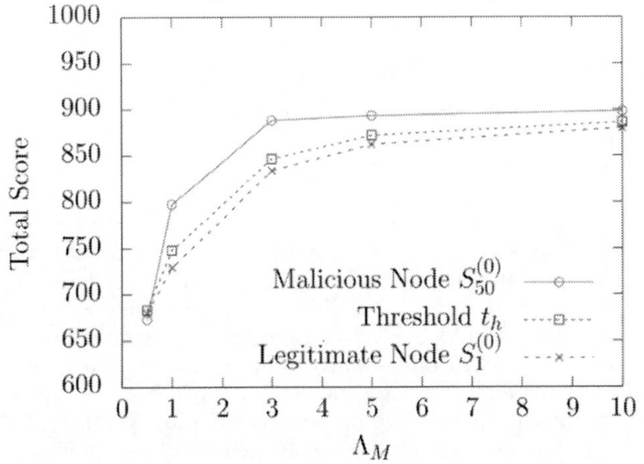

Figure 5. Total suspicious score as a function of message generation rate Λ_M of the malicious node.

V. Conclusion

In this paper, we proposed the detection method against the message flooding attacks, where the malicious node generates and distribute unnecessary messages to discard legitimate messages. In our proposed method, nodes records and exchanges the suspicious scores. After the suspicious scores are sufficiently updated, our proposed method discriminate between the malicious node and the cooperative nodes. Through simulation experiments, we showed that our proposed method can identify the malicious node if the suspicious scores are sufficiently updated. However, when malicious nodes generate just slightly more messages than cooperative nodes, in our proposed method, it is difficult to determine between malicious and cooperative nodes. We leave this problem for future work.

Acknowledgment

This work was partially supported by Grant-in-Aid for Young Scientists (B) of the Japan Society for the Promotion of Science under Grant No. 17K12679.

References

[1] Y. Cao and Z. Sun, "Routing in delay/disruption tolerant networks: A taxonomy, survey and challenges," *IEEE Communications Surveys & Tutorials*, vol. 15, no. 2, pp. 654–677, 2013.

[2] M. J. Khabbaz, C. M. Assi, and W. F. Fawaz, "Disruption-tolerant networking: A comprehensive survey on recent developments and persisting challenges," *IEEE Communications Surveys & Tutorials*, vol. 14, no. 2, pp. 607–540, 2012.

[3] A. Vahdat and D. Becker, "Epidemic routing for partially-connected ad hoc networks," *Duke Technical Report*, 2000.

[4] M. Grossglauser and D. N. C. Tse, "Mobility increases the capacity of ad hoc wireless networks," *IEEE/ACM Transactions on Networking*, vol. 10, no. 4, pp. 477–486, 2002.

[5] T. Kimura, Y Kayama, and T. Takine, "Home base-aware store-carry-forward routing using location-dependent utilities of nodes," *IEICE Transactions on Communications*, vol. 100, no. 1, pp. 17–27, 2017.

[6] T. Matsuda and T. Takine, "(p, q)-Epidemic routing for sparsely populated mobile ad hoc networks," *IEEE Journal on Selected Areas in Communications*, vol. 26, no. 5, pp. 783–793, 2008.

[7] G. Dini and A. L. Duca, "Towards a reputation-based routing protocol to contrast blackholes in a delay tolerant network, " *Ad Hoc Networks*, vol. 10, no.7, pp. 1167–1178, 2012.

[8] T. N. D. Pham and C. K. Yeo, "Detecting colluding blackhole and grayhole attacks in delay tolerant networks, " *IEEE Transactions on Mobile Computing*, vol. 15, no. 5, pp. 1116–1129, 2016.

[9] M. Alajeely, R. Doss, and V. Mak-Hau, "Packet faking attack: A novel attack and detection mechanism in OppNets," *Proc. of International Conference on Computational Intelligence and Security*, pp. 638–642, 2014.

[10] W. Khalid et al., "A taxonomy on misbehaving nodes in delay tolerant networks," *Computers & Security*, vol. 77, pp. 442–471, 2018.

[11] T. Idezuka, T. Kimura, and M. Muraguchi, "Behavior Analysis of Flooding Attacks in Sparse Mobile Ad-Hoc Networks," *Proc. of IEEE International Conference on Consumer Electronics - Taiwan*, pp. 1–2, 2018.

[12] R. Groenevelt, P. Nain, and G. Koole, "The message delay in mobile ad hoc networks," *Performance Evaluation*, vol. 62, no. 1–4, pp. 210–228, 2005.

BIG IoT – Interconnecting IoT Platforms From Different Domains – Final Results

Thomas Jell
Siemens AG
Munich, Germany
e-mail: Thomas.Jell@siemens.com

Claudia Baumgartner
VMW Berlin
Berlin, Germany

Arne Bröring
Siemens AG
Munich, Germany

Jelena Mitic
Siemens AG
Munich, Germany

***Abstract*—The Internet of Things (IoT) is today separated by different vertically oriented platforms for integration of all the different devices. Developers who aim to access other platforms and access that data are forced to manually adapt their interfaces to the specific platform API and data models. This paper highlights the work of the BIG IoT project that aims at launching an IoT marketplace and ecosystem as part of the European Platform Initiative (IoT EPI). The project finished end of 2018, so we present the setup and the final results of the integration of the use cases that have been implemented in Northern Germany, Italy and Barcelona.**

Keywords-BigIoT; Connectimg IoT; Interoperability.

I. Introduction THE PROBLEM OF MISSING IOT INTEROPERABILITY

The idea of the IoT is in widespread use since the last few years, collecting sensor data from various application domains. However, so far, these IoT platforms do not form a vibrant ecosystem. There have been lots of research and innovation projects in the context of the IoT. Nonetheless, no broadly used professional eco-systems for the IoT exist today. One reason for this is the large number of stakeholders who are involved in IoT ecosystems. Among these are providers of platforms and things, as well as application developers, and end users. Another reason for this issue are the high entry barriers for developers of ser-vices and applications. This is caused by the heterogeneity of all known IoT platforms. Developers who want to access things and additional data from different platforms need to manually access them by implementing specific adapters. Also, incentives are missing for platform providers to open their systems to third parties.

These different issues all relate to one particular challenge: the missing interoperability on the IoT. Today, various protocols and standards are available on the IoT [2]. This heterogeneity ranges from basic communication protocols such as CoAP [3] and MQTT [4], to focused standard families, such as oneM2M [5] or OGC SWE [6].

II. THE BIG IOT APPROACH

Bridging the Interoperability Gap of the IoT (BIG IoT) [6] is the project that aims at enabling the access of services and applications from multiple IoT platforms, standards and domains towards building IoT ecosystems.

Previous EC-funded projects that address such enablement of IoT ecosystems are, e.g., IoT-A, by providing a common architecture, FIWARE that offers Generic Enablers as building blocks, or projects such as compose and OpenIoT, which offer dedicated IoT platforms to aggregate other platforms and systems. BIG IoT will not develop yet another platform in order to enable cross-platform IoT applications. Instead, to reach the above outlined goal, BIG IoT builds up on 3 key pillars for an interoperable IoT ecosystem: (1) a common BIG IoT API, (2) well-defined information models, and (3) a marketplace to monetize access to resources. This approach is illustrated in Figure 1. Of central importance is the BIG IoT API, which includes functionalities such as ID management and discovery of things, access to things on platforms, tasking of things to send commands, as well as vocabulary management for handling semantics and security management. In order to interact with the marketplace, the API implemented by IoT platforms supports charging for access to things. The generic BIG IoT API as well as the underlying information models have been defined in conjunction with the Web of Things Interest Group at the W3C for standardization.

The details of this technical baseline have already been specified [8] in a comprehensive architectural design. Thereby, particular importance has been given to specific security and privacy requirements [7]. While these technical considerations build the foundation for the ecosystem to function, a crucial aspect to growing an ecosystem is the underlying business mod-el. Therefore, the BIG IoT project has analyzed various business cases and value networks [9].

III. USE CASES: OVERVIEW AND EXAMPLE

The BIG IoT project has developed a first prototype of an IoT ecosystem with overall 8 IoT platforms using all the common BIG IoT API. Among them are platforms from most of the partners: Bosch, CSI, Siemens, VMZ, and WorldSensing. The use cases to verify the interoperability span the mobility domain and include smart parking, bike sharing and traffic management. They are demonstrated and verified in pilots in Barcelona (Spain), Piedmont (Italy) and Berlin/Wolfsburg (NG, Northern-Germany).

The main focus is put on specifying services integrated and offered via the BIG IoT Marketplace. Additionally, applications based on the services that are show-cased are specified. The work is executed for all three pilots, taking into account the specific characteristics of the infrastructure as well as pilot-specific requirements.

The Northern Germany Pilot focuses in Berlin on the already installed network of parking sensors (Siemens) in dedicated areas as well as a variety of sensors throughout the city (VMZ).

Additionally a semi public parking area at VMZ's premises will be equipped with radar sensors to detect parking vehicles. Provided services and apps will be:

- smart parking,
- smart charging,
- public transport optimization,
- multimodal route optimization,
- parking and charging info and
- reservation of parking spots

The smart objects are charging stations, parking detectors and Wi-Fi probes as well as location sensors on buses, which deliver their data to availability services for further provision to the BIG IoT ecosystem. The data from those smart objects provided by the avail-ability services are used by other services or by the end user applications directly.

The services are

- Parking spot availability,
- Parking spot WMS,
- Parking reservation
- People density estimation on bus,
- People density estimation in area,
- Live bus location,
- Charging station availability and
- Charging station WMS.

The services support the different applications with offerings in terms of raw and aggregated data and functionalities.

We will present the first success story showing the integration of parking data from different sources (Berlin, Munich, Barcelona) via the already existing Marketplace into integrated end user applications.

IV. NORTHERN GERMANY PILOT

This BIG IoT Pilot makes use of innovative solutions already in place in the mobility innovation labs Berlin and Wolfsburg, the Northern Germany headquarter of automotive industry. The pilot shows how BIG IoT can contribute to mobility innovation in metropolitan areas, middle-sized towns and the connected com-muter traffic, addressing the future needs of urban and rural mobility. The pilots´ main target is to enable solutions for efficient parking, optimized public transport, better usage of e-mobility infrastructure and multimodal mobility information to support an efficient and sustainable mobility and a better environment. This is done by providing services and apps for

Smart Parking: Making use of on street Siemens parking radar sensors in Berlin and parking detectors in public car parks in Wolfsburg. BIG IoT provides a Smart Parking App to inform car drivers on location and availability of parking spots. Thus, car drivers find the closest parking spots and parking search traffic - a major cause for urban traffic stress - is reduced. The sensor data are provided by BIG IoT-enabled platforms such as Siemens APM (Advanced Parking Management) platform and BOSCH Bezirk platform. In addition to parking availability, reservation of parking spots will be provided as a service. Being BIG-IoTized enables Siemens Smart Parking App to consume any BIG IoT parking offerings, helps to extend the geographical coverage of parking information and increases business opportunities for service providers. Step one on the way to a European solution has al-ready been done with the integration of WorldSensing parking data of our co-pilot Barcelona – enabled by: BIG IoT.

Public Transport Optimization: Based on Wifi-sensors on connected buses Wolfsburg public transport operators get better information on bus occupancy and people waiting at bus stations. Wifi-sensor data is integrated in BIG IoT enabled BOSCH Smart City Platform. This helps to optimize vehicle usage and bus line planning to get more customer demand oriented public transport services.

E-Mobility: Where can I find the next free charging station to charge my e-car, e-scooter, e-van? By providing this crucial information to e-mobility users BIG IoT contributes to the success of e-mobility. E-Mobility in Berlin picked up speed in 2012 with first charging stations on public ground and has been continuously extended to presently more than 350 charging points. Location and status of more than 350 charging stations in Berlin are currently provided via BIG IoT enabled VMZ multimodal mobility platform. With higher numbers of e-vehicles the need to reserve a charging station will increase in the future. Thus, BIG IoT reservation service for charging stations is an appreciated Open Call contribution.

Multimodal Commuter App: This App consumes sensor and mobility data coming from various BIG IoT enabled platforms to inform Commuters on the route between Berlin and Wolfsburg. The App pro-vides car and public transport routing functionalities and guides car drivers to available parking spots and charging stations, includes BIG IoT offerings for real time traffic information such as traffic detectors data, incidents and traffic messages for car and public transport. Incorporating diverse data offerings of the BIG IoT Marketplace offering collection the App bridges the interoperability gap of various platforms to provide a multi-modal real-time based information system for mobility end users.

V. Results and Conclusions

BIG IoT provides the common base for enabling dif-ferent IoT platforms to access their sensors, data and services by a common BIG IoT API and the market-place behind to orchestrate exchange. The major results achieved have been:

- Subscribe to marketplace is a couple of lines of code, only
- Connect to data source is a couple of lines of code, as well

Effort for integration (as an independent docker con-tainer) of data has been reduced from days to minutes. More and more Data Sources and Services Providers joined and join allowing to choose in a rich marketplace.

Marketplace and all other source code is made avail-able open source through an eclipse license.

Acknowledgments

This work is supported by the BIG IoT project that has received funding from the European Commis-sion's Horizon 2020 research and innovation program under grant agreement No 688038. This article pre-sents the current status of work in the project. We thank the consortium partners for their feedback and fruitful discussions. The work will be further evolved as part of the ongoing architecture development in the project.

References

[1] Kubler, S., K. Främling, A. Zaslavsky, C. Doukas, E. Olivares, G. Fortino, C. E. Palau, S. Soursos, I. Pod-nar Zarko, Y. Fang, S. Krco, C. Heinz, C. Grimm, A. Bröring, J. Mitic, K. Olstedt and O. Vermesan (2016): IoT Platforms Initiative. In: Vermesan, O. & P. Friess, Digitising the Industry - Internet of Things Connecting the Physical, Digital and Virtual World. Chapter 9, pp. 265-292. River Publishers, ISBN: 978-87-93379-82-4.

[2] Bröring, A., S.K. Datta and C. Bonnet (2016): A Categorization of Discovery Technologies for the Internet of Things. 6th International Conference on the Internet of Things (IoT 2016), 7.-9. November 2016, Stuttgart, Germany. ACM. ISBN: 978-1-4503-4814-0. http://dl.acm.org/citation.cfm?doid=2991561.2991570

[3] C. Bormann, A. P. Castellani, and Z. Shelby, "CoAP: An Application Protocol for Billions of Tiny Internet Nodes," IEEE Internet Comput., vol. 16, no. 2, pp. 62–67, Mar. 2012.

[4] IBM and Eurotech, "MQTT V3.1 Protocol Specifi-cation." [Online]. Available: http://public.dhe.ibm.com/software/dw/webservices/ws-mqtt/mqtt-v3r1.html. [Accessed: 24-Apr-2014].

[5] J. Swetina, G. Lu, P. Jacobs, F. Ennesser, and J. Song, "Toward a standardized common M2M service layer platform: Introduction to oneM2M," Wirel. Commun. IEEE, vol. 21, no. 3, pp. 20–26, 2014.

[6] A. Bröring, J. Echterhoff, S. Jirka, I. Simonis, T. Everding, C. Stasch, S. Liang, and Rob Lemmens, "New Generation Sensor Web Enable-ment," Sensors, vol. 11, no. 3, pp. 2652–2699, 2011.

[7] Bröring, A., S. Schmid, C.-K.Schindhelm, A. Khelil, S. Kaebisch, D. Kramer, D. Le Phuoc, J. Mitic, D. An-icic, and E. Teniente (2017, forthcoming): Enabling IoT Ecosystems through Platform Interoperability. IEEE Software, special issue on: Software Engineering for the Internet of Things.

[8] Hernandez-Serrano, J., J.L. Munoz, A. Bröring, O. Esparza, L. Mikkelsen, W. Schwarzott and O. Leon (2017, forthcoming): On the Road to Secure and Pri-vacy-preserving IoT Ecosystems. 2nd International Workshop on Interoperability & Open Source Solu-tions for the Internet of Things (InterOSS-IoT 2016) at 6th International Conference on the Internet of Things (IoT 2016), 7. November 2016, Stuttgart, Ger-many. Springer, LNCS.

[9] Schmid, S., A. Bröring, D. Kramer, S. Kaebisch, A. Zappa, M. Lorenz, Y. Wang and L. Gioppo (2017, forthcoming): An Architecture for Interoperable IoT Ecosystems. 2nd International Workshop on Interop-erability & Open Source Solutions for the Internet of Things (InterOSS-IoT 2016) at 6th International Con-ference on the Internet of Things (IoT 2016), 7. No-vember 2016, Stuttgart, Germany. Springer, LNCS.

[10] Schladofsky, W., J. Mitic, A.P. Metzger, C. Simona-to, L. Gioppo, D. Leonardos and A. Bröring An Architec-ture for Interoperable IoT Ecosystems. InterOSS-IoT 2016 at 6th International Conference on the Internet of Things (IoT 2016), 7. November 2016, Stuttgart, Germany. Springer, LNCS.

[11] T. Jell, A. Bröring, and J. Mitic, BIG IoT – Intercon-necting IoT Platforms from different domains - First success story IEEE, Proceedings of the ITNG 2017

[12] T. Jell, A. Bröring, and J. Mitic, BIG IoT – Intercon-necting IoT Platforms from different domains - First success story IEEE, Proceedings of the ICE 2017

[13] T. Jell, C. Baumgartner, A. Bröring, and J. Mitic, BIG IoT – Interconnecting IoT Platforms from different domains – Use case Northern Germany IEEE, Pro-ceedings of the ITNG 2018

[14] T. Jell, C. Baumgartner, A. Bröring, and J. Mitic, BIG IoT – Interconnecting IoT Platforms from different domains – Final Results IEEE, Proceedings of the ICE 2019.

5G Networks: Advancement and Challenges

Christos Bouras*†, Paraskevi Fotakopoulou †, Anastasia Kollia†
*Computer Technology Institute & Press "Diophantus", Patras, Greece

†Computer Engineering & Informatics Dept., University of Patras, Greece

bouras@cti.gr, fotakopoul@ceid.upatras.gr, akollia@ceid.upatras.gr

Abstract—**Nowadays, mobile networks are an indispensable part of everyday life. Although the advent of 5G is imminent, given that the 2020 is approaching, there are still a lot of addressable questions. It becomes of great significance that the Advancements and Challenges of the 5th generation of mobile networks are presented. The Strong points and the Weak parts should be indicated so that they will be treated. In this paper, a review of the current foundational stones of the 5G networks is completed. The state of all different technologies is noted.**

***Index Terms*—5G, survey, mobile networks, SWOT analysis**

I. INTRODUCTION

It is a well-known fact that the 5G mobile networks are of great importance, since they have been discussed extensively. These networks will play an important role both for the scientific community and the everyday life in the next decade (2020-2030) at an international level. There is a worldwide race for 5G, which is currently won by China, that is prepared for the advent of the new technology.

5G mobile networks will be able to offer a wide range of technologies and services at unbelievably high speeds with lower latency. These technologies and services will support existing devices, such as smartphones, computers, tablets, new "smart" devices and Machine-to-Machine (M2M) communications and the Internet of Things (IoT). Substantial technologies are going to star in the future networks, such as Software Defined Networking (SDN), Network Function Virtualization (NFV), Cloud Computing, Massive Multiple Input Multiple Output (Massive MIMO), Cognitive Radio (CR), Ultra-dense deployments.

The main challenges concern higher data rates, ultra-low latency, high reliability, security and higher capacity than the current 4G ones. 5G will reach 1000 times the systems' capacity, 10 times the spectral efficiency, the energy efficiency and data rates and 25 times the average cell rate compared to what today's network provide.

In this paper, the main technologies that are going to star into the next generation of mobile networks authors are reviewed. The most vital parts and the most discouraging drawbacks are considered, the issues that need to be solved and the needs of the 5G networks are pinpointed. The current state of each key enabler is presented and several ideas for future investigation are listed.

The remaining part of this paper is structured as follows: In Section II, the most important points of 5G, namely the requirements, needs, advantages, disadvantages and current state and projects are analyzed. In Section III, the key 5G enablers that are the technologies that will meet the 5G goals. In Section IV, the main technologies are contrasted. In Section V, the main conclusions are summarized and future research activity in the field is proposed.

II. 5G

In this section, the most important issues, concerning 5G milestones, requirements, needs, advantages and challenges are presented.

A. Requirements

Requirements concerning the 5G mobile communication networks are:

- **High data rates:** 5G networks should support data rates around 10 Gbps.
- **Low latency:** The latency should be around 1 millisecond.
- **More intense security:** Connected devices lead to hazards for the network.
- **Low energy consumption:** of both network and devices.
- **Augmented scalability**
- **High reliability:** is critical in many 5G applications and services.

B. Needs

In contrast to previous generations of cellular networks, it is expected that the fifth generation will significantly improve the performance, allowing businesses to exploit a wide range of applications, services and possibilities, such as smartwatches, wearables, autonomous vehicles and Internet of Things (IoT).

- **Entertainment** (e.g., multiplayer gaming, real-time streaming, mobile social media, cloud gaming, in-car entertainment, etc.)
- **Virtual Reality (VR) and Augmented Reality (AR):** a person interacts with the environment in real-time, by using wearables.

- **Self-driving cars:** The 5G brings services and opportunities.
- **Smart cities:** The creation of a new digital ecosystem will benefit the citizens, as cities will function efficiently and sustainably.

C. Advantages & Disadvantages

It is widely known that people use the mobile networks on a daily basis, since the amount of the devices that use them are augmented. Some of the major benefits are:

- effectiveness and efficiency,
- more bandwidth,
- data rates of 10 Gbps or higher can be achieved, which will support more than 60,000 connections,
- the improved 5G network architecture leads to smoother handoffs.

There are some drawbacks concerning the usage of the 5th generation of mobile technology:

- security and privacy issues yet to be solved,
- less coverage distance,
- worries about possible health and safety problems.

D. Current state

There is no doubt that the 5G mobile communication technology will open a new dimension to our lives and will significantly alter our life-style. This is why many companies have started many tests of the fifth generation wireless technology. Funding will allow the country to become a major player in the development of 5G technology, as India aims to be the leader in 5G technology in Asia.

Vodafone performed the first UK trials in April 2018 using mid-band spectrum and China Telecom's initial 5G build-out in 2018 will use mid-band spectrum as well. Last but not least, the world first service of 5G was in South Korea, as the South Korean telecoms deployed it all at once on the first day of December in 2018.

Worldwide 5G commercial launch is expected in 2020, as much work remains in upgrading the current mobile infrastructure, in order to be able to accommodate 5G technologies, whereas many companies are pushing for launching 5G by 2019.

In 2019 and 2020 it is expected that several Spectrum and Band Arrangements will happen. The Radio Framework and the IMT-2020 Radio Specifications will be presented. And finally, an updated plan will be set for future network enhancement.

III. Technologies

In this section, the technologies that will contribute to the development of 5G are summarized. In Figure 1, the basic 5G key enablers are presented.

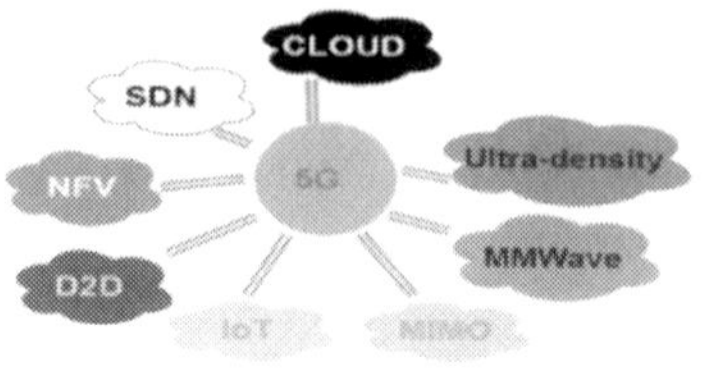

Fig. 1. The most substantial 5G key enabling technologies.

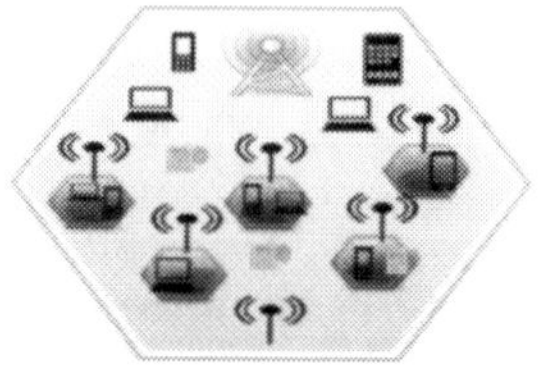

Fig. 2. An Ultra-Dense deployment architectural scheme.

A. Ultra-density

The Ultra-dense structure in the Figure 2 consists of different small cells (picocells, femtocells) that re-use bandwidth. Ultra-dense deployments offer the following benefits to end-users:

- **Higher throughput as well as lower round-trip time.**
- **Improved indoor coverage.**
- **Closed user group access.**

5G has substantial requirements, such as: 50 times more capacity, peak data rates exceeding 10Gbit/s and ultra-low latency below 1msec.

B. Software Defined Networking (SDN)

SDN splits the control and the data plane. There is the application plane, upon which a large amount of applications run. These planes are interconnected and interact with one another. The control plane is the smart part of the network and performs all the orchestration. A basic SDN architecture is presented in Figure 3. The open issues of SDN are [1]:

- **Controlling:**
  - Standardization of the control interfaces
  - Measures to avoid performance degradation
- **Reliability:**
  - Seamless connectivity/connection recovery
  - Security requirements in EPC and RAN

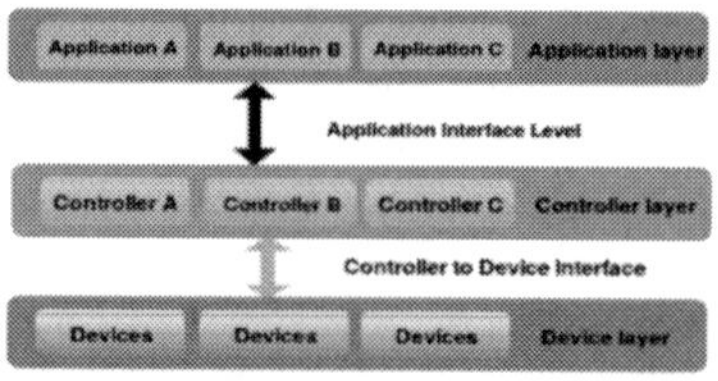

Fig. 3. A SDN deployment architectural scheme. [1]

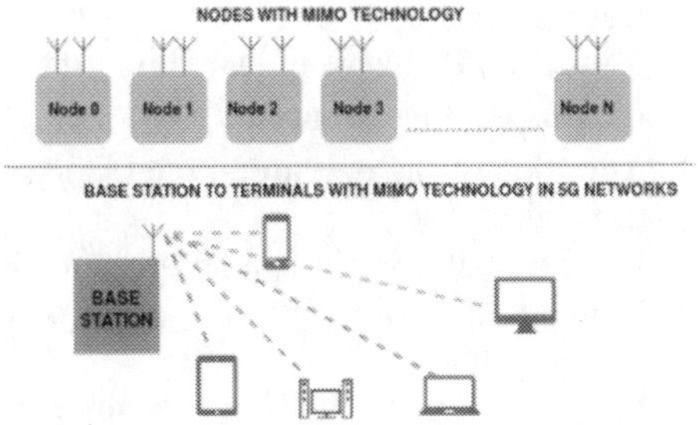

Fig. 4. A MIMO deployment architectural scheme.

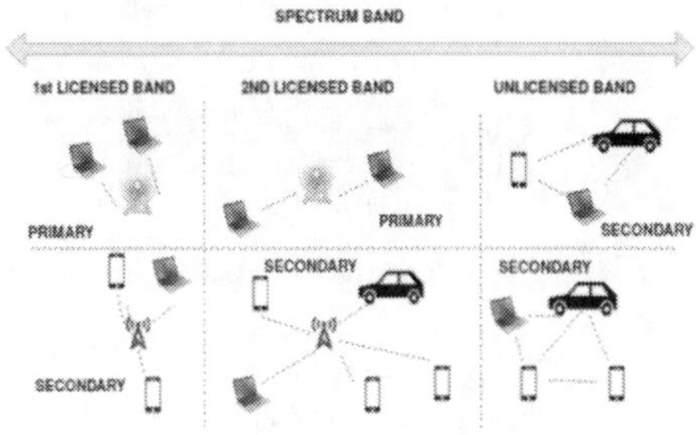

Fig. 5. A CR deployment architectural scheme.

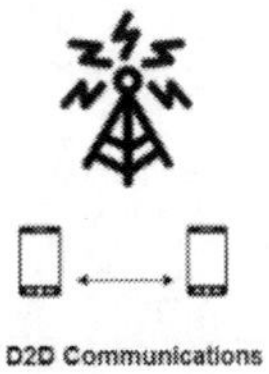

Fig. 6. A D2D architectural scheme.

- Equilibrium among performance, security and flexibility.

C. Network Function Virtualization (NFV)

NFV enables substituting hardware with software. Software or network functions are introduced into the network by using NFVs. These open issues are [1]:

- **Controlling:**
  - Seamless control and provisioning
  - Creation of network granularity policies
- **Reliability:**
  - Seamless and high quality connectivity
  - Virtualization of terminal points
- **Scalability:**
  - Carrier-grade scalability and robustness
  - Openness and interoperability

D. Multiple Input Multiple Output (MIMO)

One of the key 5G technologies is MIMO. This wireless technology includes a number of transceivers and receivers of the signal. Depending on the number of existing antennas, this technology is called MIMO or Massive MIMO. Figure 4 indicates how MIMO technology functions. This technology includes many advantages:

- **Augmented data rates & spectrum efficiency**
- **Quality of Service (QoS)**
- **Greener technology:** Lower energy consumption to the sender's side.

But its most substantial drawbacks are: **More Hardware & Complex software**

E. Cognitive Radio (CR)

On these networks, there are users, who have priority and access the licensed spectrum. There are also other users that perform real-time network status checks whether the licensed spectrum is being used or not. They use the unauthorized spectrum or the licensed spectrum if it is free. Figure 5 depicts the interaction with the network. The CR technology includes several fundamental benefits:

- **Re-usage of available resources**
- **Combination Technology**
- **Tax-free usage of spectrum zones** [2]
- **High-efficient networks** [3]
- **The sub-usage of the frequency zones**

The most important problems are listed below:

- **Need for multi-spectrum antennas**
- **Bigger safety gaps**

F. Device-to-Device (D2D)

Device-to-Device (D2D) is the communication between two mobile users without the Base Stations (BS) or the core network. Figure 6 presents the D2D architectural concept.

- **Basic Characteristics:**
  - **Trusted devices:** D2D allocate closed access to trusted devices in accordance to a list. [4]
  - **Modes:** There are a lot of different modes: Silent, Non-orthogonal Sharing, Orthogonal Sharing, Cellular. [5]
- **Advantages:**
  - **Gains:** D2D offer proximity, reuse, hop and paring gain. [5]
  - **Enables spectral reuse** [5] [6]
  - **Lower interference**
  - **Improvement of the energy consumption and throughput** [6]
  - **Combination with Wi-Fi direct:** Reduces power and delays.
  - **Short distance communication:** allow high spatial reuse.
- **Disadvantages:**
  - **User activity:** Is difficult or even impossible to be controlled.

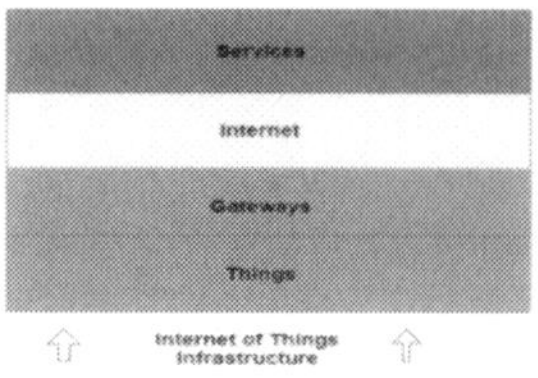

Fig. 7. An IoT abstract architectural scheme.

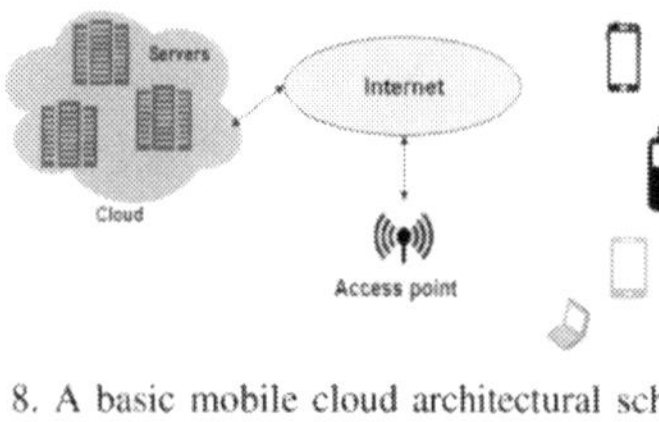

Fig. 8. A basic mobile cloud architectural scheme.

- **Device Power consumption** [5]
- **Interference Management** [5] [7]
- **Co-existence with overlay networks** [5]
- **Limited Penetration Capability** [8]

G. Internet of Things (IoT)

An IoT architecture varies enough per application. Several efforts of standardizing the infrastructure and the protocols are made. Figure 7 presents the basic IoT architectural concept. IoT is a technology that offers several fundamental benefits in terms of smart cities, e-health, smart homes, etc.

- **Health applications**
- **Specific set EU Guidelines**
- **Smart home applications**
- **Smart cities**
- **Challenges**:
  - **Privacy, Identity Management, Security and Access Control, Standardization and Interoperability, Data deluge**
  - **Security challenges:** Privacy concerns, Regulations and Policy, Violations and Criticism.

H. Mobile Cloud

The mobile cloud consists of: Terminal, Local Cloudlet and the Remote Cloudlet. Virtualization is a service approach that is widely used in Cloud [9]. Figure 8 depicts the basic mobile cloud architecture.

- **Characteristics:** Fairness, pricing approach and utilization period.
- **Types of Cloud:** Remote, Local or Hybrid [10].
- **Services:** Infrastructure as a Service, Platform as a Service and Software as a Service
- **Applications:** Individual, Group, Community, Opportunistic and Participatory Sensing.
- **Advantages:**
  - **Pay as you go**
  - **Data Storage**
  - **Reduction of Development time** [9]
- **Disadvantages/Open Issues:**
  - **Adoption of the operators:** offer cloud services to their clientele.
  - **Data security:** is debated and required by users.
  - **Cloud RAN problems:** Limited capacity, Insufficient and low utilization. [10]
  - **Base Band Unit (BBU) problems:** The BBU is low- compatible, inefficient and inelastic. [10]

I. Milimeter Wave (MMWave)

MMWave (30-300GHz) rends the under-utilized and unused bands of spectrum usable and connects more users.

- **Basic Characteristics:**
  - mmWave channel and beamforming technologies,
  - The 28 and 38 GHz will be the used bands,
  - 40 GHz is going to be the most possible one
  - The effective cell radius is 220m. [11]
- **Advantages:**
  - **More effective algorithms**
  - **MMWave communications promise to offer gigabit per second data rates**
  - **Digital Beamforming usage**
- **Open Issues:**
  - **Propagation losses**
  - **Delays:** Due to incumbent users that must be removed from the spectrum when it's licensed.
  - **Difficulty in the estimation accuracy** [12]
  - **E-band challenges:** Increased phase noise, limited amplifier gain, need for transmission line modeling of circuit components etc. [13]

IV. Compare & Contrast

In this section, the main technologies should be compared. A Strengths, Weaknesses, Opportunities and Threats (SWOT) analysis is a technique that helps indicating how several facts deriving from external or internal factors could be either helpful or harmful to achieve a goal or promote a product. Strengths and Opportunities are both helpful deriving from internal and external factors respectively. Weaknesses and Threats are both harmful and derive from internal and external factors respectively.

In the following section, a SWOT analysis Table I lists the Strengths, Weaknesses, Opportunities and Threats that are pinpointed concerning the 5th generation of mobile networks and its adoption.

Table II includes the evaluation of the 5G key enablers. The technologies are compared in terms of the following features:

- **Cost:** Although, most technologies reduce the costs, several of them include augmented Operational Expenditures (OPEX) costs. MIMO induce larger OPEX since

TABLE I. SWOT ANALYSIS OF 5G ENABLERS.

	Helpful	Harmful
Internal origin	1) **Better usage of Bandwidth (BW) (mmWave, Ultra-density, CR)** 2) **Network control & Management (CR, SDN)** 3) **Cost reduction (NFV)** 4) **Serve more users (MIMO, Ultra-density, SDN)**	1) **Interference (mmWave, Ultra-density, MIMO)** 2) **Need for Standardization (NFV, SDN, MIMO, CR, IoT)** 3) **Network attacks (SDN, IoT, D2D)** 4) **Need for marketing so that users adopt them (D2D, IoT, Ultra-dense)**
External origin	1) **5G implementation** 2) **More users imply more needs** 3) **Augmentation of data streams** 4) **Social media usage** 5) **Novelty**	1) **Augments expenditures (Ultra-dense, MIMO)** 2) **Create insecurity to users (D2D, IoT)** 3) **Difficulty to spread widely (SDN, NFV, D2D)**

an augmented number of antennas is needed, while in MMWave the BW used is more expensive.

- **Scalable:** Most technologies induce expendable characteristics, since it's very easy to add more network components or expand the network in a very easy way using less configuration. D2D and MIMO are not scalable since it's not easy to add more components (including ✓)
- **Efficiency:** Most technologies are very efficient and enhance the usage of resources in the network. (including ✓)
- **Coverage:** Most technologies cover the network offering more resources or reallocating the existing ones. (including ✓)
- **Capacity:** Most technologies offer augmented capacity. (including ✓)
- **Heterogeneous:** Some of the technologies (including ✓) cooperate well with others.
- **BW:** Some of the proposed models need more bandwidth to operate, while others are able to reallocate or better allocate the existing one. The Table II includes the: **reallocate**, which means that BW is reallocated, **need** means that more BW is needed for the network to operate properly, and the NFVs include **virtual** BW, because in these technologies the network resources are virtual, cheaper and efficient.
- **Cognitive:** Some of the technologies appear to be cognitive, namely they learn by the network's behavior and are exploiting data offering more resources in places needed. The **Statistics** are used in order to better allocate the resources. The Cognitive Secondary BSs have several capabilities and are able to check whether they can transmit to a bandwidth zone or not. **Cognitive SBSs**
- **Appeared:** The time frame in which a technology widely appeared in research.
- **Adoption:** The adoption level of each technology nowadays. **Little** means that is not widely adopted, while **Future** means that will be introduced in the future and **Large** means that it is already widely adopted in a large scale.
- **Standard:** For some technologies, standardization activities explain the solution's basic functionalities, while there are not standards for others (none). In Table II the standardization organizations are pinpointed.
- **Technology Readiness Level (TRL):** includes how "ready" is the technology to start functioning right now and follows a widely known technique, called TRL. It scales from 1 to 9 and the larger numbers mean that the technology is ready.
- **Reduced time:** Some of these solutions reduce the time needed (including ✓) in order to be introduced in the market.
- **Network management:** Some of the networking technologies are useful in order to manage the network (including ✓).
- **Interference:** The degradation of the signal happens to some technologies (including ✓).
- **Power:** The power consumption is augmented for some technologies and it induces several operational expenses (including ✓).

V. CONCLUSIONS & FUTURE WORK

Many different technologies, e.g., SDN, NFV, Cognitive Radio, MIMO, Massive MIMO, IoT, D2D, Cloud Computing, MMWave etc., are indispensable and therefore, are key enabling technologies for the 5th generation of mobile networks. These technologies have great advantages and

TABLE II. EVALUATION OF THE BASIC 5G ENABLERS.

Factor \ Solution	SDN	CR	Cloud	Ultra-dense	MIMO	D2D	IoT	NFV	mmWave
Cost	Reduced	Reduced	Reduced	Reduced	Increased	Reduced	Reduced	Reduced	Increased
Scalable	✓	✓	✓	✓			✓	✓	✓
Efficiency	✓	✓	✓	✓	✓			✓	✓
Coverage	✓	✓				✓		✓	
Capacity	✓	✓	✓	✓	✓	✓		✓	✓
Heterogeneous	✓	✓	✓	✓		✓	✓	✓	✓
BW	reallocate	reallocate	reallocate	reallocate	need	need		virtual	reallocate
Cognitive	Statistics	Cognitive SBSs							
Appeared	2011	1999	1996	2007	1970	2008	2008	2012	2017
Adoption	Little	Future	Little	Little	Large	Little	Little	Little	Future
Standard	OpenFlow	IEEE	Many	3GPP	IEEE	IEEE	None	Many	IEEE
TRL	8	7	9	9	9	9	9	8	8
Reduced time	✓	✓	✓					✓	
Network management	✓	✓						✓	
Interference				✓	✓	✓		✓	✓
Power	✓	✓	✓		✓		✓	✓	✓

there are several open issues that need to be addressed. The MMWave and MIMO technologies appear to have augmented OPEX. The MIMO and D2D technologies need more BW to be reallocated. The power consumption of the IoT, D2D and MIMO should be reduced.

Therefore, several solutions and algorithms of the new technologies need to be introduced. What is more, the CAPEX of all the technologies should be limited so that providers adopt these technologies.

REFERENCES

[1] C. Bouras, A. Kollia, and A. Papazois, "Sdn nfv in 5g: Advancements and challenges," in *2017 20th Conference on Innovations in Clouds, Internet and Networks (ICIN)*, pp. 107–111, March 2017.

[2] E. P. Iswardiani, D. Setiawan, A. Wahab, R. B. Bahaweres, and M. Alaydrus, "Techno economic approach of spectrum sharing between radar bands and lte cellular system," in *Telecommunication Systems Services and Applications (TSSA), 2016 10th International Conference on*, pp. 1–5, IEEE, 2016.

[3] P. E. Numan, K. M. Yusof, D. U. Suleiman, J. S. Bassi, S. K. S. Yusof, and J. B. Din, "Hidden node scenario: A case for cooperative spectrum sensing in cognitive radio networks," *Indian Journal of Science and Technology*, vol. 9, no. 46, 2016.

[4] M. N. Tehrani, M. Uysal, and H. Yanikomeroglu, "Device-to-device communication in 5g cellular networks: challenges, solutions, and future directions," *IEEE Communications Magazine*, vol. 52, no. 5, pp. 86–92, 2014.

[5] L. Wei, R. Hu, Y. Qian, and G. Wu, "Enable device-to-device communications underlaying cellular networks: challenges and research aspects," *IEEE Communications Magazine*, vol. 52, no. 6, pp. 90–96, 2014.

[6] X. Lin, J. Andrews, A. Ghosh, and R. Ratasuk, "An overview of 3gpp device-to-device proximity services," *IEEE Communications Magazine*, vol. 52, no. 4, pp. 40–48, 2014.

[7] A. Asadi, Q. Wang, and V. Mancuso, "A survey on device-to-device communication in cellular networks," *IEEE Communications Surveys & Tutorials*, vol. 16, no. 4, pp. 1801–1819, 2014.

[8] J. Qiao, X. S. Shen, J. W. Mark, Q. Shen, Y. He, and L. Lei, "Enabling device-to-device communications in millimeter-wave 5g cellular networks," *IEEE Communications Magazine*, vol. 53, no. 1, pp. 209–215, 2015.

[9] K. Gai, M. Qiu, L. Tao, and Y. Zhu, "Intrusion detection techniques for mobile cloud computing in heterogeneous 5g," *Security and Communication Networks*, vol. 9, no. 16, pp. 3049–3058, 2016.

[10] M. Chen, Y. Zhang, L. Hu, T. Taleb, and Z. Sheng, "Cloud-based wireless network: Virtualized, reconfigurable, smart wireless network to enable 5g technologies," *Mobile Networks and Applications*, vol. 20, no. 6, pp. 704–712, 2015.

[11] A. I. Sulyman, A. T. Nassar, M. K. Samimi, G. R. MacCartney, T. S. Rappaport, and A. Alsanie, "Radio propagation path loss models for 5g cellular networks in the 28 ghz and 38 ghz millimeter-wave bands," *IEEE Communications Magazine*, vol. 52, no. 9, pp. 78–86, 2014.

[12] S. Han, I. Chih-Lin, Z. Xu, and C. Rowell, "Large-scale antenna systems with hybrid analog and digital beamforming for millimeter wave 5g," *IEEE Communications Magazine*, vol. 53, no. 1, pp. 186–194, 2015.

[13] P. Wang, Y. Li, L. Song, and B. Vucetic, "Multi-gigabit millimeter wave wireless communications for 5g: From fixed access to cellular networks," *IEEE Communications Magazine*, vol. 53, no. 1, pp. 168–178, 2015.

A Dynamically Carpooling Dispatching Algorithm for Improving Efficiency of Self-Driving Taxis in the Connected Vehicles Environment

Hsu-Cheng Chung, Yu-Jung Chang, Kuo-Feng Ssu
Institute of Computer and Communication Engineering, National Cheng Kung University, Tainan, Taiwan
Email: q36054099@gmail.com, yjc@dcl.ee.ncku.edu.tw, ssu@ee.ncku.edu.tw

Abstract—**Since there is a great number of ride demands during the rush hour in major cities, passengers typically spend a lot of time waiting for the available taxis among the limited number of taxis. To address the issue, carpooling is a good way to reduce the waiting time of passengers. Most of the current taxi-sharing approaches have been proposed to deal with the taxi-sharing problem by utilizing traditional vehicles. In this paper, a dynamic taxi carpooling dispatching algorithm is developed in the connected vehicles environment to provide real-time taxi-sharing services. The approach schedules the proper taxis to provide the services for passengers based on the locations of taxis, the destinations of passengers, and the arranged destinations of taxis. The algorithm has been implemented and simulated by using the Simulation of Urban MObility (SUMO) simulator. The results show that the algorithm improves the service rate of taxis, the empty car rate of taxis, the average waiting time of passengers, and the driving distance when taxis are serving passengers.**

Keywords–Intelligent transportation systems; Dynamic ridesharing systems; Taxi dispatch schedule; Cooperative dispatch mechanism; Connected vehicles.

I. Introduction

With the rapid economic development of modern society, taxi is one of the important public transportation, which plays a vital role in the daily commuting for millions of passengers in urban areas. However, there is a large number of empty seating capacity of vehicles which are not fully utilized during the rush hour of major cities. For example, the survey conducted by the Federal Highway Administration (FHWA) shows that average vehicle occupancy in the US remains unchanged at 1.67 from 2009 to 2017 [1]. This result indicates the solution to under-utilized available transportation resources is still a challenging issue.

To tackle the issue, carpooling is a good way to make more efficient use of the seating capacity of vehicles to reduce the waiting time of passengers. Drivers share their trips with one or more passengers who have similar travel paths. Compared to the non-sharing scheme, the ridesharing scheme utilizes fewer transportation resources to satisfy the same quantity of ride demands. Therefore, the vehicle occupancy rate can be significantly increased by reducing the number of empty seats by using carpooling via the ridesharing scheme.

Several taxi-sharing approaches have been proposed for providing taxi-sharing services. These approaches [2] [3] can be broadly classified into two categories: static taxi-sharing scheme and dynamic taxi-sharing scheme. First, the static taxi-sharing schemes need prior knowledge of the information of taxis and passenger requests for scheduling proper taxis to satisfy passenger requests. However, the static taxi-sharing scheme cannot provide the satisfied service for the passengers that ask their rides at the varying locations and/or at different time. Second, the dynamic taxi-sharing schemes provide real-time taxi-sharing services without prior knowledge of the information of taxis and ride requests. In the most of the dynamic taxi-sharing approaches, the transport is supplied by traditional vehicles driven by human drivers to deliver passengers. Self-driving taxis will be one of the most important transportation in the future. Waymo has launched the commercial self-driving taxi service in Arizona in the Unite States [4]. Self-driving taxis can cooperate with each other to complete the tasks required from the cloud. Consequently, the dynamic taxi-sharing scheme using the self-driving taxi to transport the passengers could be a better choice to improve the whole system efficiency.

In this paper, a Dynamic Taxi Ridesharing Dispatching Algorithm is developed to provide real-time taxi-sharing services in the connected vehicles environment. With the proposed scheme, when passengers need rides, the method will dispatch the proper taxis for these passengers who need taxi-sharing services based on the location of taxis, the arranged destination of taxis, and the destination of passengers. The algorithm has been implemented and simulated by using the SUMO simulator. The results show that the proposed algorithm improves the service rate of the taxis, decreases the empty car rate of taxis, saves 30.93% of the average waiting time of passengers, and reduces 11.81% of the driving distance when taxis are serving passengers.

The remainder of the paper is organized as follows. Related work is described in Section II. The system model is presented in Section III. The dynamically carpooling dispatching algorithm is presented in Section IV. The performance of the proposed scheme is evaluated in Section V. Finally, Section VI concludes this paper.

II. Related Work

Various approaches aim to deal with taxi-sharing problems. These approaches can be broadly classified into two categories. This section describes a summary of the static taxi-sharing scheme and the dynamic taxi-sharing scheme.

A. Static Taxi-sharing Scheme

The static taxi-sharing schemes need prior knowledge of the information of taxis and passenger requests for scheduling the matches between taxis and passengers [3]. The static taxi-sharing problem can be viewed as one variant of the static Dial-a-Ride problem (DARP) [5]. In the static DARP, all transportation requests are known in advance.

Users specify pick-up and delivery requests between the origins and destinations of the vehicle services. Transport is supplied by a fleet of vehicles that provide shared services. The solution is to search for a set of minimum cost vehicle routes that serve as many user requests as possible under a set of constraints. Cordeau [6] proposed a branch-and-cut algorithm for DARP and reduced both the CPU time and the number of nodes explored in the branch-and-bound tree. This proposed method cannot be used to solve large-scale cases containing more than hundreds of users. Attanasio et al. [7] introduced a number of parallel implementations for the dynamic multi-vehicle dial-a-ride problem, based on a Tabu search for the static DARP. The proposed algorithms can meet a high percentage of user requests. Furthermore, most of the static taxi-sharing approaches focus on using either the ride reservation or the fixed-point taxi station to meet the ridesharing services [8]. Therefore, the static taxi-sharing scheme cannot meet the passenger demands in different locations and/or at different times.

B. Dynamic Taxi-sharing Scheme

The dynamic taxi-sharing schemes provide taxi-sharing services without prior knowledge of the information of taxis and ride requests. There are several dynamic taxi-sharing schemes have been studied in several previous works [9]–[16]. Most of these approaches utilize traditional vehicles to transport passengers. The approaches also consider the profit of human drivers or interpersonal trust among the drivers and the passengers. Ma et. al [5] developed a mobile-cloud based real-time taxi-sharing system which considered that the monetary constraints in ridesharing to provide incentives for passengers and taxi drivers. Although monetary constraints make the proposed model more realistic, some useful schedules are discarded even if they can significantly reduce the waiting time of passengers. Huang et. al [17] proposed the intelligent carpool system for drivers and passengers to find carpool matches at any time and in any place. The proposed system utilized a genetic algorithm-based algorithm to solve carpool service problems. The solutions typically require a greater amount of computation time.

III. System Architecture

This section describes the proposed system architecture. First, the system overview and the assumptions are presented in Section III-A. Then, the proposed scenario is illustrated in Section III-B.

A. Assumptions

Figure 1 illustrates the proposed system architecture, including a cloud, self-driving taxis, and passengers. There are three main assumptions in the system. First, each of the taxi participating in the system is the self-driving and connected vehicle, which is equipped with Internet access for mobile communication, and GPS receivers for obtaining its current location. In addition, each taxi has sufficient power and the capability of computation to perform all of the required operations for taxi-sharing services without the assistance of human drivers. Each taxi automatically reports

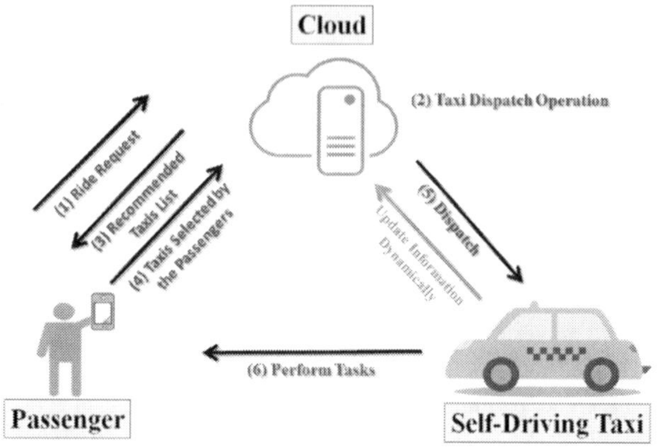

Figure 1. System overview.

it current location and the information of its status to the cloud. Second, passengers utilize the mobile application built on a handheld device to interact with the cloud system. The handheld devices with the GPS receivers provide current locations of passengers and have the capability for mobile communications. Third, the cloud has the capacity of computation, storage, and communication to conduct all of the operations for taxi-sharing services. The cloud continuously collects and updates the information of taxis and passengers. Real-time traffic conditions are provided by the connected vehicles environment.

B. Scenario

The cloud has the real-time location and status of taxis and passengers. The real-time road conditions are also available. When a passenger asks for a taxi, the passenger submits a ride request to the cloud. Each request consists of the origin and destination, the waiting time limit, the travel time limit, and the magnification rate of detour distance of the passenger's trip. The passenger can specify the origin location to be picked up, or the default location provided by his/her handheld device. The waiting time limit denotes the maximum time of the time a passenger is willing to wait. The detour distance ratio to the original driving distance cannot exceed the magnification rate. After the cloud receives the new ride request, the proper taxis are assigned by the algorithm based on the locations of taxis, the origin and destination of the passenger. The passenger thereby can check the waiting time for the taxis recommended by the cloud. After the passenger selects the desired taxi, the reply request will be sent back to the cloud. Once the cloud receives the reply request, the dispatch command is sent to the selected taxi. When the selected taxi receives the command, the taxi will pick up the passenger according to the schedule and the route given by the cloud.

IV. Dynamically Carpooling Dispatching Algorithm

This section describes the Dynamic Carpooling Dispatching Algorithm. As shown in Figure 2, the algorithm consists of three stages: 1) Preprocess Phase; 2) Inference Phase; 3) Dispatch Phase.

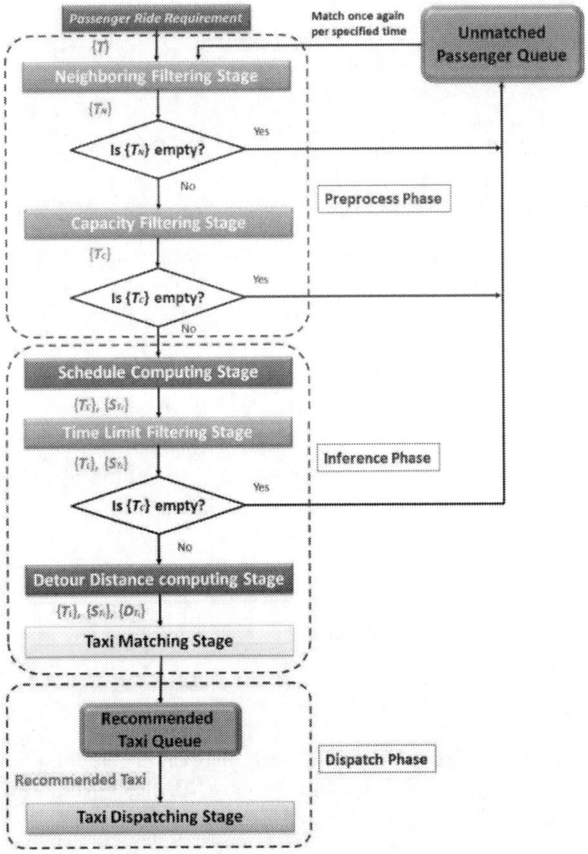

Figure 2. The flow chart of the proposed algorithm.

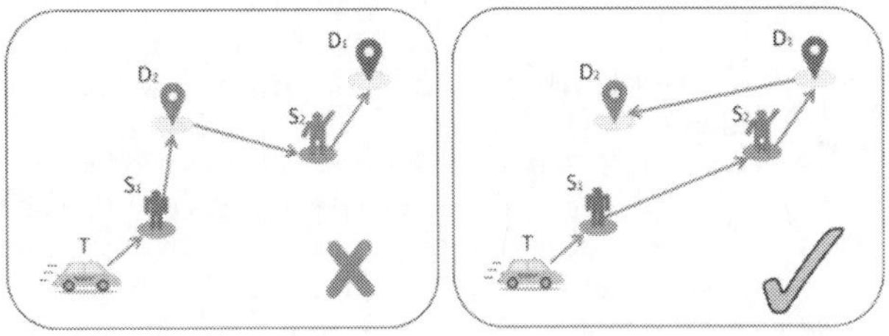

Figure 3. The examples of illegal and legal route schedules.

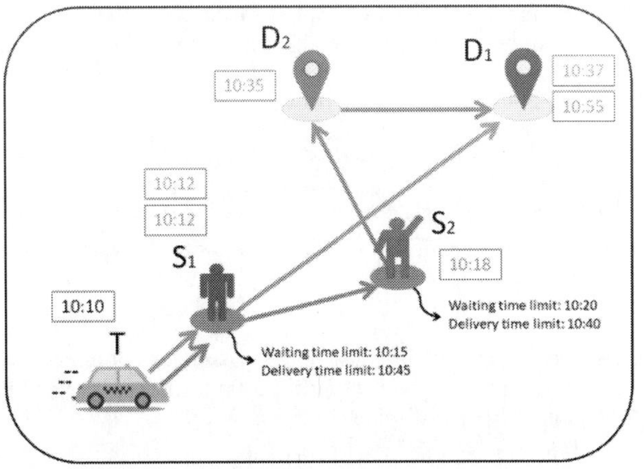

Figure 4. An example of the detour distance of ridesharing.

A. Preprocess Phase

The cloud takes the real-time information of taxis, passengers, and the traffic conditions as the input data. When the cloud receives the taxi-sharing requests, the detailed procedures of the algorithm will be conducted as follows.

Preprocess phase in the algorithm is a two-step procedure, which consists of Neighbor Filtering Stage and Capacity Filtering Stage. According to the waiting time limit of the passengers, Neighboring Filtering Stage filters out the taxis among all taxis T, which cannot arrive at the start locations of the requests in time. The eligible taxis which can satisfy the request in this step are stored in the list T_N. If there is no eligible taxi in the T_N to serve the requests, these requests will be stored into the Unmatched Passenger Queue for waiting for the next match. The match is performed every two minutes in this paper.

Capacity Filtering Stage filters out the taxis from the T_N, whose available capacity limit is less than the requested capacity. The remaining eligible taxis are stored in the list T_C. The seating capacity limit of each vehicle is set as four.

B. Inference Phase

Inference phase is a three-step procedure, which consists of Schedule Computing Stage, Time Limit Filtering Stage, and Detour Distance Computing Stage. Schedule Computing Stage schedules each legal route for each taxi in the T_C to satisfy the requirements of the requests by searching for all possible combinations of the taxis to serve all of the passengers in this match.

The examples of illeal and legal route schedules are shown in Figure 3. A taxi T is dispatched to serve two Passengers, P_1 and P_2, where S_1 and S_2 are the start locations of P_1 and P_2, respectively; D_1 and D_2 are the destination locations of P_1 and P_2, respectively. In order to satisfy the two ride demands, the taxi has to visit S_1, D_2, D_1, and D_2. Since not all of the routes are reasonable, some illegal cases are eliminated to reduce the computation in this phase. For example, the scheule $(T \to S_1 \to D_2 \to S_2 \to D_1)$ is illegal because each passenger should get on the taxi before getting off the taxi. On the other hand, the scheule $(T \to S_1 \to S_2 \to D_1 \to D_2)$ is a legal case. As a result, the number of legal route schedules can be computed as

$$\sum_{i=1}^{n} \frac{(2P_{R_i} + P_{T_i})!}{2! \times P_{R_i}}, \tag{1}$$

where n is the number of taxis in the T_C; P_{R_i} is the number of passengers who are picked up by the taxi T_i; P_{T_i} is the number of passengers who ride in the taxi T_i.

After considering each possible route schedules for each taxis T_i in the T_C to serve each combination of the passengers, the shortest distance of each legal route schedule is computed and stored in the S_{T_C}.

When a new passenger submits a taxi-sharing request for the taxi, Time Limit Filtering Stage will examine the legality of the waiting time limit and the travel time limit of those passengers who have already matched with the taxi. Some schedules passed the Schedule Computing Stage cannot satisfy the requirement of the requests. For example, the ridesharing schedule with a new passenger could increase the travel time of the original passenger who has sat in the taxi, resulting in exceeding the travel time limit of this passenger. Therefore, when a new passenger submits a taxi-sharing request, the waiting time limit and the travel time limit of the original passengers should be examined again.

Figure 4 shows an example of examining the legality of the waiting time limit and the travel time limit. P_1 is the original passenger who is served by the taxi T, and P_2 is a new passenger who wants to be served by the taxi T. The blue line is the original route of the taxi T, and the orange line is the presumed best route schedule for the taxi T to serve both P_1 and P_2. After P_2 asks for the ride request, the waiting time limit and the travel time limit of P_1 and P_2 will be calculated. The waiting time limit is expressed as

$$t_{w_i} = t_{r_i} + t_l, \tag{2}$$

where t_{r_i} is the time when the passenger submits a ride request and t_l is the waiting time limit of a passenger (the default value is 10 minutes).

The travel time is related to the travel distance d_i and the average velocity v_i of the trip. The travel time can be roughly predicted by dividing d_i by v_i. Assume that the average velocity of v_i for each taxi is set as a fixed constant. Then, the travel time limit can be expressed as

$$t_{d_i} = t_{w_i} + \alpha \frac{d_i}{v_i}, \tag{3}$$

where the detour rate of the passenger α is set as 1.5 (the maximum detour distance of the passenger trip is 1.5 times as long as the original detour distance). Algorithm 1 illustrates the pseudocode of eliminating the matches which are not suitable for the ridesharing schedule.

After examining the legality of the waiting time limit and the travel limit of each passenger in each legal route schedule in the S_{T_C}, the eligible taxis are stored in the T_L and the eligible schedules are stored in the S_{T_C}. If there is no eligible taxi in T_L to serve the requests in this stage, these requests will be stored into the Unmatched Passenger Queue, waiting for the next match.

Detour distance computing stage computes the total detour distance of the taxi, which serves all passengers in the route schedule. Specifically, Detour distance computing stage adds up each detour distance of each passenger, who is beening served by the taxi in the route schedule. The total detour distance of the taxi t denotes as d_t, which is stored in the set of D_{T_L}. The total detour distance D_T of all passengers D_p who are served by the taxi T can be expressed as

$$D_T = \sum D_p, \quad \forall p \in P_T, \tag{4}$$

Algorithm 1 : Eliminating the improper match

Definition:
- V: The set of taxi t, $\forall t \in T_C$.
- S: The set of schedule, s_v $\forall v \in V$.
- p_v: The set of passenger p in v, $\forall v \in V$.

Algorithm:

```
for all s_v in S do
  repeat
    pop mission m from s_v
    if m is start location of p ∈ p_v then
      if m does not meet the waiting time limit of p
      then
        remove s_v from S
        remove v from V
        break
      end if
    end if
    if m is destination of p ∈ p_v then
      if m does not meet the travel time limit of p then
        remove s_v from S
        remove v from V
        break
      end if
    end if
  until p is empty
end for
```

where the P_T consists of all original passengers who have been served by the taxi and the new passenger who selects the taxi for ridesharing.

$$D_p = D(T \rightarrow d_p) - D(T, s_p, d_p), \tag{5}$$

where D_p is the detour distance for a passenger p who is one of the passengers served by the taxi T. s_p and d_p are the start point and the destination of the passenger p, respectively. $D(T \rightarrow d_p)$ denotes the travel distance of the passenger p with the ridesharing scheme. $D(T, s_p, d_p)$ is the travel distance of the passenger p with the non-ridesharing scheme.

An example of computing the detour distance D_T is shown in Figure 5. In the beginning, the taxi T picks up the passenger p_1 at S_1 and delivers p_1 to his/her destination in Figure 5(a). A few moments later, another passenger p_2 asks for a ride. Figure 5(b) shows the shortest travel distance for serving both p_1 and p_2. Figure 5(c) shows the difference between p_1's driving schedules with ridesharing strategy and non-sharing strategy.

The detour distance of p_1 can be computed by subtracting the blue schedule distance from the black schedule distance, which is $D(T, s_2, s_1, d_2, d_1) - D(T, s_1, d_1)$. Similarly, the detour distance of p_2 presented in Figure 5(d) is $D(T, s_2, s_1, d_2) - D(T, s_2, d_2)$. Finally, the total detour distance D_T of the taxi T is calculated by adding up each D_p who is served by the T. Note that there might not only one passenger to be matched with the T when a new passenger asks for a ride. Algorithm 2 illustrates the pseudocode of the

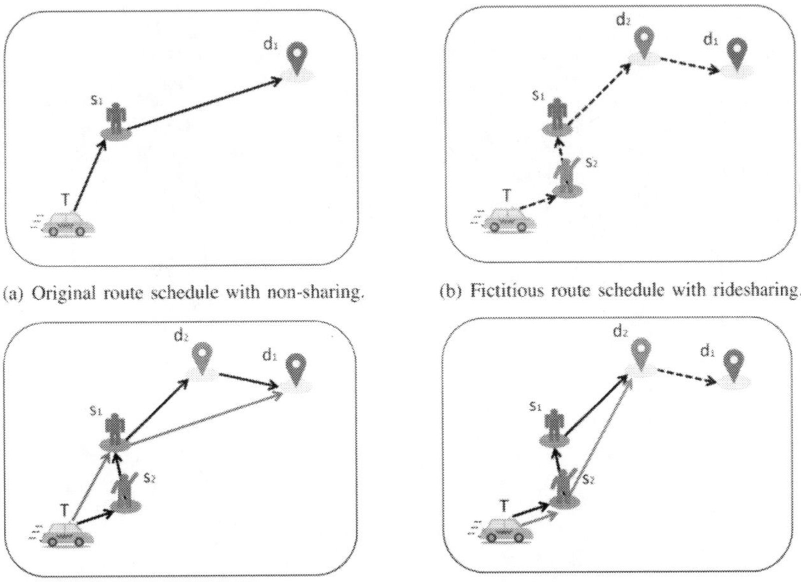

(a) Original route schedule with non-sharing. (b) Fictitious route schedule with ridesharing.

(c) p_1 detour distance illustration. (d) p_2 detour distance illustration.

Figure 5. An example of computing the detour distance D_T.

Algorithm 2 : Detour Distance Computing Stage

Definition:

T: The set of taxi t, $\forall t \in T_L$.
S: The set of schedule s_t, $\forall t \in T$.
R: The set of sorted route r_{s_t}, $\forall s_t \in S$.
M: The set of sorted mission m_{s_t}, $\forall s_t \in S$.
D: The set of total detour distance d_t, $\forall t \in T$.

Algorithm:

for all d_t in D **do**
  $d_t = 0$
end for
for all t in T **do**
  for all m_{s_t} in M **do**
    for all m in m_{s_t} **do**
      if m is the destination of a passenger p **then**
        origin_dis = $Dijkstra(v, p\_start) + Dijkstra(p\_start, p\_destination)$
        $carpool\_dis = \sum Dijkstra(r)\ \forall r \in r_{s_t}$ end when m is arrived
      end if
    end for
  end for
  $d_t = carpool\_dis - origin\_dis$
  store d_t to D_{T_L}
end for

Detour Distance Computing Stage. Note that the algorithm calculated the distance between the locations by using the Dijkstra algorithm. To reduce the computation load, the calculated distance information is stored in the database for the next utilization.

Taxi Matching Stage generates the Recommended Taxi Queue Q_{RecT}. In the Q_{RecT}, the taxis are sorted based on the following principles. First, the taxi with the smaller d_{T_L} has the higher priority. Second, when there are more than one taxis have the same d_{T_L}, the taxi closer to the passenger will have the higher priority.

C. Dispatch Phase

Dispatch Phase sends the recommended taxi requests to the passengers who need the taxi-sharing services. The recommended taxi which is pushed from the Recommended Taxi Queue definitely is the closest taxi with the shortest detour distance to the passenger. If the passenger agrees to the match, the selected taxi will be dispatched to the passenger immediately. On the other hand, if the passenger disagrees to the match and he/she sends an override reply back to the cloud, then the lower priority taxi in the Recommended Taxi Queue will be transferred to the passenger, reciprocally. The procedure will be iteratively executed until there is no taxi to be recommended in the Recommended Taxi Queue. When the Recommended Taxi Queue is empty, the requests will be pushed to the Unmatched Passenger Queue for the next match.

V. Performance Evaluation

In this section, the proposed algorithm is implemented and simulated to evaluate its performance. First, the simulation setting and evaluation metrics are introduced. Then the simulation results are presented to illustrate the effectiveness of the proposed algorithm.

A. Simulation Setting

The proposed algorithm is implemented and simulated using the SUMO simulator [18]. As shown in Figure 6, the

Figure 6. Manhattan on OpenStreetMap.

road network data is obtained through Openstreetmap [19], which is part of the Manhattan in New York City. The environment with a size of 30 square kilometers contains 4370 road segments. The time for each simulation is 7200 seconds. There are 250 taxis to serve 2,200 ride requests in the environment. In the simulation, it is assumed that the taxis will arbitrarily roam in the map if the taxis do not serve any ride request. Each taxi provides the taxi-sharing service for up to 4 passengers at the same time. The taxis must obey the maximum speed limit of the roads (60 km per hour). The trip information of all passengers, including request times, start positions, destination positions, are randomly generated. The trip distance of each passenger ranges from 1.5 km to 12 km. The maximum waiting time for each passenger is set to 10 minutes. The detour magnification in the simulation is set to 0.5.

B. Performance Results

The performance result of each metric is the average of 10 simulations. The proposed taxi-sharing algorithm was benchmarked against the non-sharing scheme.

TABLE I. OVERALL AVERAGE TRAVEL TIME OF PASSENGERS

Time Type	Non-sharing Scheme	Taxi-Sharing Scheme
Waiting Time	760.07 (675.49-819.84) (s)	239.38 (233.66-250.83) (s)
Riding Time	888.2 (884.86-895.91) (s)	899.06 (895.36-903.46) (s)
Travel Time	1648.34 (1597.91-1708.81) (s)	1138.44 (1130.26-1152.19) (s)

1) Overall Average Travel Time of Passengers: Table I shows the average waiting time, riding time, and travel time of the passengers for both the non-sharing strategy and the taxi-sharing strategy. The waiting time of the passenger is defined as the time between the passenger submits a ride request and the passenger gets on the selected taxi. The waiting time of the taxi-sharing strategy outperforms the non-sharing strategy. Since the passengers can utilize the taxi-sharing service with other passengers rather than spend time waiting for a vacant taxi. The riding time of the passenger is defined as the time between the passenger gets on the selected taxi and the passenger arrives at his/her destination. Due to the additional detour distance for

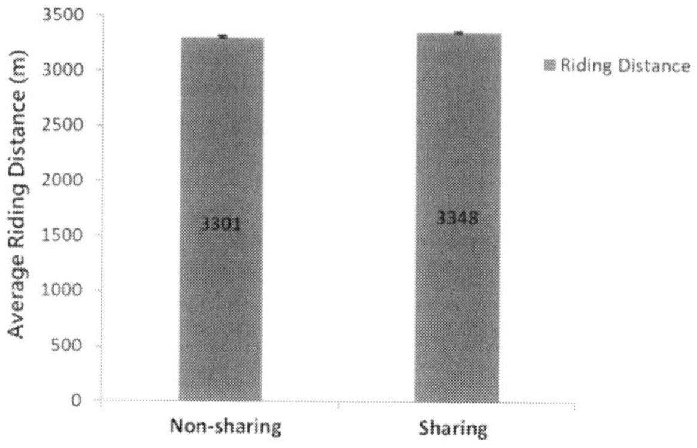

Figure 7. Average riding distance of passengers.

serving the carpooling passengers, the taxi-sharing strategy has a slightly longer average riding time than the non-sharing strategy. The travel time of the passengers is defined as the sum of the waiting time and the riding time. Based on the simulation results, the taxi-sharing method has the better travel time on average.

2) Average Riding Distance of Passengers: Figure 7 depicts that the average riding distance of the taxi-sharing approach is slightly longer than the non-sharing strategy. The main reason is that the passengers with the non-sharing approach are delivered to their destination with the shortest routes. The result also explains why the non-sharing algorithm has the better riding time.

TABLE II. COMPARISON RESULTS FOR THE SHARING AND THE NON-SHARING

Distance Type	Non-sharing	Ridesharing
Total Driving Distance	6616.07 (km)	6602.47 (km)
Driving Distance when Serving Passengers	6544.01 (km)	5771.01 (km)
Driving Distance while Carrying Passengers	4435.22 (km)	4929.27 (km)

3) Driving Distance Comparison: Table II shows that the comparison of the driving distances for both strategies. The driving distance can be divided into three types. First, the total driving distances of the two strategies are roughly the same because the taxis never take a break (except waiting for traffic lights and passengers to get on or get off). Second, the ridesharing strategy needs the shorter driving distance to serve all passengers due to its better efficiency. Third, the driving distance with carrying passengers for the ridesharing strategy is larger. The results can indicate that the taxis need the shorter distances to pick up the passengers.

TABLE III. COMPARISION OF CARPOOL RATE, EMPTY CAR RATE AND IDLE CAR RATE

Rate Type	Non-sharing	Ridesharing
Carpool Rate	0.00%	26.55%
Empty Car Rate	32.96%	25.34%
Idle Car Rate	1.09%	12.59%

4) Comparison of Carpool Rate, Empty Car Rate, and Idle Car Rate: The carpool rate, empty car rate and idle car rate are showed in Table III.The carpool rate is the proportion of the carpool participant among all passengers. The average carpool rate is 26.55% in the proposed taxi-

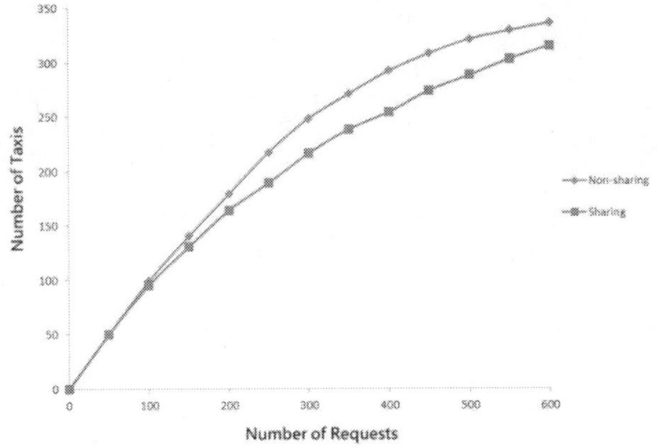

Figure 8. Number of taxis with respect to varying numbers of requests

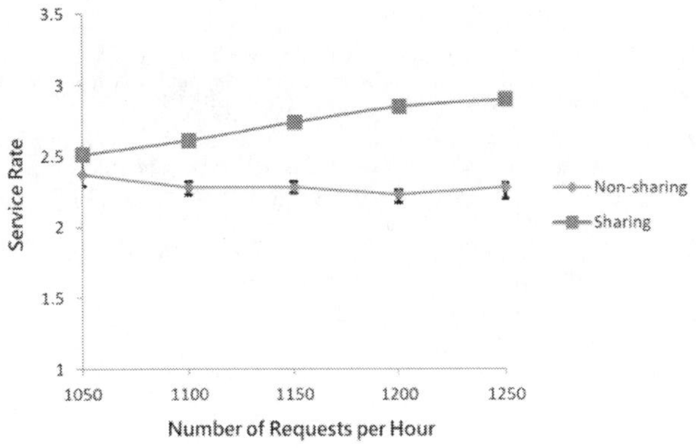

Figure 9. Service rate with the different number of passenger requests.

sharing strategy, which denotes that approximately one-fourth of passengers share rides with others. An empty car is defined as if there is no passenger in the car; an idle car is defined as the car has no ride task to perform. The non-sharing strategy has 1.09% idle car rate and 32.96% empty car rate, so the strategy is not efficient. On the other hand, with the taxi-sharing strategy, the results show that 12.59% idle car rate and 25.34% empty car rate, which demonstrate that the ridesharing system can achieve the better ride performance.

5) Number of Taxis with respect to varying numbers of requests: As shown in the Figure 8, when there are 400 ride requests, the taxi-sharing strategy can reduce 11% of the number of the needed taxis to satisfy all the requests compared to the non-sharing approach.

6) Service Rate of Taxis: Service Rate is defined as the average number of passengers who are served by a taxi per hour. Figure 9 displays the performance of the service rate with varying numbers of passenger requests. The service rate of the proposed taxi-sharing approach is always higher than the non-sharing strategy. In addition, the service rate of the proposed method continues to grow as the number of the request is increased from 1050 to 1250. The main reason is that the proposed approach can alleviate the higher ride demands during rush hour.

VI. Conclusion

This paper develops a dynamic carpooling dispatching algorithm to provide the ridesharing service in real time for improving efficiency of self-driving taxis in the connected vehicle environment. The algorithm has been implemented and simulated by using the SUMO simulator. Compared to the non-sharing strategy, the results demonstrate that the algorithm enhances the service rate, reduces 30.93% of the average waiting time of the passengers, and shortens 11.81% of the driving distance during service.

Acknowledgment

This research was supported in part by the Ministry of Science and Technology of Taiwan under Contracts 107-2221-E-006-091.

References

[1] "National Household Travel Survey," 2019, URL: https://nhts.ornl.gov/ [accessed: May 17, 2019].

[2] M. S. N. Agatz, A. Erera and X. Wang, "Optimization for dynamic ride-sharing: A review," *European Journal of Operational Research*, vol. 223, no. 2, pp. 295–303, Dec. 2012.

[3] M. Furuhata, M. Dessouky, F. Ordóñez, M. Brunet, X. Wang, and S. Koenig, "Ridesharing: The state-of-the-art and future directions," *Transportation Research Part B: Methodological*, vol. 57, pp. 28–46, Nov. 2013.

[4] "Waymo," 2019, URL: https://waymo.com/ [accessed: May 17, 2019].

[5] S. Ma, Y. Zheng, and O. Wolfson, "Real-time city-scale taxi ridesharing," *IEEE Transactions on Knowledge and Data Engineering*, vol. 27, no. 7, pp. 1782–1795, July 2015.

[6] J.-F. Cordeau, "A branch-and-cut algorithm for the dial-a-ride problem," *Operations Research*, vol. 54, no. 3, pp. 573–586, May 2006.

[7] A. Attanasio, J.-F. Cordeau, G. Ghiani, and G. Laporte, "Parallel tabu search heuristics for the dynamic multi-vehicle dial-a-ride problem," *Parallel Computing*, vol. 30, no. 3, pp. 377–387, Mar. 2004.

[8] J. Yuan, Y. Zheng, L. Zhang, X. Xie, and G. Sun, "Where to find my next passenger," in *Proceedings of ACM International Conference on Ubiquitous Computing (UbiComp)*, Spet. 2011, pp. 109–118.

[9] P. Chen, J. Liu, and W. Chen, "A fuel-saving and pollution-reducing dynamic taxi-sharing protocol in vanets," in *IEEE Vehicular Technology Conference - Fall*, Sept. 2010, pp. 1–5.

[10] S. Cheng, J. Li, and G. Horng, "Game theory based recommendation mechanism for taxi-sharing," in *Proceedings of International Conference on Advanced Information Networking and Applications Workshops*, May 2014, pp. 645–650.

[11] H. Zheng and J. Wu, "Online to offline business: Urban taxi dispatching with passenger-driver matching stability," in *Proceedings of IEEE International Conference on Distributed Computing Systems (ICDCS)*, June 2017, pp. 816–825.

[12] J. Hargrave, S. Yeung, and S. Madria, "Integration of dynamic road condition updates for real-time ridesharing systems," in *Proceedings of IEEE International Conference on Mobile Ad Hoc and Sensor Systems (MASS)*, Oct. 2017, pp. 585–589.

[13] S. Yeung, E. Miller, and S. Madria, "A flexible real-time ridesharing system considering current road conditions," in *Proceedings of IEEE International Conference on Mobile Data Management (MDM)*, June 2016, pp. 186–191.

[14] D. Pelzer, J. Xiao, D. Zehe, M. H. Lees, A. C. Knoll, and H. Aydt, "A partition-based match making algorithm for dynamic ridesharing," *IEEE Transactions on Intelligent Transportation Systems*, vol. 16, no. 5, pp. 2587–2598, Apr. 2015.

[15] J. P. Hanna, M. Albert, D. Chen, and P. Stone, "Minimum cost matching for autonomous carsharing," *IFAC-PapersOnLine*, vol. 49, no. 15, pp. 254–259, July 2016.

[16] D. Zhang, Y. Li, and F. Zhang, "Carpooling Service for Large-Scale Taxicab Networks," *ACM Transactions on Sensor Networks (TOSN)*, vol. 12, no. 3, pp. 18:1–18:35, Aug. 2016.

[17] S. Huang, M. Jiau, and C. Lin, "A genetic-algorithm-based approach to solve carpool service problems in cloud computing," *IEEE Transactions on Intelligent Transportation Systems*, vol. 16, no. 1, pp. 352–364, Feb. 2015.

[18] "Simulation of Urban MObility," 2019, URL: http://sumo.sourceforge.net/ [accessed: May 17, 2019].

[19] "Openstreetmap," 2019, URL: https://www.openstreetmap.org [accessed: May 17, 2019].

Variable Distinct l-diversity Algorithm Applied on Highly Sensitive Correlated Attributes

Zakariae El Ouazzani and Hanan El Bakkali
Information Security Research Team - ISeRT
ENSIAS-Mohammed V University
Rabat, Morocco
email: zakariae.elouazzani@gmail.com and h.elbakkali@um5s.net.ma

***Abstract*—In this information age, large amount of data is available online. These data are used by both internal and external sources for analysis and research purposes. The collected data is stored into huge data sets containing sensitive and Non—Sensitive Attributes. For the reason that attributes are generally separated, the correlation between these various attributes is lost. Thus, it will be necessary to prevent attributes from losing the correlation between them or at least reduce the correlation loss. As a solution, correlated attributes are grouped together. Although, the data utility is preserved by reducing the correlation loss between Sensitive Attributes, privacy protection remains a serious concern. The main problem here is publishing data sets without revealing the sensitive information of individuals and in the same time preserving data utility. Most of the current researches on ensuring privacy in big data are centered on data anonymization. L-diversity is an anonymization technique that can be applied on a data set with one or multiple Sensitive Attributes. This paper proposes an algorithm that deals with sensitive numerical and non—numerical attributes. The algorithm applies the principle of l-diversity technique after grouping highly correlated attributes together through a vertical partitioning. Our proposed algorithm makes a balance between privacy and data utility.**

***Index Terms*—big data; anonymization; l-diversity technique; non—numerical attributes; correlation; Pearson.**

I. INTRODUCTION

In recent years, the data collected by public and private organizations are increasing every day and stored in electronic repositories. The collected data includes various types of attributes, especially sensitive ones [1]. Besides, Big data sets can be used in different sectors, for example, biology, online banking, medical research and so on [2]. However, more challenges are rising since the collected data includes sensitive information [1]. The first challenge is preserving data utility. Because each attribute is universally separated, the correlations between different Sensitive Attributes are lost. This will be a major problem when performing analysis about data utility [3]. Thus, we have to reduce the correlation loss between attributes by grouping highly correlated attributes together. However, even if the data utility is preserved by dividing the huge data set into various data sets containing only highly correlated attributes, the challenge of ensuring privacy remains a crucial issue when sharing a data set that contains personal information [4]. Current information technologies create vast amount of data characterized by velocity, volume and veracity. So, disseminating this data increases the possibility of violating the privacy of individuals. That's why privacy protection is considered as one of the most important issues in big data processing [5]. In order to ensure privacy, data has to be sanitized and the best way of sanitization is data anonymization. There are several anonymization techniques treating Sensitive Attributes in the literature, one of them is called "l-diversity" using horizontal partitionning. The main idea behind "l-diversity" is that the values of the Sensitive Attributes are well—represented in each bucket [6]. In this paper, a new algorithm of data anonymization is proposed. It is a variable distinct l-diversity algorithm applied on highly sensitive correlated attributes whatever its type: numerical or non-numerical. The algorithm makes a balance between data privacy and data utility. Besides, it is divided into two main parts. The first one is intended for preserving data utility by grouping highly correlated attributes together in several data sets. We used "Pearson" correlation tool to determine the highly correlated attributes. Although, "Pearson" tool processes numerical values only, we used an algorithm that converts non—numerical values into numerical ones to process non—numerical attributes too. The second part used the l-diversity principle by splitting the data set horizontally into buckets including distinct values in order to ensure privacy. In this paper, we try to prove that the l-diversity principle must only be applied on data sets including highly correlated attributes; otherwise, l-diversity will not be an effective anonymization technique.

The reminder of the paper is organized as follows: in Section 2, we will make an overview of some works found in literature using l-diversity technique in order to ensure privacy in big data. Next, in Section 3, we will present the proposed technique including the algorithm. Later, in Section 4, we give our experimental results applied on a part of a real data set. Finally, we conclude our paper and give some perspectives in Section 5.

II. RELATED WORK

Generally, l-diversity technique aims to ensure privacy in huge data sets. In most of cases, l-diversity is applied on a data set while the threshold l is fixed to a specific value. Besides, the degree of correlation between attributes is not considered. For instance, Priyadarsini et al. in [7] proposed an Enhanced l-diversity algorithm able to diversify several Sensitive Attributes without dividing the data set. The proposed algorithm attempts to support multiple Sensitive Attributes for l-diversity by applying certain conditions to determine the size of the bucket. Moreover, Priyadarsini et al. in [7] accommodate the values corresponding to the sensitive categorical attributes within each bucket by setting the value of the threshold l based on the occurrence of distinct values in the whole column. Besides, Sei et al. in [8] suggested a privacy model called $(l_1, ..., l_q)$-diversity, which can deal with databases including various sensitive Quasi-Identifier (QI) attributes. The proposed method in [8] does not make any modifications on the original data set but adds various random values to each attribute in the data set to realize $(l_1, ..., l_q)$-diversity. Therefore, the threshold l is set to a fixed value. Moreover, Oishi et al. in [4] presented (l, d)-semantic diversity algorithm considering the resemblance of sensitive attribute values within each bucket by adding distances to settle the problem of impossibility to satisfy the threshold l of l-diversity. The algorithm in [4] satisfies l-diversity through a method based on adding a Boolean indicator to every sensitive attribute without generalizing the Quasi-Identifier attributes. Also, Gaoming et al. in [9] proposed a (k, l, θ)-diversity model based on clustering to reduce information loss and increase the usefulness of data. The algorithm in [9] takes as input three parameters, the thresholds k and l correspond to k-anonymity and l-diversity techniques respectively and the parameter θ corresponds to the degree of privacy preserving. Additionally, A new technique using the principle of l-diversity is presented by Y. Sei and Ohsuga in [10], which randomizes the Sensitive Attributes belonging to each individual. The method in [10] is divided into two parts; the first one concerns the data holder where $l-1$ random values are generated and added to a sensitive attribute in the whole original data set. The second one concerns the data user where the user has the possibility to identify the QI attributes that should be analyzed based on the relation between QI attributes and sensitive ones. Furthermore, Chakraborty et al. in [11] proposed (α, l) and recursive (α, c, l) diversity techniques. Both eigenvector centrality and noise node addition concepts are used in the process in order to create an anonymized network. In other sector, Tu et al. in [12] proposed a heuristic algorithm in order to get an approximate solution. The algorithm meets l-diversity principle for protecting trajectory privacy through specific generalization, while guaranteeing the smallest loss of spatiotemporal granularity. Besides, R. Yogesh Kulkarni and Murugan in [13] proposed an algorithm called, CPGEN (C-mixture based Privacy GENetic algorithm) in order to ensure privacy. The method in [13] combines the genetic algorithm with C-mixture theory for privacy measurements. The C-mixture is a new privacy measure, which integrates various privacy constrains belonging to both k-anonymity and l-diversity principles. Moreover, Susan and Christopher in [14] suggested an anonymization technique by combining the advantages of anatomization, and an improved slicing technique using both k-anonymity and l-diversity principles to treat high dimensional data sets, which include various Sensitive Attributes. The anatomization approach reduces the information loss and slicing algorithm preserves the correlation and utility.

The main idea of this paper is inspired from the previous works and we assume that l-diversity principle has to be applied only on highly correlated attributes in order to ensure privacy and preserve utility. In the next section, we will present our proposed technique including the algorithm that applies the principle of l-diversity on a data set containing attributes having strong correlation between them.

III. The Proposed Technique and Some Related Concepts

Our proposed technique ensures privacy by applying l-diversity principle on highly correlated attributes. Besides, the technique preserves data utility by grouping every two highly correlated attributes in a data set.

A. L-diversity and Correlation

1) Correlation analysis: With data analysis techniques, precious information could be extracted from big data. In data analysis, big data technologies includes data mining, machine learning and correlation analysis [15]. Correlation is a well-known mathematical and statistical method for analyzing the compatibility of huge data sets [15]. Since each attribute is generally separated and thus distinguishable, the correlation between various attributes is lost. This is considered as an inherent issue to make efficient analysis of attribute correlations [3]. In order to reduce the correlation loss, a partitioning approach is proposed in [16] based on the lexicographic and Non-Sensitive Attributes (NSAs) sorted by correlation between NSAs and Sensitive Attributes (SA). Besides, this approach preserves the published data utility [16]. Authors in [3], [16]–[18] used vertical partitioning by grouping attributes into columns according to the correlations existing between these attributes where only highly correlated ones are grouped into columns. The main idea is to break the association between columns while preserving the relationship within each column [3] and [17]. The fact of grouping highly correlated attributes together minimizes the high dimensionality of the data set [17] and [18], moreover, it preserves better utility than generalization and bucketization approaches [17]. Besides, as mentioned in [3], [14], [17], [18], slicing technique preserves data utility because highly correlated attributes are grouped together while conserving the correlations between such attributes. The evaluation of the correlations between the pairs of attributes could be realized through several correlation tools depending on the type of the treated attributes. For instance, Pearson correlation coefficient is utilized to evaluate the correlation between two continuous attributes [18], whereas mean-square contingency coefficient is a chi-square measure of correlation between two categorical attributes [16] and [18].

In this paper, we used Pearson tool to identify the highly correlated attributes whether they are numerical or not. In the case we have non-numerical attributes in the data set; we convert non numerical values into numerical ones through a proposed converting algorithm. The algorithm gives the same number to similar values in the data set. This conversion will give us the opportunity to process different types of data. The Pearson correlation tool is used to calculate the degree of linear correlation between two numerical attributes through 1 [19].

$$\frac{\sum_i (x_i - \bar{x})(y_i - \bar{y})}{\sqrt{\sum_i (x_i - \bar{x}) \sum_i (y_i - \bar{y})}} \quad (1)$$

Where $\bar{x}$= the mean of x variable.

and $\bar{y}$= the mean of y variable.

The correlation here is the sum of the multiplication between corresponding numbers related to the treated attributes. Besides, the resulting correlation values are in the range $[-1.0, +1.0]$. After calculation Pearson correlation coefficient for all the pairs of attributes existing in the data set, we identify those corresponding to the highest value in order to apply the l-diversity principle on a data set containing only highly correlated attributes.

2) L-diversity principle: Most of anonymization techniques existing in the literature are applied before publishing the data set [20]. Some of these techniques deal with quasi identifier attributes and others deal with sensitive ones. In this paper, a technique using the principle of distinct l-diversity is suggested dealing with Sensitive Attributes. Besides, the proposed variable l-diversity technique doesn't take into consideration any prior value of the threshold l. Furthermore, the principle of l-diversity has been introduced to improve traditional data mining that preserves privacy. l-diversity is considered as an important technique in privacy protection [21]. L-diversity is a group based form of anonymization used to ensure privacy in huge data sets by minimizing the huge scale of big data in term of representation [21]. The l-diversity model (Distinct, Entropy, Recursive) is an extension of the k-anonymity technique, which deal with QI attributes [22] and [23]. L-diversity ensures that an adversary needs $l-1$ values using background knowledge to deduce $l-1$ possible values of a sensitive attribute in order to violate privacy [9] and [24]. In other words, an equivalence class (EC), also called bucket is deemed to satisfy l-diversity if there are at least l "well-represented" values related to the treated Sensitive Attributes (SAs) [6], [24], [25]. Then, the whole data set is deemed to satisfy l-diversity when every bucket existing in that data set satisfies l-diversity [24] and [25]. Moreover, l-diversity helps to mitigate both homogeneity and background knowledge attacks [22] and [25]. Existing methods for l-diversity only take into consideration l "well represent" sensitive values. However, they omit the size of every bucket in the data set. Thus, the loss of information in the published data sets is much larger, which lead to a decrease concerning the data utility [9]. Our proposed algorithm applies the principle of distinct l-diversity without a prior value of the threshold "l". That means that the value of l is not fixed, so there is an opportunity to maximize this value in order to ensure privacy as much as possible. In the next part of this section, we will present our proposed algorithm, which applies the principle of variable distinct l-diversity on highly correlated attributes.

B. The proposed Algorithm

Algorithm 1 L-diversity on highly correlated attributes algorithm

```
1: procedure ANONYMIZATION
2:     OriginalTable[1 → N] struct attr1(String) attr2(String)...attrL(String) end struct
3:     D1[1 → N] struct attr1(String) attr2(String)...attrL(String) end struct
4:     D2[1 → N] struct attr1(String) attr2(String)...attrL(String) end struct
5:     RT[1 → N] struct attr1(String) attr2(String)...attrL(String) end struct
6:     Conversion(OriginalTable)
7:     hc ← 0
8:     indi ← 0
9:     indj ← 0
10:    p ← 0
11:    find ← 0
12:    i ← 1
13:    while i<L − 1 do
14:        j ← i + 1
15:        while j<L do
16:            p = pearson(OriginalTable[.].attr[i], OriginalTable[.].attr[j])
17:            if hc<p then
18:                hc ← p
19:                indi ← i
20:                indj ← j
21:            j + +
22:        i + +
23:    repeat
24:        D1.put(OriginalTable[0])
25:        i ← 1
26:        while i<N do
27:            find ← 0
28:            if D1.Contains(OriginalTable[i].attr[indi]) then
29:                find ← 1
30:                if find = 1 then
31:                    RT.put(OriginalTable[i])
32:                else
33:                    D1.put(OriginalTable[i])
34:            i + +
35:        D2.put(D1[0])
36:        i ← 1
37:        while i<D1.length() do
38:            find ← 0
39:            if D2.Contains(D1[i].attr[indj]) then
40:                find ← 1
41:                if find = 1 then
42:                    RT.put(D1[i])
43:                else
44:                    D2.put(D1[i])
45:            i + +
46:        Clear(OriginalTable)
47:        Copy(OriginalTable, RT)
48:    until RT.isEmpty()
```

Our algorithm is divided into two parts. The first one identifies the two highly correlated attributes among all the attributes in the Original Table. The second one presents the process of applying l-diversity principle. The anonymization process is applied on a Table containing N tuples and L attributes. The attributes are the fields of a structure.

In the first part, from line 6 to line 22 in the algorithm, the identification of the two highly correlated attributes is realized through a correlation tool called "Pearson". Since the data set could contain both numerical and non-numerical attributes and also Pearson tool processes only numerical attributes, we convert non-numerical attributes into numerical ones. Then, we calculate the correlation coefficient between every two attributes p in the Original Table. After that, we save the indexes *indi* and *indj* of the attributes corresponding to the highest correlation coefficient *hc*.

In the second part, from line 23 to line 48 in the algorithm, we apply *l*-diversity on the two attributes, which have the highest correlation. We start by identifying the distinct values corresponding to the first attribute, then, we put these tuples in *D1* Table, the remaining tuples are put in *RT* Table. However, Table *D1* may still contain non distinct values with respect to the second attribute. Then, we copy distinct tuples in Table *D1* with respect to the second attribute in Table *D2*, besides, we add the remaining tuples in *D1* to *RT* Table. Thus, *D2* is the *l*-diversity Table with distinct values with respect to both highly correlated attributes. Once the process ends, we clear the Original Table and we copy the content of *RT* Table in the original table and we repeat the process of *l*-diversity until *RT* Table is empty. The complexity of the anonymization part of the algorithm is of the order of $N^{2*NbBuckets}$ where *NbBuckets* is the number of buckets existing in the data set and *N* is the number of tuples in the same data set. Therefore, when we analyse the bloc "repeat-until", we find that there are two loops inside. The first while loop processes *NbBuckets* operations because we identify distinct values corresponding to the first attribute in the *OriginalTable*. Later, in the second while loop we identify distinct values corresponding to the second attribute based on the result table of the previous loop. Then, we analyse the "repeat-until" bloc and according to the algorithm, we notice that the process is repeated *N* times, which is the number of lines in the *OriginalTable*.

In the next section, we will highlight the different steps of the proposed algorithm applied on a part of real data set.

IV. Experimental Results

Now, we will implement our algorithm on a test table related to health sector. We have developed our algorithm with Java tool. Table I is a part of a real data set called "careplans" [26], which contains several attributes like "Disease", "Treatment", "Date of diagnosis" and "Cure date". I mention that I have randomly selected 9 tupes from the "careplans" real data set.

TABLE I
The Original Table.

Id	Disease	Treatment	Date of diagnosis	Cure date
1	Whiplash injury to neck	Recommendation to rest	04/09/2015	27/09/2015
2	Whiplash injury to neck	Musculoskeletal care	15/02/2008	17/03/2008
3	Fracture of forearm	Recommendation to rest	18/12/2007	04/02/2008
4	Gout	Healthy diet	18/01/1968	24/09/1975
5	Gout	Musculoskeletal care	18/01/1968	24/09/1975
6	Rheumatoid arthritis	Ice therapy	16/12/2005	13/08/2010
7	Whiplash injury to neck	Recommendation to rest	28/12/1942	05/02/1943
8	Gout	Healthy diet	18/01/1968	24/09/1975
9	Rheumatoid arthritis	Healthy diet	16/12/2005	13/08/2010

Table I represents our original test table. Besides, Table II represents Table I after the application of the conversion process. We substitute non-numerical values (String and Date types) by numerical ones.

TABLE II
The original table after anonymization.

Id	Disease	Treatment	Date of diagnosis	Cure date
1	1	5	9	15
2	1	6	10	16
3	2	5	11	17
4	3	7	12	18
5	3	6	12	18
6	4	8	13	19
7	1	5	14	20
8	3	7	12	18
9	4	7	13	19

After converting non numerical values, we calculate the correlation between every two attributes in the data set. First, we calculate the correlation between "Disease" attribute and the other attributes in the data set. In the following, we give the corresponding Pearson correlation coefficients:

$r(Disease, Treatment) = 0.8431$

$r(Disease, Date\ of\ diagnosis) = 0.5103$

$r(Disease, Cure\ date) = 0.5103$

The correlation between "Disease" and "Treatment" attributes is strong and positive. However, there is a moderate positive correlation between "Disease" and "Date of diagnosis", the same moderate correlation is between "Disease" and "Cure date" attributes.

The Pearson correlation coefficient between "Disease" and "Treatment" equals 0.8431, which is the highest value among the three correlation values calculated between "Disease" attribute and the other attributes in the data set. The *l*-diversity principle will be applied on a part of Table I, which contains only "Disease" and "Treatment" attributes.

Second, we calculate the correlation between "Treatment", "Date of diagnosis" and "Cure date" attributes. Here are the values of the calculated Pearson correlation coefficients:

$r(Treatment, Date\ of\ diagnosis) = 0.3983$

$r(Treatment, Cure\ date) = 0.3983$

We remark that the correlation value between "Treatment" and "Date of diagnosis" attributes equals the correlation value between "Treatment" and "Cure date". The relationship between the attributes is weak because the correlation value is near zero value.

Finally, we calculate the correlation between the last two attributes "Date of diagnosis" and "Cure date".

$r(Date\ of\ diagnosis, Cure\ date) = 1$

The calculation of Pearson correlation coefficient between "Date of diagnosis" and "Cure date" gives a value of 1, which means that there is a strong positive correlation between these two attributes.

Now, we will process by applying 1-diversity on Table I with respect to "Disease" and "Treatment" attributes corresponding to the highest value of Pearson correlation coefficient (0.8431).

We are going to highlight through different tables the whole steps until we obtain an anonymized table satisfying 1-diversity. Table III represents Bucket 1 where all the tuples contain distinct values when treating both "Disease" and "Treatment" attributes.

TABLE III
BUCKET 1.

Id	Disease	Treatment	Bucket
1	Whiplash injury to neck	Recommendation to rest	1
4	Gout	Healthy diet	1
6	Rheumatoid arthritis	Ice therapy	1

In the first step, we collect the distinct values from "Treatment" attribute column, which are "Recommendation to rest", "Musculoskeletal care", "Healthy diet" and "Ice therapy". Then, we put in Bucket 1 the tuples corresponding to the already mentioned distinct values with ascendant order. We can see that "Recommendation to rest" and "Musculoskeletal care" values correspond to "Whiplash injury to neck" value, then we will retain only "Recommendation to rest" attribute because it is the first value in the order. However, "Healthy diet" and "Ice therapy" correspond to distinct values, which are "Gout" and "Rheumatoid arthritis" values. Then, we obtain the first bucket satisfying 1-diversity as mentioned in Table III. In the next step, we put the remaining tuples from Table I in another table called Rest of table $RT\,1$.

TABLE IV
REST OF TABLE RT 1.

Id	Disease	Treatment
2	Whiplash injury to neck	Musculoskeletal care
3	Fracture of forearm	Recommendation to rest
5	Gout	Musculoskeletal care
7	Whiplash injury to neck	Recommendation to rest
8	Gout	Healthy diet
9	Rheumatoid arthritis	Healthy diet

Table IV is called $RT\,1$; it contains tuples other than those existing in Bucket l. This table takes the place of the Original Table in the remaining of the proposed algorithm. Table V corresponds to Bucket 2.

TABLE V
BUCKET 2.

Id	Disease	Treatment	Bucket
2	Whiplash injury to neck	Musculoskeletal Mcare	2
3	Fracture of forearm	Recommendation to rest	2
8	Gout	Healthy diet	2

Table V includes three tuples containing distinct values with respect to "Disease" and "Treatment" attributes. Consequently, Table V satisfies 3-diversity.

TABLE VI
BUCKET 3 AND REST OF TABLE $RT\,2$.

Id	Disease	Treatment	Bucket
5	Gout	Musculoskeletal care	3
7	Whiplash injury to neck	Recommendation to rest	3
9	Rheumatoid arthritis	Healthy diet	3

Table VI represents the Rest of table $RT\,2$ and in the same time Bucket 3 since all the tuples existing in this table are all of them containing distinct values. And here we obtain 3 buckets satisfying l-diversity.

TABLE VII
THE ORIGINAL TABLE AFTER ANONYMIZATION.

Disease	Treatment	Date of diagnosis	Cure date	Bucket
Whiplash injury to neck	Recommendation to rest	04/09/2015	27/09/2015	1
Gout	Healthy diet	18/01/1968	24/09/1975	1
Rheumatoid arthritis	Ice therapy	16/12/2005	13/08/2010	1
Whiplash injury to neck	Musculoskeletal Mcare	15/02/2008	17/03/2008	2
Fracture of forearm	Recommendation to rest	18/12/2007	04/02/2008	2
Gout	Healthy diet	18/01/1968	24/09/1975	2
Gout	Musculoskeletal care	18/01/1968	24/09/1975	3
Whiplash injury to neck	Recommendation to rest	28/12/1942	05/02/1943	3
Rheumatoid arthritis	Healthy diet	16/12/2005	13/08/2010	3

We notice that we will reapply all the steps of l-diversity algorithm on a Table containing "Date of diagnosis" and "Cure date" attributes since there is a strong correlation between them.

Since Tables III, V and VI satisfy the principle of distinct l-diversity, we could say that Table VII satisfies distinct l-diversity too. Besides, we remark that at least there exist three tuples within each bucket in Table VII. Consequently, the resulting table after the anonymization process is called 3-diversity table.

V. CONCLUSION AND PERSPECTIVES

This paper presents a new approach for data anonymization. The approach focuses on anonymizing data sets while preserving the data utility. First, we applied a conversion process on values in the data set by transforming non-numerical values into numerical ones. After that, we grouped the pairs of attributes with the highest correlation together into several data sets through the calculation of Pearson correlation coefficient. Consequently, the data utility is preserved by reducing the correlation loss between the grouped highly correlated attributes. Later and in order to ensure privacy, we apply a variable distinct l-diversity on highly correlated attributes algorithm throughout a horizontal partitioning until treating all the buckets in data set. Besides, our proposed algorithm makes a balance between privacy and data utility. As a perspective, we plan to compare our proposed technique with other anonymization techniques existing in the literature. In addition, we will test our algorithm on the large real data set "Careplans". Moreover, we plan to deal also with QI attributes by applying k-anonymity technique instead of l-diversity one.

REFERENCES

[1] M. Prakash and G. Singaravel, "An approach for prevention of privacy breach and information leakage in sensitive data mining," Computers and Electrical Engineering, vol. 45, July 2015, pp. 134-140. DOI: http://dx.doi.org/10.1016/j.compeleceng.2015.01.016.

[2] Y. Qu, S. Yu, L. Gao and J. Niu, "Big data set privacy preserving through sensitive attribute-based grouping" The 2017 IEEE International Conference on Communications (ICC 2017) Piscataway, N.J., 2017, pp. 4887-4892, doi: 10.1109/ICC.2017.7996330.

[3] K. Kiruthika, M.S Kavitha and S. Gayathiri, "Publishing High-Dimensional Micro Data Using Anonymization Technique," Imperial Journal of Interdisciplinary Research (IJIR), vol. 2(8), pp. 86-96, 2016, ISSN: 2454-1362.

[4] K. Oishi, Y. Tahara, Y. Sei and A. Ohsuga, "Proposal of l-diversity algorithm considering distance between sensitive attribute values" The 2017 IEEE Symposium Series on Computational Intelligence (SSCI 2017), 2017, pp. 1-8. 10.1109/SSCI.2017.8280973

[5] J. Jeyanthi and J. Antony, "Comparison and Analysis of Anonymization Techniques for Preserving Privacy in Big Data," Advances in Computational Sciences and Technology, vol. 10(2), 2017, pp. 247-253, ISSN 0973-6107.

[6] A. Shah, H. Abbas, W. Iqbal and R. Latif, "Enhancing E-Healthcare Privacy Preservation Framework through L-Diversity" The 14th International Wireless Communications and Mobile Computing Conference (IWCMC 2018), June 2018 pp. 394-399. DOI:10.1109/IWCMC.2018.8450306

[7] R. Praveena Priyadarsini, S. Sivakumari and P. Amudha, "Enhanced – Diversity Algorithm for Privacy Preserving Data Mining" Communications in Computer and Information (CSI), vol. 679, pp. 14-23, Nov. 2016, DOI:https://doi.org/10.1007/978-981-10-3274-5-2

[8] Y. Sei, H. Okumura, T. Takenouchi and A. Ohsuga, "Anonymization of Sensitive Quasi-Identifiers for l-diversity and t-closeness" The IEEE Transactions on Dependable and Secure Computing (TDSC 2017), Apr. 2017, pp(99). 1-1. DOI: 10.1109/TDSC.2017.2698472

[9] Y. Gaoming, L. Jingzhao, Z. Shunxiang and Y. Li, "An enhanced l-diversity privacy preservation," The 10th International Conference on Fuzzy Systems and Knowledge Discovery (FSKD 2013), Shenyang, 2013, pp. 1115-1120. DOI: 10.1109/FSKD.2013.6816364

[10] Y. Sei and A. Ohsuga, "Randomized addition of sensitive attributes for l-diversity," The 11th International Conference on Security and Cryptography (SECRYPT 2014), Vienna, Aug. 2014, pp. 1-11. ISBN: 978-9-8985-6595-2

[11] S. Chakraborty and B.K. Tripathy, "Alpha-anonymization techniques for privacy preservation in social networks" Social Network Analysis and Mining Journal, vol. 6(29), Dec. 2016, pp. 1-11, DOI: 10.1007/s13278-016-0337-x.

[12] Z. Tu et al., "Protecting Trajectory from Semantic Attack Considering k-Anonymity, l-diversity and t-closeness" The IEEE Transactions on Network and Service Management (TNSM 2018), Oct. 2018, pp(99). 1-1. 10.1109/TNSM.2018.2877790

[13] R. Yogesh Kulkarni and T. Senthil Murugan, "C-mixture and multi-constraints based genetic algorithm for collaborative data publishing," Journal of King Saud University-Computer and Information Sciences, vol. 30(2), pp. 175–184, Apr. 2018, https://doi.org/10.1016/j.jksuci.2016.06.001.

[14] V. Shyamala Susan and T. D. Dickman Christopher, "Anatomisation with slicing: a new privacy preservation approach for multiple sensitive attributes," SpringerPlus, vol. 5: 964, July 2016, https://doi.org/10.1186/s40064-016-2490-0.

[15] H. Jiang, K. Wang, Y. Wang, M. Gao and Y. Zhang, "Energy big data: A survey," IEEE Access, vol. 4, 2016, pp. 3844-3861. doi: 10.1109/ACCESS.2016.2580581

[16] H. Zhu, S. Tian and M. Xie, "Anonymization on refining partition: Same privacy, more utility" The 2014 2nd International Conference on Systems and Informatics (ICSAI 2014), Shanghai, 2014, pp. 998-1005. doi: 10.1109/ICSAI.2014.7009431

[17] P.Sreevani, P.Niranjan, P.Shireesha, "A Novel Data Anonymization Technique for Privacy Preservation of Data Publishing," International Journal of Engineering sciences and Research Technology (IJESRT), vol. 3(11), pp. 201-205, Nov. 2014.

[18] P.Nithyal, V.Karpagam, "Improving Privacy And Data Utility For High-Dimensional Data By Using Anonymization Technique," International Journal of Innovative Research in Computer and Communication Engineering (IJIRCCE), vol. 2(1), pp. 2874-2881, Mar. 2014, ISSN: 2320-9801

[19] W. Feng, Q. Zhu, J. Zhuang and Y. Shimin, "An expert recommendation algorithm based on Pearson correlation coefficient and FP-growth" Cluster Computing, Jan. 2018, DOI: 10.1007/s10586-017-1576-y.

[20] F. Li, X. Zou, P. Liu, JY. Chen, "New threats to health data privacy," BMC Bioinformatics, vol. 12 (Suppl 12):S7, Nov. 2011, DOI:10.1186/1471-2105-12-S12-S7.

[21] P. Jain, M. Gyanchandani and N. J. Khare, "Big data privacy: a technological perspective and review," Journal of Big Data, vol. 3(25), July 2016, DOI: 10.1186/s40537-016-0059-y.

[22] P. Dabas and S. Sharma, "Privacy and Security Issues in Social Networks with Prevailing Privacy Preserving Techniques," Journal of Network Communications and Emerging Technologies (JNCET), vol. 8(2), pp. 54-56, Feb. 2018, ISSN: 2395-5317.

[23] Z. EL Ouazzani, H. El Bakkali, "A new technique ensuring privacy in big data: k-anonymity without prior value of the threshold k," ELSEVIER First International Conference on Intelligent Computing in Data Sciences. (ICDS), Vol. 127, 2018, pp. 52-59.

[24] E. Elabd, H. Abd elkader and A. Mubarak Alhamodi, "L–Diversity-Based Semantic Anonymaztion for Data Publishing," International Journal of Information Technology and Computer Science (IJITCS), vol. 7, pp. 1-7, Sep. 2015, DOI:10.5815/ijitcs.2015.10.01.

[25] L. Philippe Sondeck, M. Laurent and V. Frey, "The Semantic Discrimination Rate Metric for Privacy Measurements which Questions the Benefit of t-closeness over l-diversity" The 14th International Conference on Security and Cryptography (ICSC 2017), Jan. 2017, pp. 285-294. DOI:10.5220/0006418002850294

[26] https://syntheticmass.mitre.org/downloads/2017_1106/synthea_sample_data_csv_nov2017.zip accessed on 15 May 2019.

Efficient Distributed Access Control Using Blockchain for Big Data in Clouds

Oussama Mounnan
Oscars Laboratory, ENSA
Cadi Ayyad University
Marrakech, Morocco
e-mail: oussama.mounnan@gmail.com

Anas Abou elkalam
Oscars Laboratory, ENSA
Cadi Ayyad University
Marrakech, Morocco
e-mail: elkalam@hotmail.fr

Abstract—**Big Data is a growing concept, offering us opportunities, that were not available before in many fields. However security and privacy issues are magnified by large amounts of heterogenous data. Ciphertext-Policy Attribute Based Encryption is a promising cryptographic primitive for the security of cloud storage system, which can bring fine-grained access control. The blockchain is a distributed ledger that records transactions in a secure, flexible, verifiable and permanent way. In this paper, we propose a distributed, scalable and fine-grained access control scheme with efficient decryption for the Big Data in clouds. Blockchain technology is used to manage identities and provide the authentication, store and execute a smart contract that incorporates the contextual and detailed access policy defined by the data owner, which is triggered by an access requester, that gives data owners the sovereign right to effectively manage their data sets and manage the policy. We also used the ciphertext-Policy Attribute Based Encryption scheme for supporting the efficient decryption outsourcing as another security layer for managing the policy. The analysis shows that our scheme is correct, complete, secure and efficient.**

Keywords-access control; encryption; blockchain; cloud; CP-ABE.

I. INTRODUCTION

Nowadays, the increase and the proliferation of large amounts of heterogenous data, also known as Big Data, generated in many fields, such as agriculture, business, finance/banking [1], education, medicine and healthcare, provide us with opportunities which did not exist before [2]. This technology opens various doors of another era of innovation and production. However, these heterogenous data are continuously increasing and pose evident challenges, which necessitate more flexible data processing tools and platforms, in order to find useful information in data [3]-[5].

The continuously increasing exchange of sensitive data has made the security of Big Data compulsory. These data are considered as a capital in its own right, and its potential is multiple. Indeed, some companies are literally creating new data-centric activities (monetizing data) while others are optimizing their supply chains or maintaining their equipments. The data is thus becoming generalized and used in all processes. Hence, these data are a valuable asset in today's economy. That is what makes us focus on its security and privacy. The latter is becoming an important issue, especially, when we deal with data in distributed cloud storage. Cloud Security Alliance (CSA) published a document that lists the top ten challenges for protecting Big Data systems [6], and granular access control is one of the stated and most critical ones.

Blockchain technology makes use of cryptography in multiple different ways, for wallets, transactions, security, and privacy-preserving protocols. It is a growing list of records, called blocks, which are linked using cryptography. Each block contains a cryptographic hash of the previous block, a timestamp, and transaction data (generally represented as a Merkle tree). In addition, it is an open, distributed ledger that can record transactions between two parties efficiently and in a verifiable and permanent way [7] [8]. The blockchain is a simple yet ingenious way of passing information from A to B in a fully automated and safe manner. The transmitted information or transactions are grouped in blocks. Each block is verified by thousands, perhaps millions of computers distributed around the net. The verified block is added to a chain, which is stored across the net, creating not just a unique record, but a unique record with a unique history. Falsifying a single record would mean falsifying the entire chain in millions of instances. That is virtually impossible. Bitcoin uses this model for monetary transactions, but it can be deployed in many others ways [9].

Ciphertext-Policy Attribute-Based Encryption (CP-ABE) is considered as one of the most applicable technologies to achieve fine-grained data access control in the cloud environment [10]. In a CP-ABE scheme [11][12], each user's key is associated with attributes and each ciphertext is related to an access policy, thus data owners can determine the access policies for their own data and control them directly. If a user's attributes satisfy the access policy in the ciphertext, the user can decrypt the ciphertext correctly. Moreover, CP-ABE has a complementary structure called key-policy Attribute Based Encryption (KP-ABE) [13], in which each user's key is associated with an access policy and each ciphertext is related to attributes. The application of CP-ABE to the cloud environment can bring data leakage prevention and access control together, which are essential requirements for Big Data security and privacy [14].

Most access control solutions adopt a centralized architecture. They outsource the control of data to trusted third parties, which prevents the user from controlling his own data. This can cause problems of ethics and confidentiality. Unfortunately, when we share our information with third parties, we immediately lose control and ownership. Our new scheme executive breaks this custom and gives people what belongs to them in a fair way. In fact, we believe that Big Data needs a new access control framework that meets its specific requirements and features, allowing users to control their own privacy. This "change" will require rethinking access control technologies and creating a new solution that addresses the security and privacy requirements of Big Data. Hopefully, we are on the threshold of a new phase of decentralization, which has resulted in the emergence of a new technology, known as blockchain, that could transform fundamentally our notions of centralized authority.

In this article, we take advantage of the consistency guarantees provided by this promising technology. Our solution consists in presenting a lightweight and privacy respectful access control scheme based on the emergent blockchain technology, to ensure access control with a strong guarantee of user anonymity and data privacy in the context of Big Data. Blockchain technology is used to manage identities and provide the authentication, store and to execute a smart contract that incorporates the contextual and detailed access policy defined by the data owner, which is triggered by an access requester, that gives data owners the sovereign right to effectively manage their data sets and manage the policy. It is also used as a new multi-authority ciphertext-Policy Attribute Based Encryption scheme for supporting the efficient decryption outsourcing.

The rest of this paper is organized as follows. Section II defines the Background and preliminaries. In Section III, We expose our system model by explaining its principle and reveal our model architecture. Afterwards, Section IV presents the features analysis of our scheme. Finally, Section V concludes this paper.

II. Background and Preliminaries

In this section, we provide a few technical backgrounds that will help ensure better understanding of our proposed work.

A. Big Data

The quantitative explosion of digital data has forced researchers to find new ways of seeing and analyzing the world. It's about discovering new orders of magnitude for capturing, searching, sharing, storing, analyzing and presenting data. So, the "Big Data" was invented as solution by the giants of the web, designed to allow everyone to access real-time databases giant. It aims to offer a choice to the classic solutions of databases and analyses.

1) Storage and analyze

Clearly, one of the biggest Big Data challenges is to store and analyze all the information. Most of this data is unstructured (documents, photos, videos and audio files...), and are difficult to analyze it. To manage the constant increase of data, companies use different technologies. In terms of storage, converged and hyperconverged infrastructures and software-defined storage make it easy to scale hardware. Technologies such as compression, deduplication or tiering also reduce the space required and the costs of Big Data storage. With regard to management and analysis, companies use tools such as NoSQL, Hadoop, Spark, and other Big Data analytical software, or artificial intelligence and Machine Learning to find the insights they need.

2) Validate the data

Data validation is also one of the major Big Data challenges. Many companies receive similar data from different systems, and this data is sometimes contradictory. Businesses can allocate a group of people to monitor data, and define rules and procedures. They can also invest in data management solutions designed to simplify governance.

3) Secure Big Data

Security is also an important concern in the field of Big Data. Business data can be attractive to hackers. However, very few companies use additional security measures for their data directories. Some of the most popular additional measures include access and identity control, data encryption, and data segregation.

4) Privacy Big Data

The confidentiality of information is about how the data is stored and how it is collected. The theft of data when transferring data via the Internet is a serious problem of data protection. Like today, the most difficult task is to secure sensitive data such as government data, medical data, space and research statistical data and military data.

B. Cloud Computing

Cloud computing has different service models, which are divided into three categories: (1) IaaS, which allows users to take advantage of the infrastructure without mentioning the hardware running behind it; (2) PaaS, which builds on IaaS and provides clients with access to basic operating software and optional services to develop and use software applications without software installation; and (3) SaaS, which enables clients to use software applications without having to install them on their personal computer, by offering these as a service through the Internet [15]. We can categorize cloud computing consistent with the deployment model into: (1) a public cloud, in which the resources are sold or rented to the public by the service provider, who is at the same time is the owner; (2) a private cloud owned or rented by an organization; (3) community clouds, in which some closed communities share the same cloud resources; and (4) a hybrid cloud, which has the characteristics of two or more deployment models [16]. Several features are available in cloud computing, for example: on-demand broad network access, self-service, measured service, resource pooling, and rapid elasticity. Self-service means that the customers can manage and request their own resources. On the Internet or in private networks, the services offered are known as broad network access. In pooled resources, the customer draws from a pool of computing resources, usually in a remote data center. The services can be scaled larger or smaller, and customers are billed according to the measured use of a service [17].

C. *Blockchain*

In 2008, a person or group of persons known under the name of Satoshi Nakamoto published a paper [18] dealing with a new decentralized peer-to-peer electronic cash system. This paper introduces the blockchain as a new data structure to store financial transactions, as well as an associate protocol to ensure the validity of the blockchain in the network.

1) *Definition*

The blockchain is a technology of storage and transmission of information, transparent, secure, and functioning without a central control body (definition of Blockchain France). By extension, a blockchain is a database that contains the history of all the exchanges made between its users since its creation. This database is secure and distributed; it is shared by its different users, without intermediaries, which allows everyone to check the validity of the chain.

Blockchain technology utilizes cryptography, namely public-key cryptography, also known as asymmetric cryptography, that is exposed in Figure 1, as a means of ensuring transactions are done safely, while securing all information and storages of value. Therefore, anyone using blockchain can have complete confidence that once something is recorded on a Blockchain, it is done so legitimately and in a manner that preserves security.

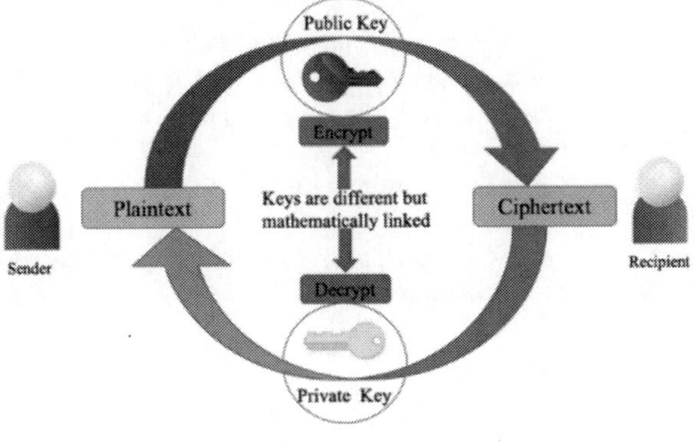

Figure 1. Public Key Cryptography

There are public blockchains, open to all, and private blockchains, whose access and use are limited to a certain number of actors. A public blockchain can therefore be likened to a large public accounting book, anonymous and unfalsifiable. As the mathematician Jean-Paul Delahaye [19] writes, one must imagine a very large notebook, which everyone can read freely and freely, on which everyone can write, but which is impossible to erase.

2) *Wallet*

Every user owns at least one wallet that stores his credentials, addresses and the transactions related to them. It contains all the keys needed to register and identify his resources, sign his transactions, ask for access.
The main functionalities of a wallet are: 1) generating keys "secrete and public" and addresses" is a cryptographic identities of users, An address is basically the hash of an ECDSA [20] public key and a user in possession of the corresponding private key is said to own the address". 2) Transforming the access control policies to a transactions and broadcast those last ones to the network. 3) validating received transactions from the network .

3) *Proof of work*

In the principle of blockchain, it is necessary to obtain the consensus of the majority of the actors in the network. And for that purpose, several methods exist. The most widespread cryptocurrency is called Proof of Work (PoW) [21]. This process was theorized in 1992, well before the arrival of Bitcoin and was implemented for the first time with HashCash, a solution that was to limit the proliferation of spam, but was never adopted on a large scale.

In the case of crypto-currencies, the miners, who make their computing power available to the network, must carry out energy-intensive operations. They must "chop" all the transactions to add to a block, as well as the hash of the previous block by respecting various constraints set by the level of difficulty requested by the network. The first step in in finding the solution to this problem diffuse it to the rest of the network, which verifies it.
Example:

A processor is asked to produce a proof of work consisting of coding a variation of "Hello, world!" using the SHA-256 hash function to find a fingerprint that starts with 4 zeros. The variation is to add a number at the end of the string. The processor will have to make 33,681 attempts to succeed.

4) *Concept of Blockchain*

In his paper, Nakamoto describes the blockchain as a database modeled by a linear sequence of blocks, each one containing cryptographic hashes corresponding to the previous and current block to ensure continuity and immutability. Bitcoin uses the blockchain to store financial transactions and contracts.

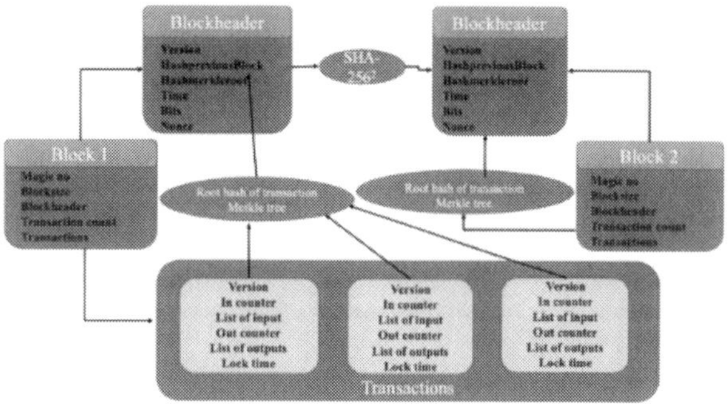

Figure 2. Blockchain infrastructure

The Merkle root of all transactions is included in the block header and then used as input for the next block in the chain. The chaining method used in Bitcoin ensures the immutability by using the hash of the previous header block hash in the current block. The header includes the root hash of the Merkle tree [22] of all transactions in the block. This way transactions cannot be changed without changing the root Merkle hash and then invalidating the block. Due to the way the blockchain is built, fork chains can append with different valid blocks storing different transactions. The Bitcoin protocol resolves this issue by selecting the longest blockchain as the correct one. Note that due to this choice, even after being included in a valid block, transactions can be considered valid only after a subsequent block has been calculated and successfully included in the blockchain by the majority of the network.

The blockchain data structure can be considered outside of its application in Bitcoin, as a generic decentralized secured data storage structure. It is possible to use any data payloads other than transactions as parts of the block. The block is then divided in two parts, (a) the block constants and header and (b) the data payloads.

A single modification in one payload of a block will change its Merkle root hash value, and then invalidate it. This solution thus provides secure and reliable storage distributed among all peers in the network. Note that this implies that the complete blockchain and all data linked to it must be duplicate on all peers.

5) Blockchain authentication and identification

New companies have now begun to harness the potential of the blockchain and develop a variety of services using the technology. The center of blockchain authentication would be a blockchain ID. This ID is essentially a block of data on the chain that can be both verified by any third and can display necessary information such as date of birth. The secret to this verification is the ECDSA (elliptic curve digital signature algorithm). When adding an ID to the blockchain, an identification issuing service binds a public key by default and then transfers ownership of the private key to the user. This allows the user, and only the user, to sign a signature that can be verified against the public key stored in the blockchain.

This identification of a user would serve as a decentralized source of authentication. It would essentially be a single-sign-on portal that can be accessed by any app while not being owned by any single entity. A protected app would only have to request a digital signature and an ID from a user requesting access. The app could then verify that the signature is valid and that the user's ID verifies who they say they are.

6) Smart contract

The Smart contract [23] is a computer protocol that allows the automatic execution of contracts whose clauses have been defined programmatically. An electronically registered contract on a distributed register (DLT) [24] cannot be altered, destroyed or contested.

One of the best things about Blockchain is that, because it is a decentralized system that exists between all authorized parties, there is not necessary to pay intermediaries, which saves money, time and conflict. Blockchains are undeniably, faster, cheaper and safer than traditional systems. These are some of the reasons why banks and governments are turning to them. In Figure 3, there are some use cases of smart contract.

Contracts can be converted into computer code, stored and replicated on the system and supervised by the network of computers running the blockchain.

Figure 3. Use cases of smart contracts

a) Characteristics of smart contracts

Smart contracts have the following characteristics:

- they're self-verifying due to automated possibilities;
- they're self-enforcing when the rules are met at all stages;
- they're tamper-proof, as no one can change what's been programmed.

b) Advantages

Autonomy: Thanks to the smart contract, it is not necessary to rely on a broker, a lawyer or other intermediaries to confirm. Moreover, this also strikes the danger of manipulation by a third party, because the execution is managed automatically by the network, rather than by one or more individuals possibly with bad intentions which can deceive you.

- ***Trust:*** Data is encrypted on a shared ledger. There is no way anyone can say that they lost it.
- **Backup:** The data is duplicated many times, there is no risk of being lost, With the Blockchain, the data is in several nodes in various places in the world.
- ***Security:*** Document encryption keeps data safe. There is no hacking. In fact, it would take an abnormally intelligent hacker to crack the code and infiltrate.
- ***Speed:*** for manual contract processing you have to spend more time. Smart contracts use software code to automate tasks, reducing work hours in no time.
- ***Savings*** :Smart contracts save money by eliminating the presence of an intermediary.
- ***Accuracy***: Automated contracts are not only faster and less expensive, but also avoid errors that result from manually filling a bunch of forms.

D. Attribute based Encryption ABE

In traditional cloud storage, attribute-based encryption technology [25] can achieve fine-grained access control over data. In this technique, attributes are used instead of identities. Data owner can assign the users groups that can access the data by setting an access policy. Only the users whose attributes set meet the access policy can access the data. Since attribute-based encryption technology was proposed, many research works have been done in many ways driving by actual needs, and have achieved many significant research results. For example, in a practical application, if the users attributes change, the corresponding users secret key must also be changed accordingly, so attribute revocable attribute-based encryption schemes [26]–[27] are proposed; as access policies may be revealed important privacy information of users, attribute-based encryption schemes with hidden access policy [28], [29] were proposed; in many commercial application scenarios, multiple attribute authorities are required for attribute distribution and management, so multi-authority attribute-based encryption schemes [30]–[31] has been developed. In addition, with the widespread application of mobile devices with limited computing and storage resources, outsourced decryption in attribute-based encryption schemes [32], [33] are proposed. At present, attribute-based encryption technology has been well developed and applied in traditional cloud storage systems.

1) Access structure

Definition: Let $U = \{a_1, a_2, .., a_n\}$ be a set of attributes. For $a_i \in U$, $S_i = \{v_{i,1}, v_{i,2}, \ldots, v_{i,ni},\}$ is a set of possible values, where n_i is the number of possible values for a_i. Let $L = [L_1, L_2, .., L_n]$ $L_i \in S_i$ be an attribute list for a user, and $W = [W_1, W_2, .., W_n]$ $W_i \varepsilon S_i$ be an access policy. The notation $L \models W$ express that an attribute list L satisfies an access policy W, namely $L_i = W_i$ $(i=1,2..,n)$. The notation $L \not\models W$ implies L not satisfying the access structure W.

2) Ciphertext-policy attribute based access control

A cipher text policy attribute based encryption scheme consists of four fundamental algorithms: Setup, Key Generation, Encryption and Decryption.

Setup: The setup algorithm takes no input other than the implicit security parameter. It outputs the public parameters PK and a master key MK.

Key Generation (MK,S): The key generation algorithm takes as input the master key MK and a set of attributes S that describe the key. It outputs a private key SK.

Encrypt (PK,A, M): The encryption algorithm takes as input the public parameters PK, a message M, and an access structure A over the universe of attributes. The algorithm will encrypt M and produce a ciphertext CT such that only a user that possesses a set of attributes that satisfies the access structure will be able to decrypt the message. Assume that the ciphertext implicitly contains A.

Decrypt(PK,CT,SK): The decryption algorithm takes as input the public parameters PK, a ciphertext CT, which contains an access policy A, and a private key SK, which is a private key for a set S of attributes. If the set S of attributes satisfies the access structure A then the algorithm will decrypt the ciphertext and return a message M.

3) Security Model for CP-ABE

Init. The adversary sends the two different challenge access structures W_0^* and W_1^* to the challenger.

Setup. The challenger runs the Setup algorithm and gives the public parameters, PK to the adversary.

Phase 1. The adversary sends an attribute list L to the challenger for a Key Gen query, where ($L \not\models W_0^*$ and $L \not\models W_1^*$) or ($L \models W_0^*$ and $L \models W_1^*$) The challenger answers with a secret key for these attributes.

Challenge. The adversary submits two equal length messages M0 and M1. Note that if the adversary has obtained SK_L where ($L \models W_0^*$ and $L \models W_1^*$) then M0 = M1. The challenger chooses d randomly from {0,1} and runs Encrypt(PK, M_d, W_d^*). The challenger gives the ciphertext CT* to the adversary.

Phase 2. Same as Phase 1. Guess. The adversary outputs a guess d' of d.

The advantage of an adversary A in this game is defined as

$$Pr[d'=d] - 1/2 .$$

Definition: A ciphertext-policy attribute based encryption scheme is secure if all polynomial time adversaries have at most a negligible advantage in the above game.

III. SYSTEM MODEL

In this section, we will present our system model by explaining its principle and entities.

A. System model

As shown in Figure 4, our system model is made of four main entities, i.e., the data owner (DO), data consumers (users), cloud server and Blockchain including other own entities.

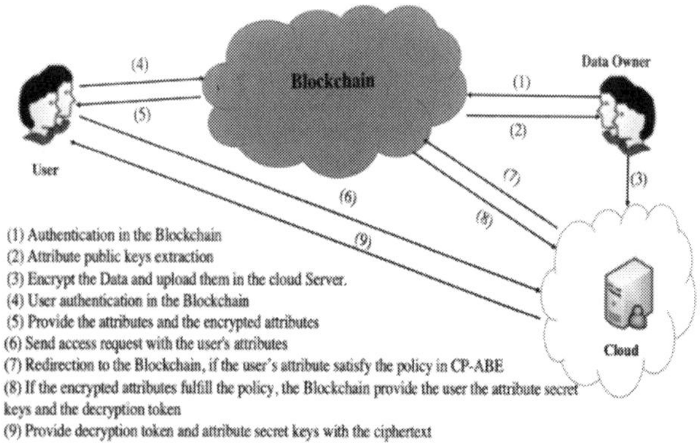

Figure 4. System model of distributed access control for Big Data

1) The main entities

Data Owner: One who sets access policies for these resources identified by different addresses generate through his wallet to ensure pseudo-anonymity.

User: A user in our infrastructure is the one who requests access to a resource identified by an address and stocked in the cloud.

Server. The cloud server is assumed to be semi-trusted. More specifically, the server is curious and honest, that is, the server is curious about the encrypted data stored on it and executes the assigned tasks properly. The server is responsible for storing the ciphertexts and providing data access service to users. It also obtains the user's attributes secret key from the Blockchain. When the server receives a ciphertext access request from a user, it searches the user's attributes secret key from the blockchain and generates a decryption token (TK) for the user.

Blockchain: The blockchain is considered as a database that stores all processed transactions and access control policies for each pair (owner, requestor) as a smart contract in chronological order shared by all participating users or nodes. A blockchain is a specific path in a tree structure of generated blocks, each referencing exactly a previously generated block.

2) Blockchain entities

The wallet: Each user has at least one wallet containing their identifiers, addresses and transactions. It contains all the keys needed to register and identify its resources, sign transactions, request access. In our framework, we consider a wallet as an Authorization Management Point (AMP), whether it is a web or mobile application, through the wallet, the system manager could record its resources to protect and define its access control policies. Then, the main features of a wallet are:

1) Generate keys and addresses.
2) Attributes Extraction and encryption.
3) Transform access control policies into transactions and broadcast them to the network.

Address: In our framework, users are either a DO (data owner) or a requestor and their resources can have an almost unlimited number of cryptographic identities, called addresses. The addresses are public and shared on the network. They are used to grant and request an access token. An address is basically the hash of an ECDSA public key and a user in possession of the corresponding private key is the address owner.

Transaction: A transaction in our framwork is considered as a communication form between network nodes. In fact, all the nodes of the network: minors, DO, Rq and their resources are identified by addresses and interact with each other via transactions. Each transaction has an identifier, at least one input and one output and a value to transfer from the sender of the transaction to its recipient. The input can be seen as an address source, it refers to the address of the entity that creates the transaction. The output can be viewed as the target or destination of the transaction value stream and is an address itself.

Our infrastructure introduces four types of transactions:

1) GetAccess Transaction: Created by an DO, it is used to deploy a smart contract in the blockchain. Then, its address source corresponds to an address of a DO and its address destination corresponds to an address of a SmartContract.

2) RequestAccess Transaction: is created by a requestor to interact with SmartContract. Then, its address source corresponds to an address of a Rq and its address destination corresponds to an address of a SmartContract. We trigger an intelligent contract by sending this requestAccess transaction. It then runs independently and automatically as follows on each node of the network, depending on the input included in the trigger transaction. In the data included in the RequestAccess transaction corresponding to the access control policy defined in SmartContract, a token is generated and included in a list of authorization tokens. Otherwise, access to the application is rejected

3) AllowAccess Transaction: Uses the authorization token. Then, its address source corresponds to an address of a Rq and its address destination corresponds to an address of a resource.

SmartContract: we use a SmartContract called PolicyContract. It is a representation of an access control strategy defined by an DO, to manage access to one of its resources. It's a script stored on the blockchain. Since he lives on the channel, he has a unique address. This SmartContract is triggered by addressing a RequestAccess transaction type. It then automatically executes on each node of the network according to the data included in the trigger transaction. If the data completes the access control policies, the policy contract will be executed correctly, and then generate and assign an authorization token to the sender of the RequestAccess transaction. For each data, the DO defines a PolicyContract that is responsible for managing its access control functions. The way in which authorization tokens are generated will be explained in detail in the next chapter.

Authorization token: In our infrastructure, an authorization token represents the right of access or right defined by the owner of the policy contract to the sender of the RequestAccess transaction who successfully triggered the policy agreement in order to access to a specific resource identified by its address. Each applicant has a list called Auto Tokens List.

Block: Blocks are types of data used to store data permanently in the blockchain. The main reason for permanently storing data on the network is the way transactions are verified by the network, always keeping all information about them open to the public. A block consists of several transactions and SmartContracts that should not be contained in another block. Each block always refers to exactly one previous block by containing a hash of the referenced block. This characteristic is what creates the blockchain which consists of several blocks. The most recent block contains some or (ideally) all transactions and SmartContract that have been broadcast on the network but are not so far stored in the previous blocks that are already part of the blockchain.

B. *Our solution description*

Our framework consists of two processes. The first concerns the data owner, who encrypts their data with CP-ABE before outsourcing it to the cloud, and the second concerns the access requester who wants to have to access a resource stored in the cloud.

1) *The process of the Data Owner:*

The data owner authenticates with his wallet in the blockchain, which provides him with the necessary keys (public and secret, and attribute public key) for encrypting data with the CP-ABE system. the Data Owner defines the access policy and the wallet takes charge of encrypting the attributes in the policy. So that they are not visible in the blockchain and transforms it into the smart contract, then it broadcasts it as a transaction in the Blockchain until it reaches the minors, and then the transaction will be stored in the Blockchain, otherwise it will be rejected.

2) *The process of the user:*

Before the user submits an access request to desired resource in the cloud, he first authenticates with his wallet, the user retrieves their attribute keys and their encrypted attributes and sends them with his request to the cloud. If the requester's attributes satisfy the security policy, then the cloud redirects the request to the blockchain, which in turn verifies the encrypted attributes, whether they are authentic or not. if so, it provides the cloud with the secret attribute keys and generate a decryption token, which is sent to the cloud which in turn provides the requester access with the secret attribute keys, authorization token and the encrypted text and the latter one will combine them to decrypt the data.

C. *Discussion*

Numerous efforts have been emerged in adapting traditional access control models to meet new requirements in terms of security. Xiao et al [34] proposed a decentralized multi-authority CP-ABE scheme, which can support efficient decryption outsourcing and user revocation by leveraging a key separation technique. In this scheme, each Attribute Authority is independent and can dynamically join and leave the system. They also apply the scheme to achieve efficient and scalable distributed access control for Big Data in clouds. Unfortunately, those typical security and access control standards today are built around the notion of trust where a centralized trusted entity is always introduced, which harm user transparency and privacy. In addition, access control becomes a distributed problem. We therefore turn our attention to blockchain, the technology behind bitcoin protocol, to conceive our new framework as efficient solution that solve all challenges extensively highlighted in [35]-[37]. Actually, the blockchain is a technology breakthrough that has fundamentally changed our notions of centralized authority. It is a universal digital ledger that functions at the heart of decentralized financial systems, such as bitcoin, and increasingly, many other decentralized systems. The main contributions of this work can be summarized as follows.

1) We construct an efficient and scalable distributed access control scheme using Blockchain for Big Data in clouds, in which there is no need of a central authority and no entity is capable of decrypting ciphertexts individually. The scheme is more efficient than existing schemes and provably secure in the generic group model.

2) We design a decentralized CP-ABE scheme with efficient decryption outsourcing, as another security layer for managing the policy defined by the Data owner.

This framework is efficient and more suitable for Big Data access control than existing solutions, because it relies on the two security factors, which improve and increase the security level in this context.

IV. THE FEATURES ANALYSIS OF OUR SCHEME

Our framework is composed of 7 phases which are: system initialization, attributes extraction and Encryption, grant access, access request, access decision making, obtaining access and validation of authorization token .

Phase 1: Initialization of the system:

The data owner retrieves their attribute public keys by his wallet after authentication process, then encrypts their data with CP-ABE system before outsourcing them in the cloud. In addition, the data owner defines the security policy for these resources.

Phase 2: Extraction and encryption of attributes:

In this phase the wallet extracts the attributes from the predefined policy, encrypts each attribute, and puts these encrypted attributes into the policy.

Phase 3: Grant Access:

Reload the access control policy as a smart contract in the blockchain with GetAccess Transaction: After setting the access policy and encrypting the attributes, the DO wallet transforms these policies with encrypted attributes into SmartContract called PolicyContract and broadcasts it in the Blockchain via the GetAccess transaction, which is signed with the owner's private key. Then, the wallet broadcasts the GetAccess transaction to the Blockchain, as shown in Figure 5.

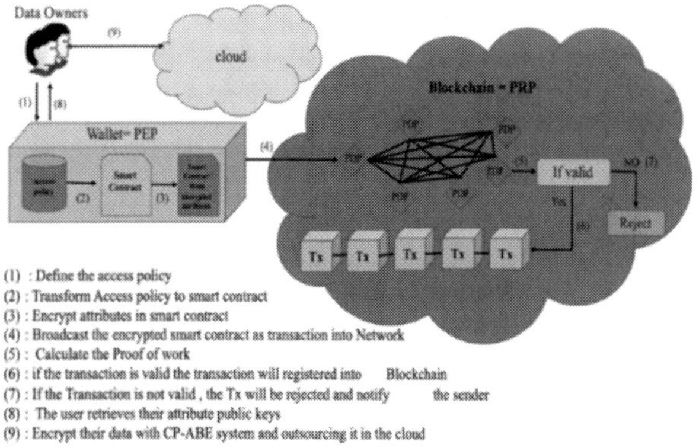

Figure 5. Reload access policies process

Peer-to-peer nodes check the transaction and save it to the Blockchain if successful. At this point, the policy contract, managing access to the resource in cloud, is deployed in the blockchain and ready to be triggered by the requestor who wishes to access a resource in the cloud.

The GetAccess transaction sequence can be displayed as follows:

- The DO (data owner) defines for his resource identified by the address Rs an access control policy:

  Policy (R*s*)

- The wallet transforms this access control policy into a subscription agreement:

  Policy (Rs, Rq) $\rightarrow \pi x$

- The wallet generates a GetAccess transaction to deploy this PolicyContract in the blockchain.

The GetAccess transaction is in the following form:

$Tx = (m, sigRs\ (m))\ where\ m = (IDx, from\ (Rs), to\ (\pi x))$

- Each node verifies the transaction in the process of validating the transaction. If the transaction is valid, the access control policy is saved in the blockchain as SmartContract. Otherwise, the transaction will be rejected.

At the end of this phase, if the transaction appears in the blockchain, it means that the network is witnessing that the data owner (DO) is protecting access to his resource through this policy agreement. As a result, anyone wishing to access this resource must unlock the access condition by successfully running the deployed PolicyContract after an encrypted attribute check in the access policy and in access request, if the encrypted attribute are identical. To do this, the requestor must trigger the policy contract and prove to the network that it actually fulfills the access requirements in a new transaction called RequestAccess transaction, which is the goal of the next phase.

Phase 4: RequestAccess: triggering the policy contract

In this phase, the user creates a new transaction, which he will call a RequestAccess transaction. The RequestAccess transaction triggers the PolicyContract if the user's attributes fulfill the policy in ciphertext stored in the cloud and follows the access control policy defined in PolicyContract (Figure 6).

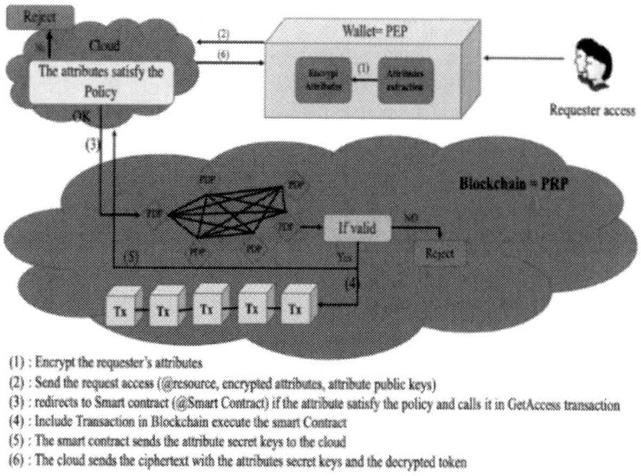

Figure 6. Request access process

The RequestAccess transaction sequence can be displayed as follows:

1) The access requester's wallet retrieves the attributes and encrypts them.

2) The user sends an access request to a resource in the cloud by enclosing the access request with the attribute public keys and the encrypted user's attributes.

3) The cloud redirects the requestor to the policy contract in Blockchain as a transaction, if the user's attributes satisfy the policy in the ciphertext and broadcasts the transaction to network nodes until it reaches minors. They check the transaction and run PolicyContract.

4) The smart contract runs automatically if the access requester attributes and the policy attributes in the smart contract are identical. In this case, the transaction will stored in the blockchain and places its response as entries in the RequestAccess transaction.

$$\text{MeetAccessControlPolicy}\ (\pi x_x) \rightarrow \psi$$

The RequestAccess transaction type is in the following form:

$$Tx = (IDx, from\ (Rq, \psi), (\pi x))$$

5) Provide the cloud with the attribute secret keys and generate an authorization token.

6) The cloud provide the requestor access with the ciphertext, attribute secret keys and the authorization token in order to combine them to decrypt the ciphertext.

Phase 5: Evaluating the Access Control Policy by Running PolicyContract

Each minor receives a signed transaction in the following form:

$(Tx, sigA\ (Tx))$ *where* $Tx = (\mathrm{ID}x, from\ (A.pk, \psi), to\ (B.\mathrm{pk}, \pi x))$

where A represents the access requester, Tx represents the transaction, IDx represents the transaction identifier, $A.pk$ represents the access requester's public key, and ψ represents the policy verification response, B.pk represents the public key of the target and πx represents the address of the smart contract.

To validate the transaction and evaluate the access control policy, the node performs the following functions:

1) CheckIdentity: This function provides the following properties:

- Authenticate the sender.
- prove his property to the resource
- prove his non-repudiation.

This function is performed by verifying the sender's signature using this procedure:

$Check\mathrm{A}\ (Tx, \sigma) = \mathrm{True}$

where σ is the signature of the requester.

2) CheckIntegrity(Tx): chop the transaction and compare it by its ID to make sure that the transaction has not been modified when it was propagated in the network. This function is performed by performing this procedure: Compare (H (Tx). $IDx) = True$

3) Checkattribute (Att): checks if the encrypted attributes in the policy and in the user request are identical.

Compare (Enc (Att (A) .Enc (Att (πx)) = True

where Att represents the attributes and Att (πx) represents the attributes in the smart contract.

CheckPolicy: Checks whether the sender follows the access control policy by running PolicyContract, an identifier that is permanently registered in the blockchain. This function is provided by the execution of these procedures:

a) Address GetPolicyContract $(Tx) \rightarrow \pi x$

b) GetRequestAcess entry: $(Tx) \rightarrow \psi$

c) Execute $(\psi, \pi x) = \mathrm{True}$

If a result other than "True" remains after performing the described function, the transaction is considered invalid. It will be rejected, access will be refused and a notification will be sent to the sender. If successful, PolicyContract triggers another SmartContract named CreatTokenContract, identified by this $\pi'x$ address, to generate an authorization token and assigns it to the requester via an AllowAccess transaction in the following form.

Tx = (m, sigA (m)) *where* m = (IDx, $from\ (\pi'x)$, to (Rq, TKN (Rq, $\pi'x$))

1) CreateToken Contract Releases AllowAccess Transaction

2) The nodes of the network validate the transaction

3) If the transaction is valid, the unspent transaction output: TKN (Rq, $\pi'x$) is saved in the Blockchain and added to the requestor's token list.

Phase 6: Token generation

When the requester wants to access this resource, he creates a GetAccess transaction that uses the authorization token and the attribute secret keys obtained in the previous phase and sends them to the cloud. The GetAccess transaction has the following form:

Tx = (m, sigA (m)) *where* m = (IDx, $from$ (Rq), to (Rs, TKN (Rs, $\pi'x$))

Phase 7: Access to resource target

The cloud provides the user with the authorization token, attribute secret keys and ciphertext in order to decrypt this latter and obviously access to the resource.

V. Conclusion and Perspectives

We created an efficient access control system in a Big Data environment using Blockchain. Our system allows granular access control based on the Blockchain scheme. The latter uses transactions to guarantee authentication, non-repudiation and integrity. We have demonstrated the feasibility of using blockchain technology to manage access control process for Big Data through the description of our proposed framework. The latter leverages the salient features of Blockchain that are, distribution, full-fledged and append-only ledger to make a promising solution for addressing the access control challenges in Big Data. However adopting the blockchain technology to handle access control functions is not straightforward and additional critical issues emerge that are: The public aspect of the blockchain versus the private aspect of some access control policies and the inherent traceability problem. To address these issues, the encryption was used to encrypt attributes in the data owner's security policy and access requester's attributes to mask the transparency and visibility of the attributes to the public. Regarding the problem of traceability, we planned to ensure it in our next work.

We also used the ciphertext-policy Attribute Based Encryption (CP-ABE) scheme in order to add another security layer in our framework. This technology is a promising cryptographic primitive for the security of cloud storage system, which can bring fine-grained access control. In the future, we envision implementing our model using access control tools and Multichain for the blockchain. The results of this implementation would help us to evaluate the security level and performance of our proposed infrastructure.

References

[1] S. Hosseinzadeh , P. Hosseinzadeh, and S. E. Najafi, " introducting a hybrid model of DEA and data mining in evaluating efficiency. Case study: BankBranches," Acad; J; Res. Econ. Manag. , vol. 3, no. 2, 2015

[2] P. Cato, P. Gölzer, and W. Demmelhuber, "An investigation into the implementation factors affecting the success of big

data system," in 2015 11th International Conference On Innovations Technologiy (IIT), 2015, PP. 134-139

[3] D. Xia, Z. Rong, Y. Zhou, B. Wang, Y. Li, and Z. Zhang, "Discovery and analysis of usage data based on hadoop for personalized information access," in Proceedings - 16th IEEE International Conference on Computational Science and Engineering, CSE 2013, 2013, pp. 917–924.

[4] V. N. Gudivada, R. Baeza-Yates, and V. Raghavan, "Big data: Promises and problems," Computer, vol. 48, no. 3, pp. 20–23, 2015.

[5] P. Kassani, A. Teoh, and E. Kim, "Evolutionary-modified fuzzy nearest-neighbor rule for pattern classification," Expert Syst. Appl., vol. 88, pp. 258–269, Dec. 2017.

[6] Big Data Working Group, "Expanded top ten big data security and privacy challenges : Cloud Security Alliance.", [Online]. Available:https://downloads.cloudsecurityalliance.org/initiatives/bdwg/Expanded_Top_Ten_Big_Data_Security_and_Privacy_Challenges.pdf. [Accessed: 06-Jun-2019].

[7] W. Meng, E. Tischhauser, Q. Wang, Y. Wang, and J. Han, "When Intrusion Detection Meets Blockchain Technology: A Review," IEEE Access, 2018., vol. 6, PP. 10179-10188, Jan. 2018.

[8] M. Samaniego and R. Deters, "Internet of Smart Things - IoST: Using Blockchain and CLIPS to Make Things Autonomous," in Proceedings - 2017 IEEE 1st International Conference on Cognitive Computing, ICCC 2017, PP. 9-16. 2017.

[9] K. Yang, X. Jia, and K. Ren, "Dac-macs: effective data access control for multi-authority cloud storage systems," in IEEE INFOCOM'13, 2013, pp. 2895-2903.

[10] J. Bethencourt, A. Sahai, and B. Waters, "Ciphertext-policy attribute-based encryption," in IEEE S&P'07, 2007, pp. 321-334.

[11] B. Waters, "Ciphertext-policy attribute-based encryption: An expressive, efficient, and provably secure realization," in PKC' II, 2011, pp. 53-70.

[12] V. Goyal, O. Pandey, A. Sahai, and B. Waters, "Attribute-based encryption for fine-grained access control of encrypted data," in ACM CCS'08, 2006, pp. 89-98.

[13] C. Tankard, "Big data security," Network Security, pp. 5-8, 2012.

[14] H. Qian, J. Li, Y. Zhang, and J. Han, "Privacy-preserving personal health record using multi-authority attribute-based encryption with revocation," Int. J. Inf. Secur., vol. 14, no. 6, pp. 487–497, Nov. 2015.

[15] F. Lombardi and R. Di Pietro, "Secure virtualization for cloud computing", *J. Netw. Comput. Appl.*, vol. 34, no. 4, pp. 1113-1122, 2010.

[16] S. Zawoad and R. Hasan, Cloud forensics: A meta-study of challenges approaches and open problems, Feb. 2013.

[17] D. Kumar and K. Morarjee, "Survey on insider data theft misuse attacks in the cloud", *Int. J. Comput. Sci. Mobile Appl.*, vol. 2, no. 2, pp. 26-29, 2014.

[18] Satoshi Nakamoto, "Bitcoin: A Peer-to-Peer Electronic Cash System,". Oct. 2008. [online]:Available: https://bitcoin.org/bitcoin.pdf [Accessed: 03-Jun-2019].

[19] J.-P. Delahaye, "Les blockchains, clefs d'un nouveau monde," Pourlascience.fr. [Online]. Available:https://www.pourlascience.fr/sd/informatique/les-blockchains-clefs-daposun-nouveau-monde-8354.php. [Accessed: 03-Jun-2019].

[20] D. Johnson, A. Meneze, and S. Vansto, "The Elliptic Curve Digital Signature Algorithm (ECDSA)," certicom. [Online]. Available:http://www.cs.miami.edu/home/burt/learning/Csc609.142/ecdsa-cert.pdf. [Accessed: 05-Jun-2019].

[21] A. Gervais et al, "On the Security and Performance of Proof of Work Blockchains," in *Proceedings of the 2016 ACM SIGSAC Conference on Computer and Communications Security*, New York, NY, USA, 2016, pp. 3–16.

[22] "What is a Merkle Tree? Beginner's Guide to this Blockchain Component." [Online]. Available: https://blockonomi.com/merkle-tree/. [Accessed: 06-Jun-2019]

[23] "How Do Ethereum Smart Contracts Work? - CoinDesk." [Online]. Available: https://www.coindesk.com/information/ethereum-smart-contracts-work. [Accessed: 06-Jun-2019].

[24] D. Mills et al, "Distributed ledger technology in payments, clearing, and settlement," Distributed ledger technology in payments, clearing, and settlement, 2016. [Online]. Available: http://ccl.yale.edu/sites/default/files/files/Mills%20et%20al%20Distributed%20Ledger%20Technologies.pdf. [Accessed: 05-Jun-2019].

[25] A. Sahai and B. Waters, ''Fuzzy identity-based encryption,'' in Proc. Annu. Int. Conf. Theory Appl. Cryptograph. Techn. Berlin, Germany: Springer, 2005, pp. 457–473.

[26] L. Zu, Z. Liu, and J. Li, ''New ciphertext-policy attribute-based encryption with efficient revocation,'' in Proc. IEEE Int. Conf. Comput. Inf. Technol. (CIT), Sep. 2014, pp. 281–287.

[27] J. Li, W. Yao, J. Han, Y. Zhang, and J. Shen, ''User collusion avoidance CP-ABE with efficient attribute revocation for cloud storage,'' IEEE Syst. J., vol. 12, no. 2, pp. 1767–1777, Jun. 2018.

[28] A. Kapadia, P. P. Tsang, and S. W. Smith, ''Attribute-based publishing with hidden credentials and hidden policies,'' in Proc. NDSS, vol. 7, 2007, pp. 179–192.

[29] Y. Zhang et al, "Ensuring attribute privacy protection and fast decryption for outsourced data security in mobile cloud computing," Inf. Sci., vol. 379, pp. 42–61, Feb. 2017.

[30] M. Chase, ''Multi-authority attribute based encryption,'' in Proc. Theory Cryptogr. Conf. Berlin, Germany: Springer, 2007, pp. 515–534.

[31] H. S. G. Pussewalage and V. A. Oleshchuk, ''A distributed multi-authority attribute based encryption scheme for secure sharing of personal health records,'' in Proc. 22nd ACM Symp. Access Control Models Technol., 2017, pp. 255–262.

[32] J. Li, Y. Wang, Y. Zhang, and J. Han, ''Full verifiability for outsourced decryption in attribute based encryption,'' IEEE Trans. Services Comput., to be published.

[33] J. Li, X. Lin, Y. Zhang, and J. Han, ''KSF-OABE: Outsourced attributebased encryption with keyword search function for cloud storage,'' IEEE Trans. Services Comput., vol. 10, no. 5, pp. 715–725, Sep. /Oct. 2017.

[34] M. Xiao, M. Wang, X. Liu, and J. Sun, "Efficient distributed access control for big data in clouds," in *2015 IEEE Conference on Computer Communications Workshops (INFOCOM WKSHPS)*, 2015, pp. 202–207.

[35] U. Feige, J. Killian, and M. Naor, "A Minimal Model for Secure Computation (Extended Abstract)," in *Proceedings of the Twenty-sixth Annual ACM Symposium on Theory of Computing*, New York, NY, USA, 1994, pp. 554–563.

[36] A. Ouaddah, H. Mousannif, A. Abou elkalam, and A. Ait Ouahman, "Access control in The Internet of Things: Big challenges and new opportunities," *Comput. Netw.*, vol. 112, Nov. 2016.

[37] H. Wang, X. Jiang, and G. Kambourakis, "Special Issue on Security, Privacy and Trust in Network-based Big Data," *Inf Sci*, vol. 318, no. C, pp. 48–50, Oct. 2015.

Collaborative Cloud-based Application-level Intrusion Detection and Prevention

Omar Iraqi*†, Meryeme Ayache*, and Hanan El Bakkali*
*Rabat-IT Center, ENSIAS, Mohammed V University, Rabat, Morocco
†School of Science and Engineering, Al Akhawayn University, Ifrane, Morocco
Email: o.iraqi@aui.ma, meryeme.ayache@um5s.net.ma, h.elbakkali@um5s.net.ma

Abstract—**The recent years have witnessed an increasing number of coordinated and large-scale attacks. This comes at no surprise as data processing, transfer and storage have got and continue to be faster and cheaper. A standalone Intrusion Detection System (IDS) may only be exposed to a narrow subset of such attacks, which could be too insignificant to raise suspicion. In contrast, a Collaborative Intrusion Detection System (CIDS) leverages collaboration among its members across multiple networks and organizations. In this work, we extend our Application-level Unsupervised Outlier-based Intrusion Detection and Prevention framework by leveraging the benefits of CIDSs. More specifically, we design a collaborative intrusion detection architecture made of three levels: the organization level, the domain level and the overarching root level. This hierarchical architecture combined with streaming and clustering offers very good privacy, scalability, accuracy and resilience tradeoffs. Moreover, the adoption of the cloud as a cost-effective and elastic platform allows us to handle big data generated by millions of applications as alarm streams. We also specify a lightweight Application Alarm Message Exchange Format (A2MEF) to support collaboration among the different stakeholders. Finally, we design a reputation-based alarm correlation algorithm that manages the iterative and bidirectional relationship between the reputation of involved parties and the accuracy of their reported alarms.**

Keywords*—*Collaborative Intrusion Detection; Application-level Intrusion Detection; Hierarchical Architecture; Alarm Correlation; Cloud Computing; Big Data.

I. INTRODUCTION

With the ever growing and affordable processing power and network bandwidth, coordinated and large-scale attacks are steadily prevailing. For example, adequately-equipped attackers may launch Internet-wide scans, discover and infect vulnerable systems to finally use them in Distributed Denial of Service (DDoS) attacks worldwide. A standalone IDS may only be exposed to a narrow subset of such attacks, which could be too insignificant to raise suspicion [1]. In contrast, a *Collaborative Intrusion Detection System (CIDS)* leverages collaboration among its members, which may spread over multiple networks or even different organizations. This global, cross-network and cross-organizational approach does not only reduce false negatives, but it also reduces false positives thanks to alarm correlation and filtering [1]. Moreover, CIDSs improve overall performance while reducing the overhead on each node thanks to load sharing [2].

In this work, we extend our Application-level Unsupervised Outlier-based Intrusion Detection and Prevention framework [3] by leveraging the benefits of CIDSs. In our initial framework, methods to be instrumented are selected statically/manually by the application owner. Indeed, when applying our framework to immunize a target application [3], the owner has to explicitly specify methods or entire packages to intercept, monitor and analyze using unsupervised outlier detection. Such a choice may not be well-informed or may even be arbitrary. Some irrelevant methods may be instrumented, incurring an unjustified overhead, while other pertinent methods may be missed, causing some critical intrusions to go undetected.

Therefore, we aim at empowering our application-level intrusion detection and prevention framework to make well-informed, risk-based and adaptive decisions about methods to (un)instrument. Risk identification, or at least threat identification, shall be supported through collaboration. Peer applications (instances of the same application running in different nodes and different organizations eventually) would start by instrumenting seed methods that can be downloaded from the collaborative system, manually selected by the node owner, or even based on information gathered from external sources, such as Computer Emergency Response Teams (CERTs) and security advisories. Then, as an application instance detects an intrusion at the level of a method, related information propagates through the collaborative system, ultimately making the other instances activate the monitoring of that method. Peer applications may be further narrowed under communities and alliances based on the geopolitical context, business sector, causes and interests, as well as other criteria to be defined. Once these communities are designated, their application instances shall be considered as *community members*. This allows our initial framework to evolve from empowering applications with immunity like the *human body*, to providing them with a sense of belonging like in *human societies*.

This work makes the following contributions:

- A collaborative cloud-based framework for application-level intrusion detection
- A hierarchical architecture for collaborative application-level intrusion detection
- An application alarm message exchange format
- A reputation-based alarm correlation algorithm

This paper is organized as follows. Section II reviews the related work in terms of application-level intrusion detection and collaborative intrusion detection, as well as collaboration-specific threats and countermeasures. Section III describes our Collaborative Cloud-based Application-level Intrusion Detection framework in terms of architecture, alarm exchange format and alarm correlation algorithm. Finally, we conclude our paper by stating future work and direction.

II. Related Work

A. Application-level Intrusion Detection

This work leverages and extends our Application-level Unsupervised Outlier-based Intrusion Detection and Prevention framework [3]. The ultimate goal is to empower software applications with artificial immunity against cyber attacks. We contributed to the fulfillment of such a goal by allowing applications themselves to play a central and active role in the intrusion detection and response processes. While traditional network and host intrusion detection systems have access to raw strings and bytes through I/O operations only, our framework allows tracking application domain objects all along the processing lifecycle. Thanks to unsupervised learning, our framework leverages the application business context and learns from production data, without creating any training burden on the application owner. Moreover, as our framework uses runtime application instrumentation, it incurs no additional cost on the application provider.

More specifically, we built a fine-grained and rich-feature application behavioral model that gets down to the method level and its invocation context. We consider the call stack as a key indicator of such a context. Indeed, under different call stacks, the same method may take completely different sets of inputs, follow different control flows, and yield different sets of outputs. Unsurprisingly, the call stack is extensively used in the current work. As a matter of fact, the main purpose of the collaborative framework proposed in this paper is to identify, prioritize and share call stacks to monitor per application.

Other approaches to application intrusion detection have been proposed. A useful review is given by [3] - Table 1. It classifies and compares different works in terms of *what* data is collected, *who* collects it, from *where* it is collected, *when* it is collected and *how* it is analyzed.

B. Collaborative Intrusion Detection

The main artifacts related to CIDSs are challenges and requirements, architecture, analysis target, technique and timeline, shared information and interoperability.

1) Challenges / Requirements: While collaborative intrusion detection offers several benefits, it also introduces several challenges, which drive the main requirements of CIDSs. These are privacy, scalability, accuracy, resilience and incentive [4]. As explained below, these requirements are oftentimes conflicting, e.g., privacy and scalability vs. accuracy.

1) Privacy: as the collaborating members need to share information with each other, privacy becomes a concern. While secure channels can protect shared data from eavesdropping by external parties, sensitive information may still be divulged to other CIDS members. Therefore, shared data shall be carefully specified in order to abide by the security policy, legal obligations and contractual agreements of involved parties.
2) Scalability: collaboration creates a network overhead that depends on the amount of exchanged data, as well as the number of nodes. The adopted architecture too has a direct impact on scalability. For example, in a centralized architecture, central servers may be overloaded, affecting system scalability. However, in a distributed / P2P architecture, higher scalability is supported as nodes play a symmetric role, but network overhead grows quadratically with the number of nodes [4].
3) Accuracy: while collaboration is supposed to enhance intrusion detection accuracy, hiding some data to preserve privacy or reducing it to support scalability may have a negative impact on accuracy. Moreover, in distributed / P2P architectures where higher scalability is supported, accuracy is negatively impacted as no member holds complete knowledge about the system [4]. Therefore, tradeoffs between data privacy and system scalability versus detection accuracy shall be made depending on organizational priorities and operational constraints.
4) Robustness / Resilience: attacks against CIDSs may have disastrous consequences since protected networks, systems and applications become directly exposed to subsequent threats. This is why CIDSs shall avoid single points of failure (SPoF) and be resilient to both external and internal attacks [1]. These are described below along with corresponding state of the art countermeasures, such as membership, trust and reputation management.
5) Incentive: why would an organization join a CIDS? Why would it offer its processing power and network bandwidth, and maybe sacrifice its privacy in the name of collaboration? Organizations have mainly two incentives: coercion incentive and benefit incentive [4]. Coercion incentive means that nodes have *no choice* to "survive" but collaborate. This could be due for instance to their insufficient processing power or their incapacity to detect intrusions without external help. As opposed to coercion incentive, benefit incentive means that members are *encouraged* to join the collaborative sytem and if they do, they will gain benefits from the CIDS. More specifically, these are "merit-based", which means that higher contributions lead to higher benefits.

2) Architecture: A CIDS is made of monitoring units, correlation units and decision units [4]. A monitoring unit gathers data locally and, depending on the node capability and design choices, may partially or fully process it. Raw, partially processed or fully processed data is then passed over to a correlation unit. This latter is what really characterizes CIDSs. It communicates with other correlation units and exchanges security-relevant information with them according to a protocol, such as the Intrusion Detection Exchange Protocol (IDXP) [5] or a common data exchange format, such as the Intrusion Detection Message Exchange Format (IDMEF) [6]. Finally, the decision unit collects and processes shared information to make a decision. Where these units are deployed and how they integrate with each other depend on the adopted architecture. Tradeoffs made in fulfilling the requirements stated above lead to different architectures. In addition to the aforementioned centralized and distributed / P2P architectures, a hierarchical architecture is also suggested and used [1] [4].

1) Centralized architecture: whereby a central server collects and analyzes information shared by monitoring nodes. The central server hosts the unique decision unit along with a correlation unit. As mentioned earlier, centralized architectures promote intrusion detection accuracy since there is a central decision unit to which all shared information converge. However, the central server creates a Single Point of Failure (SPoF) and a bottleneck against scalability [1] [4].
2) Distributed / P2P architecture: whereby all nodes of the CIDS play a symmetric role. Hence, each and every node hosts a monitoring unit, a correlation unit and a decision unit. As previously mentioned, a peer-to-peer architecture does not suffer from any SPoF, scales to increasing numbers of nodes, but at the expense of intrusion detection accuracy. To avoid overloading the underlying network by peer-to-peer traffic, peer selection criteria need to be defined in order to narrow the number of peers that each node communicates with.
3) Hierarchical architecture: whereby a compromise between the centralized and the distributed architectures is sought. To this end, the centralized architecture is enhanced by inserting additional (tree / hierarchical) layers between monitoring nodes and the root central server. Thanks to these layers, monitoring nodes communicate with the central server via their parents. These may gather and aggregate information shared by their children, before sharing it with their own parents. At higher levels, in addition to communicating with their parents, nodes may also communicate peer-to-peer.

Table I summarizes the architecture support for privacy, scalability, accuracy and resilience requirements. Incentive has not been included as it is not directly affected by the architecture.

TABLE I. Architecture Support for Requirements

Architecture	Privacy	Scalability	Accuracy	Resilience
Centralized	⬤	•	⬤	•
Distributed	•	⬤	•	⬤
Hierarchical	●	●	●	●

3) Analysis: This is the core process in intrusion detection. It targets specific data and processes it using a specific technique in a specific timeline.

1) Target – *what* data is analyzed: network packets, system logs, other host data, or application-level data.
2) Technique – *how* data is analyzed: signature-based or anomaly-based: (semi-)supervised, unsupervised.
3) Timeline – *when* data is analyzed: offline or online.

4) Shared Information: Collaboration units may share raw, partially processed or fully processed data [4] depending on node resources and capabilities, as well as design choices.

1) Raw data: whereby low-capability nodes send gathered data "as is" to higher-capability nodes. This practice affects data privacy and causes a higher network overhead.
2) Partially processed data: whereby capable nodes perform some data preprocessing, filtering, and/or compression in addition to sensitive data hiding. These practices reduce network traffic and strive to preserve data privacy.
3) Processed data: whereby nodes perform full data processing and analysis to identify intrusions locally and send corresponding alarms to other nodes for further correlation and/or final decision.

5) Interoperability: An underlying collaboration mechanism needs to be defined and implemented at the level of CIDS nodes. This mechanism can be a communication protocol, such as the Intrusion Detection Exchange Protocol (IDXP) [5], a data exchange format, such as the Intrusion Detection Message Exchange Format (IDMEF) [6] or even a collaboration framework, such as JXTA, Pastry, Scribe, GNUnet and FreeNet.

6) Taxonomy: A detailed taxonomy of research-oriented and commercial CIDSs based on their architecture, as well as their support for privacy, scalability, accuracy and resilience requirements is given by [1] - Table III and by [4] - Table VII. An equally useful taxonomy of CIDSs based on their analysis target and timeliness, architecture, shared information and interoperability is given by [4] - Table IV.

C. Collaboration-specific Threats and Countermeasures

While IDSs are subject to DDoS and mimicry attacks in general, we focus here on attacks that specifically target the collaboration aspect of CIDSs. First, we will identify collaboration-specific threats, as well as their compensating baseline controls in terms of trust/reputation management and shared information protection. Then, we will describe popular attacks against these baselines and their countermeasures.

1) Collaboration-specific Threats and Baseline Controls: These can affect the confidentiality, as well as the integrity of shared information, hence exposing the CIDS and protected systems to a host of risks. Confidentiality-related threats take advantage of shared information to divulge sensitive data to attackers. Examples include exposing monitors location and target like networks, systems, applications and data, as well as their vulnerabilities. Integrity-related threats can be summarized as having rogue or compromised nodes "telling lies" or "not saying the whole truth" when sharing information, in addition to malicious parties tampering with such information in transit. Examples include nodes spreading fake alerts and/or selectively forwarding received information. In particular, a so-called *Sybil* attack – named after the famous dissociative identity disorder case and book – consists of using an army of pseudonymous nodes to influence CIDS decisions [7].

To address confidentiality-related attacks, information hiding, e.g. hashing, is needed. As far as integrity-related attacks are concerned, *trust/reputation management* has been introduced. It consists of managing a trust/reputation value for each node, as well as to identify, penalize and ultimately kick off rogue and compromised nodes. Trust/reputation management requires node identification and authentication. Moreover, Sybil attacks can only be addressed through a certification authority (CA), which scrutinizes and validates nodes [7].

2) Attacks against Trust/Reputation Management and Countermeasures: Trust/reputation management can be compromised by several attacks. A so-called *Betrayal* attack consists of compromising a trusted node and using it to expose the confidentiality and/or integrity of the CIDS. A variant called *Sleeper* attack uses a rogue node that spends an initial period faking a normal behavior to gain a higher trust/reputation value before exploiting it against the CIDS. The *Newcomer* attack tries to make the CIDS "forget" about the bad reputation of a rogue node by joining it again under a new, clean identity.

To counteract these attacks, several enhancements have been suggested. More specifically, the impact of both Betrayal and Sleeper attacks can be reduced through fast degradation of trust against nodes that exhibit a malicious behavior, while the Newcomer attack can be controlled through a probation period for newcomers. Table II summarizes attacks against trust/reputation management and their countermeasures.

TABLE II. ATTACKS VS. COUNTERMEASURES

Attack	Trust/Reputation Management
Sybil	CA
Betrayal / Sleeper	Fast degradation of trust
Newcomer	CA, Probation period

D. Cloud-based Intrusion Detection

Cloud computing provides organizations with computing resources featuring easy deployment, connectivity, configuration and scalability. There are three cloud service delivery models and IDS cloud deployment differs from one model to another.

- Software as a Service: in SaaS users merely depend upon their providers to deploy their services. Hence, the SaaS cloud provider is responsible of deploying the IDSs. In this case, the users may only get some logs or configure some cosutoms monitoring alerts.
- Platform as a Service: in PaaS, IDSs are deployed outside applications by the cloud service provider. However, users can configure their applications and platforms to log out onto a central location to be used by a central IDS.
- Infrastructure as a Service: this delivery model is more flexible in term of IDS deployment. In fact, the IDS can be deployed at several levels in the IaaS cloud layer: the virtual machine, the hypervisor and the network.

As listed and compared in table III, we can classify the deployment of IDSs in the cloud into five categories:

- In-Guest agent based approach, which consists of deploying the IDS at the Virtual Machine (VM) level. The advantage of this approach is that it does not require any modification of the hypervisor and runs as an application in a tenant VM, which is configured and controlled by the tenant. Moreover, the IDS has a good visibility of the monitored VM. Hence, it can perform deep scanning of packets leaving or entering the VMs and can perform host audit log analysis, system call analysis and program analysis of the VMs. One limitation of this approach is that it fails to detect collaborative attacks.
- In-VMM agent based approach, which consists of deploying the IDS at the hypervisor level in IaaS environments. The hypervisor acts like a central location for intrusion detection. In fact, it can monitor both the hypervisor and data traveling between the hypervisor and the virtual machine (for any VMM attacks). However, just like the In-Guest agent based approach, the In-VMM agent based approach fails too in detecting collaborative attacks.
- Network-monitor based approach, which allows monitoring the network traffic between VMs and the host machine and between VMs themselves. IDSs are deployed at network points, such as the core switch or other network switches. However, this approach yields a poor visibility of the monitored VMs and can not detect host-based anomalies, such as VM escapes, rootkits, viruses, worms and collaborative network attacks.
- Collaborative agent based approach, which places IDS components at different locations, such as at the VM, VMM or network points. These components collaborate to detect various attacks including collaborative attacks.
- Distributed approach, which runs IDS instances over tenant VMs (TVMs) on a Cloud Compute Server but are controlled by a Cloud Controller Server (CCS).

TABLE III. INTRUSION DETECTION SYSTEMS IN THE CLOUD

References	Year	IDS Method	IDS Type
Lee et al. [8]	2011	In-Guest Agent (A)	Anomaly-based
McGee [9]	2013	In-Guest Agent (A)	Prevision-based
Shi et al. [10]	2016	In-VMM Agent (B)	Anomaly-based
Maiero et al.[11]	2011	In-VMM Agent (B)	Intrusion-based
Chiba et al. [12]	2018	Net. Monitor (C)	Anomaly-based
Bharadwaja et al. [13]	2011	Collab. Agent (D)	Anomaly-based
Lo et al. [14]	2010	Collab. Agent (D)	Attack-based
Gupta et al. [15]	2014	Disributed (E)	Attack-based

E. Comparison of our Framework with Existing CIDSs

As opposed to existing CIDSs that use either the client-server model or the peer to peer model for synchronous and tightly-coupled communication, we adopt a hierarchical architecture that leverages cloud-based, clustered, and brokered streaming for asynchronous, loosely-coupled and scalable communication. Another unique aspect of our framework is the integration of social, news and security advisories feeds to enhance collaboration. We also define a lightweight JSON message exchange format to share alarms as fully processed data among nodes hidden behind brokers, hence avoiding sensitive information leakage. Finally, we design an alarm correlation algorithm that manages the iterative and bidirectional relationship between the reputation of involved parties and the accuracy of their reported alarms.

III. Our Collaborative Cloud-based Application-level Intrusion Detection

A. Collaborative Cloud-based Intrusion Detection Architecture

As shown in Figure 1, we adopt a hierarchical collaborative intrusion detection architecture leveraging the cloud. The choice of a hierarchical architecture is motivated by the privacy, scalability, accuracy and resilience tradeoffs it offers in comparison with the centralized and distributed architectures. Moreover, the cloud is a key element in our architecture thanks to its cost-effectiveness, elasticity and capacity to handle alarm streams generated by millions of applications as big data.

In the proposed architecture, organizations can have their applications running on premise or in the cloud. These applications are instrumented to dynamically (un)select methods for raw data extraction and secure streaming to the organization-level Kafka cluster through Kafka Streams API. These data streams are continuously consumed by the Organization-level Application Intrusion Detection Nodes (OAIDNs). These are managed by Kafka Streams API as a group/cluster (OAIDC) and implement our unsupervised, application-level intrusion detection framework [3]. Moreover, we distribute the load among the OAIDNs while making sure each OAIDN receives a coherent and complete stream. To this end, we create a single Kafka topic for all applications, with a separate partition for each call stack of each selected method within each monitored application. This way, the whole stream of data extracted from a method call in a given call stack will be processed by the same OAIDN. Other streams may be assigned to other OAIDNs in the cluster for load sharing.

Intrusions detected at the level of an organization are streamed as alarms to the domain-level correlation and decision cluster (DCDC) through the domain-level Kafka cluster. We would like to underscore that while alarms are shared with the DCDC, applications remain hidden behind the OAIDC. Without using other offline techniques like social engineering, it is not possible to reveal which application generated which alarm. As previously mentioned, to defend against Sybil attacks, the organization-level intrusion detection cluster needs to present a trusted certificate to the DCDC. With its broader cross-organizational view, the DCDC is responsible for correlating alarms generated by all organizations under its domain. Here again, we define a single Kafka topic and we partition it based on the application identifier. Then, the DCDC propagates the aggregated scores to higher levels up to the Root Correlation and Decision Cluster (RCDC) for decision making and information sharing with other CIDS branches. Moreover, the DCDC may make decisions at its own level and share related alarms with organizations under its domain.

Finally, the DCDC may leverage news, social and security advisories feeds to augment correlated data with geopolitical and cyber trends. Here, we consider authoritative security advisories, such as the National Vulnerability Database (NVD), as well as feeds from trusted security product vendors. We also consider other general-purpose feeds, such as news and social feeds from sources that are not necessarily trusted. Nevertheless, such sources can bring valuable information timely. AI and text mining techniques shall be applied to filter corresponding feeds and extract meaningful information.

B. Application Alarm Message Exchange Format

We define an Application Alarm Message Exchange Format (A2MEF) that maps a list of alarms to an application. A2MEF is specified as a lightweight JSON object whose schema is exhibited in Listing 1. The *app* property consists of SHA-512 hash of the application software ID (SWID) in compliance with the ISO/IEC 19770-2 standard. According to this standard, the SWID specifies the software name, edition, version and publisher in XML format [16]. The *alarms* property is an array of alarms described each by the *method* and specific *call stack* that raised it. It is worth mentioning that the *app* property may be omitted if it can be inferred from the queue to/from which the alarm message is streamed, e.g., Kafka stream topic or partition. The same format can be used to propagate information upward the hierarchy for alarm correlation and decision making, as well as downward the hierarchy for alarm feedback and response. In the latter case, the *alarms* array shall represent an *ordered* list of correlated alarms.

```
{
  "$schema": "http://json-schema.org/schema#",
  "title": "Application Alarms",
  "type": "object",
  "properties": {
    "app": {
      "type": "string",
      "description": "SHA-512 hash of the ISO/IEC 19
          770-2 SWID"
    },
    "alarms": {
      "type": "array",
      "description": "Alarms bound to app",
      "items": {
        "type": object,
        "properties": {
          "method": {
            "type": "string",
            "description": "Fully qualified method
                name"
          },
          "callstack": {
            "type": "string",
            "description":  "SHA-512 hash of the
                call stack"
          }
        }
      }
    }
  }
}
```

Listing 1. JSON Schema of A2MEF

C. Reputaion-based Alarm Correlation

We aim here at designing a correlation algorithm that, given a stream of alarms reported by different parties, emits an *ordered* list of methods and call stacks per application. This

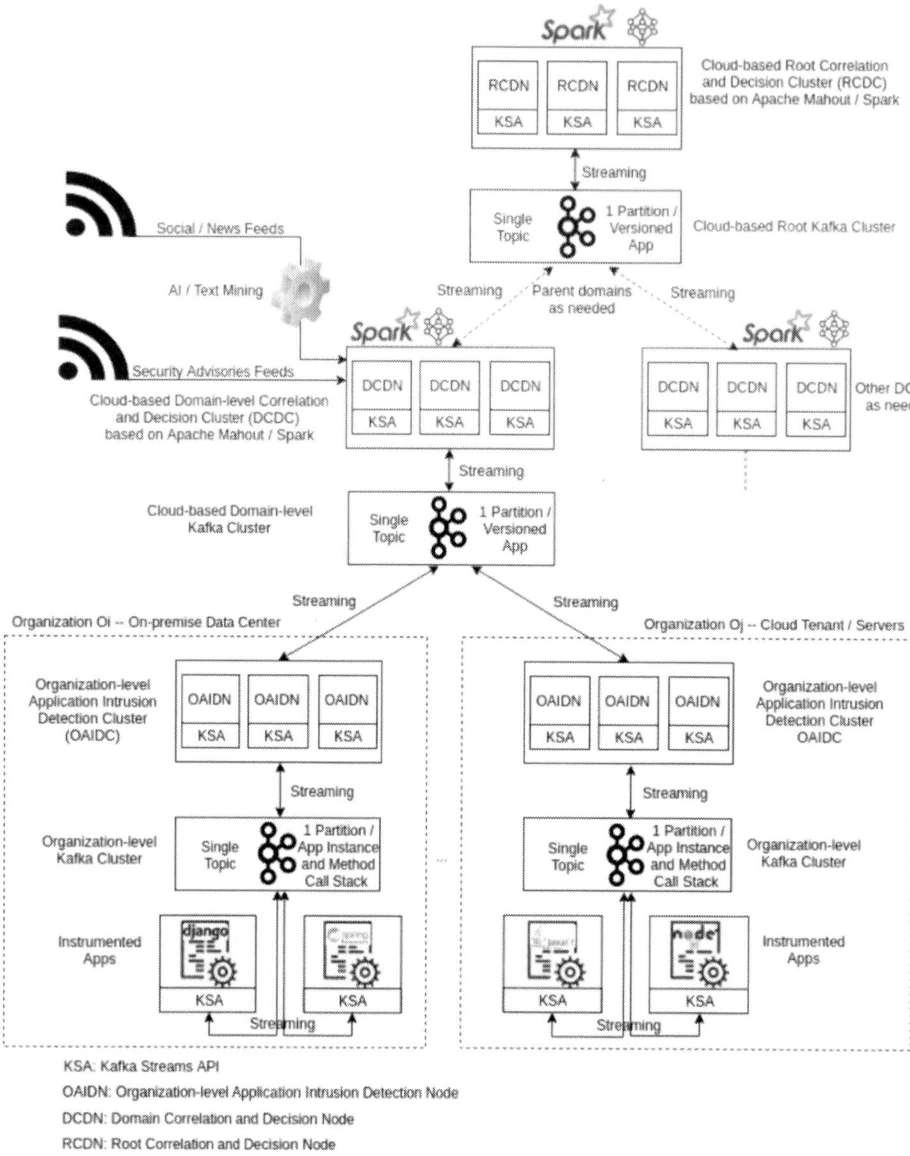

Fig. 1. Collaborative Cloud-based Intrusion Detection Architecture

list can be used by concerned/subscribed parties to prioritize and optimize their application monitoring. Our algorithm shall manage the bidirectional relationship between the reputation of each party and its reported alarms. Indeed, while reputation shall be based on the accuracy of reported alarms, it shall also reflect on the correlation weight of these alarms.

We could base our alarm correlation on a score aggregation technique from the Multiple Attribute Decision Making (MADM) field. As an example, the spectral method [17] could be a good starting point. We would model our call stacks as candidates that are scored or ranked by our parties, considered in this context as sources of information, voters or judges. This requires specifying a score for each alarm or at least a rank from which a score can be derived. It would be a good fit for our application-level unsupervised outlier-based intrusion detection framework [3] as it already provides such a score.

However, MADM methods suppose that every judge provides a score for every candidate. Other improved methods alleviate this constraint, but still require a minimum overlap between candidates scored by different judges [18]. Since in our case we may have thousands of applications with thousands of call stacks to score by thousands of judges, finding those minimum overlaps would not be guaranteed, or at least not in a linear time. Moreover, each aggregated score must be continually recomputed as new alarms are received. Therefore, we had to design a new correlation method.

For a given application with an internal identifier (*aid*) mapped to the SHA-512 of its SWID, we consider a matrix $A^{\mathrm{aid}}_{\mathrm{c,p}}$ that represents the alarms received from p parties about c call stacks. So $A^{\mathrm{aid}}_{\mathrm{ij}}$reflects alarms reported by party j about call stack i. A^{aid} evolves through time with the alarm input stream. Part of A^{aid} evolution, p and c are supposed to grow as new parties related to the given application join the system or alarms about new call stacks are reported. We also consider a $R^{\mathrm{aid}}_{\mathrm{p,1}}$ vector that represents the reputation of the p parties and evolves through time depending on the accuracy of alarms reported by each party about the given application. Finally, we consider a vector $S^{\mathrm{aid}}_{\mathrm{c,1}}$ that represents the scores of the c call stacks. Based on these scores, call stacks are sorted before being sent back to the p parties. For simplicity, $A^{\mathrm{aid}}_{\mathrm{c,p}}$, $R^{\mathrm{aid}}_{\mathrm{p,1}}$ and $S^{\mathrm{aid}}_{\mathrm{c,1}}$ will be referred to as A, R, S respectively.

As shown in Algorithm 1, we create three observers: O_1, O_2 and O_3. O_1 is an event observer that updates S and R for each predefined number of received alarms. O_1 also sends the updated ordered list of call stacks (*SortedCS*) to concerned parties. O_2 is a stream observer that updates A for every received alarm. O_3 is a time observer that updates A periodically to take account of aging.

1) Reputation and Score Manager: Our method is based on an iterative, bidirectional, never-ending relationship between the reputation of parties and the accuracy of their reported alarms. Lines 10 and 11 of Algorithm 1 reflect such a relationship. Each element of S, representing the score of a call stack, is computed as a weighted sum of reported alarms. The weights reflect the reputation of parties that have reported these alarms (A x R). The other parties will be naturally excluded from giving any judgement as their corresponding A cells are null. Likewise, each element of R, reflecting the reputation of a party, is computed as a weighted sum of reported alarms. The weights are the scores of call stacks that have been reported by these parties (A^{T} x S). The intuition here is that the more a party reports about a higher-score call stack, the higher its reputation will be. Nevertheless, there is a pitfall that could be exploited by parties to easily acquire a good reputation. Indeed, as ordered lists of call stacks are published to all subscribers, any party could just "vote on the winner(s)" by echoing top-ranked call stacks back to the system. This will be addressed in the next subsection. Otherwise, our method allows parties to join or leave at any time, as well as to report or not alarms about any call stack at their own discretion.

2) Alarm Observer: The alarm observer is responsible for initializing A, R and S elements, as well as continually updating A elements. As shown on line 18 of Algorithm 1, whenever a new party joins the system, the alarm observer sets its reputation to 1. Similarly, whenever an alarm is reported about a call stack for the first time, it sets the score of the call stack to 1 as shown on lines 25 of Algorithm 1. It also sets the alarm cells of the same call stack to 0, except for the current alarm cell that is set to 1 as shown on lines 28 and 30 of Algorithm 1 respectively. Line 35 is the most important line of the alarm observer. It determines how an A cell gets

Algorithm 1 Reputaion-based Alarm Correlation

1: $A \leftarrow$ [][]
2: $R \leftarrow$ []
3: $S \leftarrow$ []
4: *SortedCS* $\leftarrow$ []
5: $c \leftarrow 0$
6: $p \leftarrow 0$
7: *changed* $\leftarrow$ false
8: **procedure** REPUTATION AND SCORE MANAGER: O1
9:     **if** *changed* **then**
10:         $S \leftarrow A$ x R
11:         $R \leftarrow A^{\mathrm{T}}$ x S
12:         *SortedCS* $\leftarrow$ Sort call stacks based on S
13:         **if** *SortedCS* has changed since last time **then**
14:             encapsulate *SortedCS* as A2MEF and stream
15:         *changed* $\leftarrow$ false
16: **procedure** ALARM OBSERVER: O2(*callstack*, *party*)
17:     **if** new *party* **then**
18:         *R[p]* $\leftarrow$ 1
19:         *bindParty(party, p)*
20:         *pi* $\leftarrow p$
21:         $p \leftarrow p + 1$
22:     **else**
23:         *pi* $\leftarrow$ *getPartyIndex(party)*
24:     **if** new *callstack* **then**
25:         *S[c]* $\leftarrow$ 1
26:         **for** index in 0..p-1 **do**
27:             **if** index != pi **then**
28:                 *A[c][index]* $\leftarrow$ 0
29:             **else**
30:                 *A[c][index]* $\leftarrow$ 1
31:         *bindCallStack(callstack, c)*
32:         $c \leftarrow c + 1$
33:     **else**
34:         *ci* $\leftarrow$ *getCallStackIndex(callstack)*
35:         *A[ci][pi]* $\leftarrow$ *A[ci][pi]* + 1/*S[ci]*
36:     *changed* $\leftarrow$ true
37: **procedure** TIME OBSERVER: O3(*agingFactor*)
38:     $A \leftarrow$ *agingFactor* . A

updated when the corresponding call stack has already been reported, either by the same party or other parties. The idea here is to favor "breaking news". An alarm about a call stack whose score is already high does not "help much". This is why we update the cell by adding a component as a decreasing function of the call stack score (*1/S[ci]*). More importantly, this addresses the shortcoming highlighted in the previous section. Echoing top-ranked call stacks back to the system will not help parties grow their reputation any faster.

3) Time Observer: The past is important, but the present is more relevant. While learning from previous events, live information should be given a higher weight. The time observer fulfills this objective by introducing an aging factor. By multiplying A by an *agingFactor* on line 38 of Algorithm 1, we increase the relative effect of live updates by the alarm observer. It also reflects on R and S when they are updated by the reputation and score manager. The *agingFactor* is to be tuned through experiments. A typical value would be 0.8.

IV. Conclusion and Future Work

In this paper, we presented our framework for Collaborative Cloud-based Application-level Intrusion Detection and Prevention, which extends our Application-level Unsupervised Outlier-based Intrusion Detection and Prevention framework by leveraging the benefits of CIDSs. We designed a collaborative intrusion detection architecture made of three levels: the organization level, the domain level and the overarching root level. This hierarchical architecture combined with streaming and clustering offers very good privacy, scalability, accuracy and resilience tradeoffs. Moreover, the adoption of the cloud as a cost-effective and elastic platform allows to handle big data generated by millions of applications as alarm streams.

We also specified a lightweight Application Alarm Message Exchange Format (A2MEF) to support collaboration among the different stakeholders. Finally, we designed a reputation-based alarm correlation algorithm that, given a stream of alarms reported by different parties, emits an ordered list of methods and specific call stacks per application. This list can be used by concerned parties to optimize their application monitoring. Our algorithm manages an iterative, bidirectional, never-ending relationship between the reputation of parties and the accuracy of their reported alarms. It also aims at coping with known attacks against CIDSs.

We have started the implementation of our framework in order to evaluate its effectiveness and efficiency. This will allow us to fine tune the proposed architecture, the message exchange format, as well as the alarm correlation algorithm. We are faced with two main challenges: dynamically (un)instrumenting application methods without creating an unacceptable overhead, as well as using the right AI techniques and tools to mine the unstructured social and news feeds.

References

[1] E. Vasilomanolakis, S. Karuppayah, M. Muhlhauser, and M. Fischer, "Taxonomy and survey of collaborative intrusion detection," *ACM Computing Surveys*, vol. 47, no. 55, pp. 1–33, 2015.

[2] C. V. Zhou, C. Leckie, and S. Karunasekera, "A survey of coordinated attacks and collaborative intrusion detection," *Computers and Security*, vol. 29, pp. 124–140, 2010.

[3] O. Iraqi and H. E. Bakkali, "Application-level unsupervised outlier-based intrusion detection and prevention," *Security and Communication Networks*, 2019.

[4] G. Meng, Y. Liu, J. Zhang, A. Pokluda, and R. Boutaba, "Collaborative security: A survey and taxonomy," *ACM Computing Surveys*, vol. 48, no. 1, pp. 1–42, 2015.

[5] B. S. Feinstein and G. A. Matthews, "The intrusion detection exchange protocol (idxp)," *The Internet Engineering Task Force (IETF)*, 2007.

[6] H. Debar, D. A. Curry, and B. S. Feinstein, "The intrusion detection message exchange format (idmef)," *The Internet Engineering Task Force (IETF)*, 2007.

[7] J. R. Douceur, "The sybil attack," in *Revised Papers from the First International Workshop on Peer-to-Peer Systems*, IPTPS '01, (London, UK, UK), pp. 251–260, Springer-Verlag, 2002.

[8] J. Lee, M. Park, J. Eom, and T. Chung, "Multi-level intrusion detection system and log management in cloud computing," in *13th International Conference on Advanced Communication Technology (ICACT2011)*, pp. 552–555, Feb 2011.

[9] W. G. McGee, "System and method for intelligent coordination of host and guest intrusion prevention in virtualized environment," May 14 2013. US Patent 8,443,440.

[10] J. Shi, Y. Yang, and C. Tang, "Hardware assisted hypervisor introspection," *SpringerPlus*, vol. 5, no. 1, p. 647, 2016.

[11] C. Maiero and M. Miculan, "Unobservable intrusion detection based on call traces in paravirtualized systems," in *Proceedings of the International Conference on Security and Cryptography*, pp. 300–306, IEEE, 2011.

[12] Z. Chiba, N. Abghour, K. Moussaid, A. El Omri, and M. Rida, "Novel network ids in cloud environment based on optimized bp neural network using genetic algorithm," in *Proceedings of the 3rd International Conference on Smart City Applications*, p. 26, ACM, 2018.

[13] S. Bharadwaja, W. Sun, M. Niamat, and F. Shen, "Collabra: a xen hypervisor based collaborative intrusion detection system," in *2011 Eighth International Conference on Information Technology: New Generations*, pp. 695–700, IEEE, 2011.

[14] C. C. Lo, C. C. Huang, and J. Ku, "A cooperative intrusion detection system framework for cloud computing networks," in *2010 39th International Conference on Parallel Processing Workshops*, pp. 280–284, IEEE, 2010.

[15] S. Gupta and P. Kumar, "System cum program-wide lightweight malicious program execution detection scheme for cloud," *Information Security Journal: A Global Perspective*, vol. 23, no. 3, pp. 86–99, 2014.

[16] "ISO/IEC 19770-2:2015 - Software Identification Tag," tech. rep., ISO/IEC, 2015.

[17] M. Xiao and Y. Wang, "Score aggregation via spectral method," in *Proceedings of the Twenty-Sixth International Joint Conference on Artificial Intelligence, IJCAI-17*, pp. 451–457, 2017.

[18] C. Dwork, R. Kumar, M. Naor, and D. Sivakumar, "Rank aggregation methods for the web," in *Proceedings of the 10th International Conference on World Wide Web*, WWW '01, (New York, NY, USA), pp. 613–622, ACM, 2001.